Feminism's New Age

Feminism's New Age

Gender, Appropriation, and the Afterlife of Essentialism

KARLYN CROWLEY

Cover art of *Water Skiing Witches* courtesy of Gilly Reeves-Hardcastle

Published by State University of New York Press, Albany
© 2011 State University of New York

For information, contact State University of New York Press, Albany, NY
www.sunypress.edu

Production by Diane Ganeles
Marketing by Michael Campochiaro

Library of Congress Cataloging-in-Publication Data

Crowley, Karlyn, 1968–
  Feminism's new age : gender, appropriation, and the afterlife of essentialism / Karlyn Crowley.
    p. cm.
  Includes bibliographical references and index.
  ISBN 978-1-4384-3625-8 (hardcover : alk. paper)
  ISBN 978-1-4384-3626-5 (pbk. : alk. paper)
  1. Feminism—United States—History—21st century. 2. New Age movement—United States—History—21st century. I. Title.
  HQ1421.C76 2011
  305.420973'0905—dc22

                                                      2010032065

10 9 8 7 6 5 4 3 2 1

To my parents, Ann Varnon and Ronald Crowley

Contents

Illustrations

Acknowledgments

So many people along the way believed in this project and helped me think it through even when others thought—New Age culture, really? My parents, to whom this book is dedicated, have been my first champions and encouraged every wild idea and intellectual longing even when they should have squashed them. I am me because of you.

This project began at the University of Virginia (UVA), where I had great support from professors and peers. Thanks to Eric Lott and Rita Felski, in particular, whose intellectual influence is all over this book; your unwavering engagement and enthusiasm have humbled me consistently. I also appreciate the years of camaraderie from the UVA American studies group—you know who you are—including Bryan Wagner, whose encouragement and initial ideas about race in this subculture were indispensable. Even earlier, I want to acknowledge my wonderful professors at Earlham College, especially Paul Lacey and Barbara Ann Caruso, who started me down the path of critical thinking and feminist criticism.

A shout-out to "Lady Professor," my women's studies scholar posse, who made my thinking life a joy and gave me oodles of support. Catherine Orr, Ann Braithwaite, Astrid Henry, Alison Piepmeier, Diane Lichtenstein, and Annalee Lepp, I turn to you for renegade thinking about the field and for late nights at the National Women's Studies Association (NWSA) conferences. I also want to thank my editor at State University of New York (SUNY) Press, Larin McLaughlin, for nurturing the book along the way—your faith increased mine at every turn.

My colleagues and friends at St. Norbert College gave me a home to complete this work. Thank-you to the English Department (Ryan Cordell, Deirdre Egan, Laurie MacDiarmid, John Neary, John Pennington, and Ed Risden) and especially to the women's and gender studies program. Kudos to all who attended faculty libation night at Nicky's bar—those many conversations kept a soul going. My appreciation goes to the library staff and to all those interlibrary loaned books. I also relied heavily on Stacey Wanta and Kelly Krummel to hammer out production details that would have driven other less patient souls crazy. Equally, a number of undergraduate teaching assistants (TAs) helped me with parts of this manuscript: Paige Caulum, Meghan Engsberg, Christine Garten, Kellie Herson, Gretchen Panzer, Kristen Susienka, Cassandra Voss, and Sasha Zwiefelhofer, you have made my work and teaching life a delight; Shane Rocheleau helped in the final hour with images; and Amy Macdonald was my buddy. Gratitude goes to my dear friend Bridget Burke Ravizza for cheering emails and long walks.

Thanks to my YaYas (Helen Lodge, Danielle Pelfrey Duryea, and Kim Roberts), a group of friends who bolstered me more than I could have dreamed. You are sisters and a smarty-pants women's community all rolled into one. Helena, you read every line of it, just like you've known everything about me from before the moment I met you. Misty, your cakes, wisdom, and faith in all of us have guided me through every turn. Kimba, I wouldn't have written this project without you, since we wrote sitting next to one another in carrels—I aspire to be the "shero" that you are.

A particular thank-you to the artist Gilly Reeves-Hardcastle (http://www.properpaintings.com) who generously shared her wonderful painting *Water Skiing Witches* for the book's cover art. I also would like to thank several presses for permission to reprint some portions of this book that were previously published. An abbreviated early version of chapter 3 appeared as "Gender on a Plate: The Calibration of Identity in American Macrobiotics," in *Gastronomica: The Journal of Food and Culture* (Berkeley: University of California Press, 2002). Portions of chapter 1 appear in "New Age Feminism? Reading the Woman's 'New Age' Non-fiction Bestseller in the United States," in *Religion and the Culture of Print in Modern America*, ed. Charles L. Cohen and Paul S. Boyer (Madison: University of Wisconsin Press, 2008); "New Age Soul: The Gendered Translation of New Age Spirituality on *The Oprah Winfrey Show*," in *Stories of Oprah: The Oprahfication of American Culture*, ed. Trystan T. Cotten and Kimberly Springer (Jackson: University Press of Mississippi, 2010).

Thanks also to John Pennington for all of his jokes, voices, songs to the cats, intellectual sparring, and deep loyalty and love. And, finally, thanks to Ada Mae Varnon Crowley-Pennington: welcome to the world and to the wonkiest and goofiest of households. A blessed new chapter begins.

Introduction

"It's Power without the Anger": Spirituality, Gender, and Race in the New Age

I went to what I thought was a fairly innocent women's weekend at a commune outside of Charlottesville, Virginia, because I needed a break from graduate school and thought it would be a lark. But the mud baths and spirit circles had far more in store for me than I could have anticipated. What I discovered was more informed by a conglomeration of spiritual practices that could be called "New Age" than anything feminist, yet many of the women that weekend found it fortifying in feminist fashion. The fireside dance and drumming rituals were as empowering to them as were the mud baths and health food. Wasn't this what feminists longed for? Women healed their bodies, bonded, rebelled, expressed themselves, and communed, frequently in various states of disrobe around a fire. For me, this was the first of many such experiences in which the crossing of cultures—feminist and spiritual, academic and popular, public and private—proved fascinating, disturbing, and intriguing. It made me ask: why were New Age bookstores popping up everywhere I turned? Why did I always seem to know someone who was into crystals or Reiki or Goddess worship? And what was the appeal of these practices for white women, especially, and why were they turning to crystals when they could just as easily enact public forms of feminist protest? Where does a crystal get you?

The Gender of American New Age Culture: Critics Meet the Public Sphere

Some say that for the past thirty years the United States has been in the midst of a "spiritual revival" or another "Great Awakening," as religious

1

historians call periods of extensive spiritual crisis and reorientation.[1] In every period of religious revival, there have been movements, credos, and rituals that are seen as bizarre by some critics but in retrospect can be recognized as generating important elements of American religious and cultural life. In the present instance, these various movements are often known by the umbrella term "New Age culture," a term that names diverse spiritual, social, and political beliefs and practices that promote personal and societal change through spiritual transformation. Once relegated to the cultural fringe, the New Age movement is now at the cultural center in the United States: with a billion-dollar book industry, popular shows ranging from *Medium* to *Oprah*, and personal growth seminars in businesses and schools, New Age has become a synonym for a surprisingly popular form of spirituality that includes crystals, aliens, and angels. This explosion of New Age spirituality has baffled critics on both the Left and the Right who see the New Age as infantile, regressive, and superstitious. On the Right, many traditional religious thinkers scoff at the New Age as "spirituality-lite"; on the Left, few feminist academics, for example, have been willing to grant New Age practitioners any form of agency. Indeed, for those bemoaning the end of 1960s activism, it seems that "true" politics has turned into rampant individualism, and reason has turned into New Age quackery. In short, while immensely popular, the New Age is also critiqued and derided from all sides.

Skepticism toward movements such as the New Age one is not new. In 1848, when the Fox sisters supposedly discovered unaccountable "rappings" in their parents' New England home, modern spiritualism was born. In spite of widespread popularity, a cynical counter-audience not only pronounced the rappings fake but also declared it improper for women to experience such spirits directly. Such opinions did not prevail: in fact, women have played an increasingly public role in alternative religions, spiritualism, and occultism in the United States—all practices that continue currently, though under different names. Clearly these spiritual practices hold a specific allure for women, who are drawn in record numbers to the "New Age." But why? When one female practitioner says about her New Age beliefs, "It's power without the anger," what "power" does it provide that feminism does not (Robb 32)? While this particular project focuses on white women in New Age subcultures of the last forty years, it also seeks to answer a broader question relevant to the study of gender and American religious culture generally: exactly what kind of authority do white women find in the spiritual? Furthermore, in what ways is the New Age movement a continuation of earlier American religious and cultural "Awakenings," and, more particularly, why is it that white women are the leading figures and consumers of New Age culture and spirituality?

By illuminating why New Age beliefs appear so empowering to some, and so naïve to others, this project remedies the lack of scholarship on gender and American New Age culture. In the field of religious studies, New Age spirituality is frequently seen as emanating from the consumer market rather than from religious tradition. Consequently, critics such as Wendy Kaminer, Harold Bloom, and Gary Wills draw strict distinctions between established religions or even religious sects and a diffuse New Age spirituality. Thus the study of New Age culture frequently drops out of religious inquiry. Even within the handful of academic books that examine the New Age primarily, such as Paul Heelas's *The New Age Movement: The Celebration of the Self and the Sacralization of Modernity* (1996) and *Spiritualities of Life: New Age Romanticism and Consumptive Capitalism* (2008), Wouter Hanegraaff's *New Age Religion and Western Culture: Esotericism in the Mirror or Secular Thought* (1996), Steven Sutcliffe's *Children of the New Age: A History of Spiritual Practices* (2003), David Tacey's *The Spirituality Revolution: The Emergence of Contemporary Spirituality* (2004), and Leigh Schmidt's *Restless Souls: The Making of American Spirituality* (2005), gender is not considered integral to understanding the philosophical foundations or the practical demographics of the culture. While there are a few studies of New Age culture generally that include sections on gender—such as Sarah M. Pike's *New Age and Neopagan Religions in America* (2004) and Catherine L. Albanese's *A Republic of Mind and Spirit: A Cultural History of American Metaphysical Religion* (2007)—it is not necessarily the central focus for what is usually a sociological and religious analysis rather than an interdisciplinary one. Though Paul Heelas notes perceptively that the lingua franca of the New Age can be summed up in the term "Self Religiosity," he does not move on to point out that such a concept could be liberatory for women, who have struggled to have a self all along (*New Age Movement* 18).

In more recent studies of various aspects of New Age culture, such as Michael Brown's *The Channeling Zone: American Spirituality in an Anxious Age* (1997), Kimberly Lau's *New Age Capitalism: Making Money East of Eden* (2000), Sarah Pike's *Earthly Bodies, Magical Selves: Contemporary Pagans and the Search for Community* (2001), and Jeffrey J. Kripal's *Esalen: America and the Religion of No Religion* (2007), gender is once again examined briefly but is not the focus of a sustained account. Catherine Tumber's *American Feminism and the Birth of New Age Spirituality: Searching for the Higher Self, 1875–1915* (2002) is the lone full-length monograph that begins to demonstrate the interconnectedness of

New Age culture and feminism but limits its analysis to the turn of the century. "Self-help" is the only area of New Age culture where gender has been examined in depth, though interestingly Micki McGee observes in *Self-Help, Inc.: Makeover Culture in American Life* that "among the most striking features of the 'unisex' literature of self-improvement is the poverty of the solutions offered to women in their quests for self-made success" (79). In spite of this, Wendy Simonds and Elayne Rapping argue against the popular belief that women simply consume self-help ideologies uncritically, and believe that self-help aids women in making nascent feminist claims—even if ultimately they are contained by individualistic rhetoric. Simonds and Rapping see women as not simply passive consumers, and read New Age culture as neither entirely hegemonic nor entirely liberatory.[2]

However, other than in discussions of self-help books, most examinations of gender in New Age practices are both cursory and bleak. Kimberly Lau, for example, believes that women, along with everyone else, are duped into purchasing New Age products by the illusory promise that such products will change their identity; for Lau, women are simply shifting their consumption habits from buying products sold in women's magazines or at perfume counters to New Age products. Lau argues that New Age practices such as macrobiotics, aromatherapy, yoga, and t'ai chi "push women into the modes of consumption required to sustain New Age capitalism" (45). Essentially, she makes the case that New Age culture is entirely commodified and thus entirely inauthentic; the final commodity is the self, or, as she says, in New Age cultures "identities become commodities to buy" (13). Moreover, Lau argues that purchasing products that are marketed as politically or spiritually radical signals a threat to the health of American democracy because it channels desires for change into further consumerism (14). While Lau is right to some extent that New Age culture sells identity, I disagree with her assumption that women are the mindless pawns of New Age commodification; she overlooks the ways in which women consume products for their own spiritual satisfaction. However, Lau's negative assumptions about the New Age movement and New Age consumption are typical of most critics. Trysh Travis notes that "few observers are so foolish as to blame the recovery movement outright for the 'postfeminist' turn of the late 1980s and 1990s," but it is clear from her statement that there are those who are at least tempted to do so (189). Travis explains why "recovery" gets blamed for ruining future feminist empowerment this way:

> In part because it still bears the traces of feminist consciousness-raising, but seems not to push its devotees toward collective

action for social change, recovery has become a favorite scape-
goat, seen as a narcissistic consumer lifestyle that lured women
away from the movement and/or a corrupting virus that under-
mined it from within. (189)

Beryl Satter raises the stakes further: "Self-help and New Age writings
are attacked as an escape from rationality and critical thinking, and as a
mind-numbing form of self-indulgence that signals the end of America as
an enlightened democracy" (252).

In this book, I aim to not only observe how the New Age movement
configures gender but to also move beyond observation to interpretation.
In my extensive reading on New Age culture, I have found that there are
three common gender beliefs: (1) Women and men are essentially different from one another and act out of these cultural/biological differences
(as in "difference feminism," where women are held up as superior
because of innate spiritual and emotional sensibilities); (2) Women and
men need to integrate their masculine and feminine sides to be whole, or
to reach the goal of "divine androgyny"; and (3) Women and men should
move "beyond gender" to inhabit a spiritual plane devoid of these
"earthly" distinctions. What seems like a contradiction between a desire
for gender balance here on earth and a longing to leave gender behind is
better described as a tension—a tension common to New Age culture,
where practitioners try to bridge the gap between the material plane of
everyday life and the more ethereal plane of the spiritual one.

To illustrate how these beliefs play out in New Age culture, I briefly
look at two studies that show gender dynamics at work. In his book on
channeling, Michael Brown observes that either channelers appeal to
"notions of inherent differences between the sexes," or "they emphasize
the important role that spiritual gender-crossing can play in broadening
people's views of their own internal multiplicity" (95, 93). That is, while
channelers believe that those with "feminine qualities" are superior, more
receptive channelers, they also believe that channeling one's "opposite
sex" gives one an experiential sense of another gender that helps balance
one's own gender. The latter practice leads to "sacred androgyny," where
"highly developed spiritual beings encompass male and female principles
in fruitful complementarity" (103). Finally, some channelers wish to
bypass gender altogether to channel "genderless spirits" who may even
be from "different dimensions or galaxies that have either evolved past
gender or never experienced it in the first place" (104).

In contrast to the channeling world, with its emphasis on the body as
a conduit for a numinous spiritual presence, Sarah Pike's book on neo-
pagan rituals examines how practitioners foreground the body as a site of

play and gender experimentation. Neo-paganism is defined as "a return to pre-Christian ideals and religious practices characteristic of several branches of thought including primarily witchcraft, nature religion, and earlier occult traditions" (Campbell and Brennan 159; Pike xiv). Neo-pagan practitioners try to get "beyond gender" through costuming the body: from medieval, science fiction, and fantasy costuming to animal heads, body paints, and piercings, neo-pagans purposefully create visually ambiguous and mysterious creatures that are not always identifiable by species, let alone gender (198). Pike notes in her ethnography that "more than anything else, Neopagans use appearance to raise questions about their nature—who they are in terms of gender and religious identity" (202). And yet Pike finds that in the moments where gender is challenged, it is also reified. For example, at the important ritual space of the "festival fire," neo-pagan men and women "play with gender distinctions, reveal tattoos, cross-dress, exaggerate femininity and masculinity, or try to look androgynous" (202). However, these ritual fires also "replicate gender roles in the outside society": "Men tend to be more aggressive dancers and drummers, dominating ritual space and taking more risks, such as jumping over the fire, while women dance more slowly and sensuously" (206). Just as in the nineteenth century, when particular "feminine traits" such as purity and goodness became a vehicle for women to enter religion with greater authority, so too do neo-pagans play on gender stereotypes of the woman as more "sensuous" and "earthy" and the man as more "aggressive" and "primal" while enacting their spiritual experience (206).

    In all of these various analyses—from those that ignore the centrality of gender to the New Age, to those that suggest that gender is solely a vehicle for New Age commodification, to those that examine different kinds of gender roles in New Age subcultures—the category "gender" is still conceived relatively narrowly, and almost always without the benefit of an intersectional lens that sees gender in relationship to race and/or other identities. While examining gender and interrelated oppressions is fundamental to feminist analysis, it is also important to examine the visual, cultural, and symbolic gender terrain, as well as the particular everyday life practices of millions of New Age women. Instead, the two main questions that have emerged thus far from critiques of gender and the New Age are: Do New Age women ultimately step outside of seemingly restrictive roles? Do the practices of New Age women translate into political activism? This project tries to go beyond these questions into a richer, more probing investigation of gender in New Age culture by applying an intersectional, interdisciplinary women's and gender studies lens. And, as we shall see, while it is true that in the nineteenth century women's rights and alternative religions overlapped extensively, more overlap between feminism and New Age culture occurs in the twentieth and twenty-first centuries than has been previously perceived. Whether wearing an animal mask, channeling a spirit, or purchasing a crystal, New Age women are claiming spiritual desires unavailable to them elsewhere.

Whiteness, Appropriation, and Intersectionality: The New Age Meets the Field of Women's and Gender Studies

Given the centrality of gender in New Age culture, why haven't more women's and gender studies scholars investigated this phenomenon? I believe it comes down to one word: disgust. Feminist academics view the New Age movement as reviving essentialist notions of gender, supporting egregious ideas about race and primitivism, and promoting irrational, loopy practices that set women back. As a women's and gender studies scholar, I share many of these concerns. I came to this project in part because I watched the New Age bookstore in my town take over what had once been the feminist bookstore. In the 1980s and 1990s, I observed many white women turn toward spiritual exploration predicated on bizarre race fantasies and away from feminist protest. The more I asked why, the more I realized that I needed to complete a fair though critical study of New Age women. No one was asking: why angels and not activism? This study attempts to answer that question.

Still, when I would tell people my project, I could see them hold their nose and try to scoot away. It has not been popular party conversation. How could I blame them? But as I got this reaction, it made me even more determined to get underneath what feminist academics and others were finding so abject. So I began the nearly impossible task of trying to be fair to my subject knowing that my audience might be unwilling to entertain an evenhanded examination of the subject. Women's and gender studies as a field has been accused so often of being ideological that it does not bear repeating; I have spent my career defending the field against those accusations. And suddenly I felt that the unwillingness of gender scholars to even look at New Age practices seemed not just shortsighted but hindering. In order to understand better why some white women fetishize Native culture or black Goddess figurines or Orientalist diets, you have to grasp how these despicable practices work. To not understand how gender operates in appropriation is to lose an entire body of analysis central to the field.

I am an academic and also a spiritual seeker. I began this project asking why New Age practices matter to women, and to white women in particular. My answers when I began my search are no longer the answers I posit now, by their publication. I began with more sympathy for white women's seeking (wasn't I like them?) and by the end of the project had to work hard to maintain a fair, critical lens when my patience had all but run out. While I am a bit younger than many of the women I study here, my own time line mirrors what first intrigued me: the rise of the New Age movement has run parallel to the rise of the second-wave feminist movement from the late 1960s to the 1990s. I have observed both movements in their later incarnations—I was a feminist activist in the early 1990s at the same time that I was curious about spiritual dabbling. I have been involved in women's and gender studies since 1988, when the field itself was undergoing interrogation for its whiteness, in particular. I have become a women's and gender studies scholar who is interested in the meta-critique of the field. Simultaneously, New Age culture has become a set of practices here to stay in American culture, though now sometimes called "New Spiritualities." Someone once said that all academic projects are autobiographical. The questions of this project have been deeply shaped by all of these locations. I believe that nothing is out of bounds in women's and gender studies scholarship; this project takes up a set of taboo or disdained practices to ask: why? Why spirituality and not feminism? Or why not recognize how they interrelate?

A central argument of this book is that white women participate in New Age culture in part to negotiate the long, complex, and some would say failed political alliances with women of color. Just when women of color challenged feminism and women's and gender studies for its racist foundations in the 1980s and 1990s, many white women turned toward New Age spiritual practices that "allowed" them to live out fantasy unions with women of color that were disrupted in the public, feminist-political sphere. The New Age spiritual turn toward a fantasy multiracial sisterhood occurred as that sisterhood was interrogated, dismantled, and reconstituted in the academy. I argue that the gendered racial formation of New Age culture has been unexplored and is essential to understanding the history of feminism in the United States.

White New Age women have a deep investment in their "racial innocence" (Srivastava 30). In " 'You're calling me a racist?' The Moral and Emotional Regulation of Antiracism and Feminism," Sarita Srivastava describes how "colonial and contemporary representations of virtue, honesty, and benevolence have been a historical foundation of whiteness, bourgeois respectability, and femininity," and adds that her goal "is to show further that the history of Western feminist movements adds another layer of moral imperative to these historical constructions of *racial innocence*" (30, emphasis added). In New Age culture, white women report feelings of ennui, limitation, lack of immediate spiritual experience, emptiness, and inauthenticity. While these feelings are real, they are also predicated on a white culture that benefits from privilege and norms of universalism with one of the concomitant costs being the absence of specific ethnic/racial spiritual traditions. I cannot count the times my students have said to me, "But there is nothing interesting about my white background." It is this presumed lack of anything "interesting" that sets the stage for future spiritual and cultural appropriation. Many white New Age women have had a rudimentary consciousness-raising that depends on socially constructed gendered notions of "relating," "empathy," and "dialogue" that they translate to identifying with, emulating, joining, and then ingesting the Other as the sign of ultimate respect. "Romantic racialism," or romanticizing the Other, leads practitioners to recover their racial innocence through various New Age practices that bring whites "to life."

My ideas about racial appropriation as they relate to New Age culture are indebted especially to Eric Lott's groundbreaking study *Love and Theft: Blackface Minstrelsy and the American Working Class*. Lott departs from the standard wisdom about blackface minstrelsy (a practice wherein whites caricatured blacks), which assumed that blackface was formed out of hatred and was purely agonistic. He suggests instead that "it was cross-racial desire that coupled a nearly insupportable fascination and a self-protective derision with respect to black people and their culture practices, and that made blackface minstrelsy less a sign of absolute white power and control than of panic, anxiety, terror, and pleasure" (6). To understand the full import of blackface minstrelsy on the color line demands "a much more sensitively historicist look at the uneven class, gender, and racial politics of forms such as the minstrel show" and "a subtler account of acts of representation" (8). For Lott, "the minstrel show was less the incarnation of an age-old racism than an emergent social semantic figure highly responsive to the emotional demands and troubled fantasies of its audiences" (6). While white women's New Age practices may seem profoundly dissimilar to blackface minstrelsy, there are striking similarities in terms of appropriation, of "love and theft."

White women's participation in New Age culture is formed, most would argue, through racial appropriation. Simply put, appropriation is taking—taking another's culture, beliefs, style, and/or ways of being. Appropriation is built on a complex set of popular practices related to essentialism and is often founded in longing for the Other. So far, accusations of appropriation have been the stopping point for most critics. For me, it is the starting point. Is appropriation always bad? Is it actually stealing, or can appropriation have a mutually beneficial outcome? If we believe appropriation is always wrong, is that belief founded on an essence—that is, that something essential can be taken—or is it possible that the process of appropriation may involve more exchange, pastiche, and remaking? James O. Young and Conrad G. Brunk note that "we need criteria for distinguishing wrongful from benign appropriation" (5). For some time, theorists have broken down binary categories of insider/outsider and appropriator/appropriated. However, when we turn to white women's participation in New Age practices, the consensus has been that white women are purely appropriative and steal practices as a mode of cultural imperialism. While I agree that white female New Age practitioners engage in colonizing acts of appropriation that are often shocking in their naïveté, I would argue that these acts are not simply theft, as they also involve affection, incarnation, and reattribution. That never means that racial appropriation is "okay." But it does mean that white women simultaneously obtain "gendered satisfactions" from these New Age appropriations, and it is more fruitful to understand than to simply reject them.

White women's longing for the female power that can be found in some cultures of color has many cultural antecedents. Margaret Jacobs indicates that by the 1920s in the United States, white women looked to Pueblo cultures because in Pueblo culture "women enjoyed high status and a great deal of power" (2). Jacobs explains:

> Having rejected female moral reformers' version of feminism and their vision of womanhood, [Mary] Austin and many other white women journeyed to the Southwest in search of a new womanhood. Here, as they attended Pueblo dances and purchased Pueblo arts and crafts, Austin and her friends concluded that they had discovered what writer Mary Roberts Coolidge called the "land of women's rights." Among the Pueblos, they shaped and articulated a new type of antimodern feminism. (2)

Antimodern feminism also describes what white women seek from New Age culture, a culture that they suppose to be, as the white women fascinated with the Pueblo named it, "far superior to modern American society" (2). This white spiritual longing is centered in the belief that these female cultures, based in the authenticity of people of color, offer white women a better gender identity than public forms of feminism. Indigeneity can save white culture from its own apocalypse. However, Jacobs notes that while American Indian policy during this time of white women's fetishism "seemed to accord Native Americans greater self respect and self-determination," "the underlying assumption of many whites and of the Bureau of Indian Affairs (BIA)—that they knew what was best for Indians—remained virtually unchanged" (3, 4). The historical déjà vu is striking, though white women in the 1920s were obviously grappling with different feminist issues than white women of the 1980s and 1990s. Nevertheless, white women's "good intentions" toward women of color do not lessen the pain of colonialism or alter material conditions of existence. Shannon Sullivan notes that even with "the conscious intent to honor . . . diversity is simultaneously a vehicle for white unconscious habits of ownership" (135).

For white New Age women, spiritual transcendence may be easier to achieve than a difficult dialogue or a contested ideology. Jean Wyatt, in "Toward Cross-Race Dialogue: Identification, Misrecognition, and Difference in Feminist Multicultural Community," explains how white women's racial fantasies of black women create a false idealization:

> The unconscious processes of idealization and identification can generate cross-race misrecognitions and misunderstandings. Idealizing identifications tend to obstruct a perception of the other as the center of her own complex reality—as, in a word, a subject. And as black feminists' commentaries on white women's idealizing fantasies of them make clear, they do nothing to change actual power relations or to bring about economic and social justice. Indeed, white feminists' focus on the individual power of a black woman obscures and distorts the power differential between white and black women. (882)

Wyatt explains further, "When I idealize you, I see in you the qualities that I lack, the qualities that I would like to have" (885). One racial logic for white New Age women is that because white women feel they suffer through sexism, they analogize sexism to racism, which implicitly justifies spiritual appropriation. Again, Wyatt unpacks how white women's fantasies of black women "have more to do with the ideologically constructed position of the white middle-class idealizer than they do with the African-American object of idealization" (884). From the perspective of the larger culture, I have sympathy for the spiritual longing and gender empowerment that white New Age women desire; but within New Age women's culture, distorted cross-racial identification disrupts the potential political gains based on gender.

My argument is situated in critical whiteness studies and looks at how gender and race function intersectionally in these various New Age practices. Michele Berger and Kathleen Guidroz describe how scholars who use intersectional methods "examine how both formal and informal systems of power are deployed, maintained, and reinforced through axes of race, class, and gender" (1). We need new terms to understand gendered participation in New Age culture. Spiritual terms change both gender identity and notions of appropriation. If feminist identity does not look traditionally "activist" or "overtly feminist," then it is not read as a proper feminist subject. What if that identity looks different? Obviously, appropriation of the oppressed has radically different stakes. "The appropriation of one more remaining fragment—spiritual and religious practice and ritual—has an impact that it would not have if the appropriation acted in the reverse direction, from the dominant to the struggling, colonized culture" (Young and Brunk 94). Though intersectionality has become "*de rigueur* in feminist studies," Rachel Luft warns that there is a "risk of flattening difference" if race and gender are analyzed without their specific historical underpinnings (100). She suggests that "today's intersectional, tactical repertoire should include within it the periodic use of single-issue tactics" in order to not collapse some crucial race/gender distinctions because they have "different ruling logics" (101). Uncovering these various "logics" reveals new configurations of New Age white women's theory and practice.

Fin de Siècle and Fin de Millennium: A Short History of Gender and New Age Culture's Antecedents

This project examines New Age culture as the most recent manifestation of a long history of women's alternative spiritual expressions in the United States, particularly within the last two centuries. Alternative spiritualities and especially women's role in them have usually been given short shrift by scholars. In the past, religious scholars have often either suggested that alternative religions are not a part of American religious history and therefore dismissed them entirely, or have seen the influence of alternative religions on mainstream religions as largely negative. New work in religious studies is changing both of these earlier views.[3] Scholars Harry Stout and D. G. Hart note that "one major theme in virtually all religious histories of the past two decades has been the discovery of religious 'outsiders' " (4). Increasingly, scholars now argue that even the most established religions contain the seeds of later marginal practices, and vice versa. For example, scholar Brett Carroll makes the bold claim that Spiritualism, an occult religion in which one channels spirits, stems from Protestantism. Carroll says that Spiritualism fits within a reform tradition beginning with Puritanism in the United States because Spiritualism "was an expression of a powerful restorationist or primitivist impulse by which many American Protestants of the early nineteenth century tried to revitalize Christianity" by "restoring its original purity and eliminating perceived institutional and doctrinal incrustations" (9). In this way, Carroll and other progressive historians of American religious history, such as Catherine Albanese, Stephen Prothero, Sally Promey, Leigh Schmidt, Robert Orsi, and Mary Farrell Bednarowski, argue that there is a more permeable barrier between "established" religions and "marginal" ones than previously realized.

The history of alternative religions has often been narrated as a story about how canonical Protestant religions became infected by marginal foreign influences such as Swedenborgianism, Asian religions, Theosophy, and mesmerism. Now, however, American religious history is reconceived as being mutually constitutive: the so-called marginal religions inform the canonical ones, even as the marginal religions are shaped by more traditional religious forms. "The language of outsiders-become-insiders, and peripheries-become-centers, is now a commonplace in the literature on religion in America," note scholars Stout and Hart (4). Indeed, "marginal" religions have a long history within the United States, beginning in the seventeenth century with practices and traditions such as American Indian Sun Dances and African American spirituals—both of which were outlawed in certain states—to radical reformers of Christianity such as Baptists, Disciples of Christ, Shakers, Mormons, and, later, Spiritualists (Carroll 9). This shifting historiographical terrain opens up the possibility that women's participation in marginal religions and spiritualities will begin to be considered not just as a curiosity but as essential to understanding how religion functions in the United States.

While alternative religions that came from outside the United States had a strong influence domestically, it was not until the 1840s, with the rise of transcendentalism, that America produced its own "homegrown" form of mystical, romantic, individualist spirituality. Though transcendentalism began as a "marginal religion," it soon entered public philosophy and letters and affected established religions.[4] By now, transcendentalism is generally acknowledged as not only one of the most important religious and philosophical movements created in the United States but also as the "forerunner to several nineteenth-century occult and metaphysical movements, such as New Thought and Christian Science" (Kyle 66). Famous transcendentalists such as Emerson, Thoreau, Bronson, Alcott, and Fuller suggested that religion could be as much if not more a private experience than a public one, and they began to focus less on doctrines and religious institutions than on individual experience.

When Catherine Albanese notes that for transcendentalists, "external miracles . . . emanated from spirit powers within," she marks an important national historical shift that would have profound gender implications ("Republic of Mind" 164). For many women who did not have a sustained way to participate in the religious public sphere, validating personal experience from "within" as religious experience made it possible at least to claim authority in a private arena. Susan Warner's 1850 *The Wide, Wide World*, for instance, depicts a heroine whose "intense personal piety not only elevates private feeling as the primary source of genuine spirituality, but also allows her to triumph over an extraordinarily unpleasant domestic situation" (Lippy 97). It is this elevation and acceptance of feeling that critic Ann Douglas marks as leading to a "feminization" of religious culture.

As religion was "privatized" by moving out of the pulpit and into the heart and home, it provided a way for women's voices, and those of white women in particular, to gain greater authority. Women's voices were especially prominent in practices that involved contacting the dead, such as Spiritualism. Spiritualism, which was influenced by transcendentalism, Swedenborgianism, and mesmerism, is defined as "a belief in communication with spirits through human mediums" (Moore xii). Spiritualism has been vitally important in American religious history not only for its wide-reaching effect on many late nineteenth-century institutions such as abolitionism and suffrage but also for its influence on spin-off religious groups. The many spiritual practices that evolved from Spiritualism include Christian Science, Seventh-Day Adventists, the Oneida Perfectionists, and a wide range of occult practices, ranging from New Thought and Theosophy to divination, astrology, witchcraft, and Satanism (Kyle 67). Religious groups proliferated in the nineteenth century at a rate that would not be matched again until the end of the twentieth century. Although Spiritualism had a particular "middlebrow" appeal (similar to New Age culture), a number of prominent figures were involved in the 1850s: William Lloyd Garrison, Harriet Beecher Stowe, Lydia Maria Child, William Cullen Bryant, and James Fenimore Cooper, among others, as R. Laurence Moore notes (3).

Politically, Spiritualism had a radical tendency and supported free love, feminism, and abolition. While these positions were not dominant within Spiritualism, it was often stereotyped as being composed of nothing but such radicals. Because "most radical reformers were intensely religious," Spiritualism gave them a way to challenge both conservative religion and conservative culture at the same time (Braude 62). Not surprisingly then, Spiritualists were often portrayed in novels as those "aiding and abetting some radical social cause"—Orestes Brownson's *The Spirit Rapper* (1854),

Bayard Taylor's *Hannah Thurston: A Story of American Life* (1863), John Hay's *The Breadwinners* (1884), and James's *The Bostonians* (1886) are just a few examples (Moore 72). In particular, Spiritualism attracted women's rights leaders, who were drawn to a religion that "reinforced the self-ownership of women" (193). Indeed, the experience and self-esteem gained in Spiritualism were crucial for the suffrage movement. As Ann Braude has pointed out in her groundbreaking study, *Radical Spirits: Spiritualism and Women's Rights in Nineteenth-Century America*, "Woman suffrage benefited more than any other movement from the self-confidence women gained in Spiritualism. During the last quarter of the nineteenth century, Spiritualism and suffrage engaged in a two-way exchange" (193). Women gained their voices in Spiritualism and then continued to speak out on overtly political matters.

The most prominent women in Spiritualism, though, continued to be mediums.[5] As Ann Braude observes, "Spiritualism embraced the notion that women were pious by nature. But, instead of concluding that the qualities that suited women to religion unsuited them to public roles, Spiritualism made the delicate constitution and nervous excitability commonly attributed to femininity a virtue and lauded it as a qualification for religious leadership" (83). Though men were also mediums, the movement was perceived as entirely feminine, and male mediums were called "addle-headed feminine men" (Moore 105). By drawing on essentialist stereotypes of womanhood, women used their bodies as the spiritual message conduit. As Braude notes, female spirit mediums "bypassed the need for education, ordination, or organizational recognition, which secured the monopoly of male religious leaders" (84). It is notable that the reception and validation of the famous Fox sisters' readings came in part from the sisters' perceived feminine purity, goodness, and beauty. At a Spiritualism session with the Fox sisters, which included famous writers such as Horace Greeley, William Cullen Bryant, and James Fenimore Cooper, one of the striking comments is on the attractiveness of Kate and Maggie, who were "'considerably prettier than the average'" (Brown 116). However, even though the Fox sisters were described in the language of stereotypical femininity, they continued to claim power by channeling messages directly from the dead. Direct communication with spirits not only gave women an experiential and private sense of their own authority but also provided a way for them to gain public authority as well. Mediumship was "one of the few career opportunities open to women in the 19th century," claims Moore, while trance-lecturers took on anti-Victorian roles as they left the house for the public stage (106). Thus "spirit mediums formed the first large group of American women to speak in public or to exercise religious leadership" (Braude xix). While this claim may seem overly bold, and while there are excellent studies that indicate that women did participate at earlier moments in public religious life (two good examples are Rebecca Larson's work on eighteenth-century Quaker women and Catherine Brekus's work on early American female preachers), it appears that Braude's assertion still stands: spiritualism was the first "*sustained* moment of public participation" by women in the religious public sphere (Braude xix, xx, emphasis added). Indeed, Spiritualism made it possible for the controversial Victoria Woodhull, who linked Spiritualism to communism (even suggesting to Marx that Spiritualism and communism were one and the same), to be the first woman to run for president in 1872 (Moore 71).

However, even as female mediums gained a certain authority, they were also trapped by Victorian notions that the "natural lot" of white women is "sickness, suffering, and self-sacrifice" and punished for assuming new roles (Moore 106). For example, if female mediums traveled and were away from their family temporarily, their children were sometimes taken away from them (Braude 124). When, years after their first popularity, the Fox sisters were exposed as complete frauds when one of the sisters confessed that they had made up their revelations from the dead, the media turned against them as "bad women" as eagerly as they had once lauded them as "good women." Their plight represents a textbook feminist "double bind": women are either pure vessels, ripe to receive a divine message, or corrupt containers, overly sexual conduits of the metaphysical. Still, in spite of such instances, Spiritualism provided "a model of women's unlimited capacity for autonomous action to the men and women of nineteenth-century America" (201). That model made it increasingly difficult for women to see men as the only source of spiritual authority.

After Spiritualism's heyday, it continued to influence other new religions such as the New Thought movement. New Thought, or "the power of thought to alter circumstances," like Spiritualism, was largely made up of women (Satter 6). As Beryl Satter observes in her excellent study, *Each Mind a Kingdom: American Women, Sexual Purity, and the New Thought Movement, 1870–1920*, "the majority of late-nineteenth-century New Thought authors, healers, teachers, patients, and congregants were white middle-class women" (8). These women imagined "themselves to be part of a women's religious movement that would herald a new 'women's era,'" and it is not surprising that many New Thought women were also women's rights reformers (8). By "purifying the self" through New Thought practices such as meditation, women believed that they could improve society by improving the self. Even into the twentieth century, the New Thought movement continued to support new kinds of feminism even as that feminism changed. Whereas in the nineteenth century, New Thought women were also women's rights activists who emphasized how "womanly spiritual virtues" of "love, service, cooperation, and self-sacrifice" would heal society, by the beginning of the twentieth century, New Thought women and women's rights activists emphasized instead how men and women were similar, and "were equally fueled by desire and oriented toward growth, self-expression, and willful intelligence" (222, 233). For example, Satter notes that Helen Wilmans, a twentieth-century New Thought believer and women's rights supporter, believed that "true love and maternity were dependent upon strengthening the ego rather than sacrificing it" (233). Being involved in New Thought allowed white women to find both a private spiritual strength and a foundation for political action.

By touching on a few of the most important instances of the complex relationship between gender and alternative religions in the United States, we can begin to see a continuous history of white women's participation in alternative religions, from nineteenth-century practices such as Spiritualism to twenty-first century New Age religions. Suddenly, a feminist project emerges in which a number of fragmented and unrelated moments make sense under one narrative: women become empowered by moving from the private to the public sphere; women who have been socialized to be more intuitive, feeling, and empathic than their male counterparts make strategic use of these qualities to function as moral authorities; women create alternative models to the confining "cult of domesticity." Of course, the nuances of each historical moment as well as particular race and class antinomies factor into this narrative, and while white women have been consumers and producers in what can be seen as a continuous history of alternative religions, my aim is not to reify narratives that offer one image of "the spiritual woman." Instead, by focusing on gender, I wish to understand what Satter so provocatively notes:

> Popular writers of self-help books are among the most aggressive participants in the complex process of fashioning new forms of gendered selfhood to fit a changing political and economic order. Future historians might find in the messy, ambiguous, unsophisticated but massively popular writings of today's self-help authors the clues to how gendered selfhood was renegotiated in the closing years of the twentieth century. (254)

Indeed, this project takes seriously the "messy, ambiguous, unsophisticated but massively popular writings" of New Age culture and examines just what they tell us about the construction of gender at our current historical moment.

New Age Culture as "Women's Culture"

This book is divided into five topical chapters, each focusing on one facet of New Age culture and its particular appeal to white women. The initial theoretical chapter makes the claim for New Age culture as primarily a white women's culture because it is constituted, produced, and consumed by white women. Because New Age culture is a women's culture, it has been perceived as negatively feminizing American culture. Taking off from Ann Douglas's landmark study on women's influence on religion in the nineteenth century, *The Feminization of American Culture*, I claim that the fear of the New Age woman as a marker of ubiquitous irrational, marginal spiritual beliefs replicates an earlier fear about women's involvement in religious culture. By examining critics of New Age culture, such as Harold Bloom, Andrew Ross, Elaine Showalter, David Brooks, Robert Bellah, and Mel D. Faber, this chapter uncovers just how women's participation and influence in New Age culture are understood. These critics constitute a "reaction formation" in relation to New Age culture.[6] This "reaction formation" conceptualizes New Age culture as a negative feminizing influence and perpetuates egregious gender, cultural, and national ideologies, even while it misses exactly how women engage in New Age beliefs and practices. By looking at the construction of certain female types who present some of the most disarming aspects of New Age culture—from "Sheila" who names her religion after herself, to the female bourgeois bohemian or "Bobo" who buys her spirituality in the marketplace, to Carol White in Todd Haynes's film *Safe* who contracts environmental illness (a New Age disease) that makes her allergic to the twentieth century—we discover just what it is these women articulate that critics find so alarming, titillating, and indicative of cultural decline.

The second chapter turns from the sympathetic investigation of misogynist rants against New Age culture as "women's culture" to an examination of white women's suspect racial fantasies inside New Age culture. It investigates why and how American Indian rituals, images, icons, and indeed personas have played such a foundational role in New Age culture. In particular, it is in the arena of New Age culture that Native wisdom and tradition have, however clumsily, been interpreted as canonical American sites of spirituality and healing. Whenever American Indian practices are at issue in popular or mainstream culture, valid charges of appropriation, distortion, and exploitation emerge. However, simply assuming that New Age practitioners co-opt sacred American Indian spirituality for their own purposes ignores why white women emphasize the culture of a group that has been relatively powerless in American history. This chapter examines how women frequently use the trappings of "Indianness"—sage, drums, and feathers, for example—to gain "feminine power" as they usurp particular Native rites. Tracing cultural events, such as the American Indian movement's blacklisting of best-selling authors Lynn Andrews and Mary Summer Rain, and also looking at a host of representations, references, and texts, the chapter uncovers how gender operates in the longing for indigenous spirituality.

The third chapter examines how New Age beliefs support certain ideas about the female body and its relation to diet and food. Several critics, including Caroline Walker Bynum, Joan Jacobs Brumberg, Rosalind Coward, and Carole Counihan, have written about the historical connection between diet, women's bodies, and spiritual purification. Drawing on this work, the chapter concentrates on the New Age food cultures in the macrobiotic diet and asks why women believe that this "New Age diet" does not reinforce gender stereotypes but seems to offer a way out of them. For example, female macrobiotic practitioners believe in the diet's spiritual philosophy, often grounded in Orientalist sensibilities, to such a degree that it changes not only their cosmology but their orientation to their gender. While New Age versions of diets are not a corrective to self-abnegating body images in Western religion, it is crucial to understand the way women's bodies intersect with contemporary spiritual and religious discourse.

The fourth chapter explores Goddess worship, a subculture that arose in the 1970s from both the New Age and feminist movements. Goddess worshippers believe that roughly 10,000 years ago, women ruled the earth peacefully, and that in a future time, women will rule again. The Goddess movement and its literature, read by a larger audience than one might expect, have grown to such a degree that it has been called "one of the most striking religious success stories of the late twentieth century" (Davis 4). Goddess worship has created a space outside of mainstream religions for white women and lesbians to found their own "churches" and participate in alternative sacred commitments, such as marriage ceremonies. Though worshippers support the Goddess hypothesis by drawing on interpretations of prehistorical figurines, archaeological data, and mythology, many feminist scholars, such as Cynthia Eller and Micaela di Leonardo, argue that not only is there no proof of such a history but also that perpetuating this myth, founded on essentialist notions of gender and race, hurts contemporary feminism. Rather than argue about competing narratives of history, this chapter suggests ways of rereading prehistorical accounts of the female body and its longings. My goal is to understand why Goddess worshippers go into the past to search for power rather than claim rights in the present.

In the fifth chapter I examine Oprah Winfrey's raced and gendered translation of the New Age. While Oprah has been written on from many different angles, few have remarked on her spirituality, which is a unique combination of New Age authors and beliefs mixed with historical gestures from African American church traditions. From this mix, she has come to a spirituality that works for her as a black woman and works for her audience, made up largely of white women. Thus Oprah is essential to figuring out just why and how middle-class white American women, in particular, have turned toward certain kinds of spirituality and turned away from certain kinds of feminism. Indeed, Oprah combines perfectly all of the things that New Age culture critics love to hate: she commodifies everything, even her own self; she draws on "feel-good" therapies with no sustained political action or critique of institutions; and it has been claimed that she lowers the aesthetic tastes of an American reading public through her book club choices. Yet white women in particular view her as a cult figure. Why? This chapter examines this phenomenon and analyzes the "empowerment" that white women feel; even as it is grounded in a suspect revival of essentialism and primitivism, it continues to be crucial to document as a particular spiritual articulation in this American popular cultural moment.

Clearly, feminism has not gone underground only to emerge as New Age culture. However, this book documents why and how white women are so captivated by the language and affect of New Age spirituality. While the New Age is critiqued for its hallmark "spiritual fluidity," or the facility to be both a part of and stand adjacent to more traditional religious affiliations, I argue that this fluidity enlarges rather than restricts the sphere of religious expression and the formation of democratic modes of worship for women. Practitioners see nothing contradictory in attending a Protestant service and having a healing altar in their home; indeed, in accounts of their spiritual journeys, New Age women narrate a conversion experience from feeling aimless and ineffective in traditional religions to feeling strong through their newfound ability to communicate with the "otherworldly" on their own terms. Though some feminists in the religious community, such as Rosemary Ruether and Mary Daly, say that one should transform traditional religious language to open churches to full female participation, other women are creating genuinely female-centered spiritual communities outside of traditional religions in New Age culture. Women have themselves devised the images, practices, rituals, and values of New Age culture. While one of the most prevalent accusations against the New Age is that it is religiously vacuous, this book uncovers a genuine mode of spirituality that can foster agency and empowerment for women even as it rests on suspect racial logics. Ultimately, I propose that America's long-standing obsession with the religious fringe, in this case all things "New Age," reflects a powerful and intricate connection between white women's authority, race, and alternative spiritual expressions in America.

1

"Touched by an Angel"

The Feminization of the New Age in American Culture

> Everything she touches, she changes,
> and everything she changes she touches.
> —*Wiccan ritual chant celebrating
> female empowerment*

In the twenty-first century, if you asked most Americans what they imagine when they think of "someone who is New Agey," chances are good that you will get a response something like this: she is a white woman who wears long flowing clothing and ethnic jewelry, believes in angels, and makes her living as a channeler or Reiki master (a Japanese energy healing technique). This "New Age type" is typically caricatured as painfully earnest, self-righteous, and sanctimonious about her belief that women have special animal energy to cleanse the earth. She uses sage to smudge her home, which is arranged by feng shui principles and littered with power crystals. At her metaphysical potlucks, she has tarot card readings and relives her past lives. In short, she is the embodiment of New Age culture. Because she is so lampooned, few want to self-identify as this abject figure: after all, she is naïve and superstitious, almost infantile in her irrational beliefs in wholeness and goodness. The New Ager is the figure critics love to hate. According to most academic, religious, and popular critics, "everything she touches"—rational, democratic culture, mainstream religion, or 1960s political activism—she ruins.

If the New Age figure is a contemporary phenomenon, the ways in which she is read are not. White women were also seen as having "ruined" religion and culture during the last century in America, as Ann Douglas argues in her foundational study, *The Feminization of American*

Culture.[1] Douglas claims that there had been a previously "masculine" focus on damnation and original sin that was trumped by such "feminine" virtues as church attendance and moral piety. Or, as historian Bryan LeBeau describes it, "Religion entered a process whereby it became more domesticated, more emotional, softer and more accommodating—more feminine" (130). According to Douglas, the move from a more masculine Calvinism to a more feminine Protestantism was so pronounced that "by 1875, American Protestants . . . define[d] their faith in terms of family morals, civic responsibility, and above all, in terms of the social function of churchgoing" (7). This process of feminization reads as a story of cultural decline: the hard virtues of men were overtaken by the less vigorous "female virtues." Women and sentimental novelists, such as Harriet Beecher Stowe, formed a mass culture and moved affect out of the private sphere and into the public one. For Douglas, this new mass culture was an emotive, feminized force that overwhelmed high art, strong national identity, and vital religious experience.

Douglas's theory has been critiqued rightly for reifying the separate spheres of gender and for demonizing the sentimental and all things "feminized," but it still provides a powerful framework for understanding how the process of feminization is conceived and produced.[2] While several critics have made a historical connection between nineteenth-century spiritual practices such as mesmerism and Spiritualism and contemporary New Age practices such as channeling and aromatherapy, they have not recognized how women's participation in religious practices has been stigmatized both in the past and present. By not accounting for how these New Age practices and beliefs are gendered, we miss the ideologies at work in the denigration of New Age culture.[3] Instead, critics unwittingly duplicate Douglas's argument and contend that once again the sentimental, the feminine, and the spiritual (rather than the religious) transform a masculine public political culture for the worse. This chapter focuses on contemporary New Age culture and the criticisms it has provoked in order to uncover the not-so-latent misogyny that motivates these critiques as well as the ways that misogyny gets mapped onto New Age values. By looking at Douglas to see how her theory of feminization so closely mirrors what is happening in New Age culture, I hope to bring into sharper focus the errors of these supposedly neutral critiques. By tracing this conflation of women and New Age culture, this project uncovers a powerful genealogy from the nineteenth to the twenty-first century, one in which white women's participation in alternative spiritual practices has been both widespread and heavily critiqued.

In other words, I believe that we are at another turning point in the "feminization of American culture." Feminized values—values that are supposedly emotive, spiritual, and irrational and include such beliefs as "honoring" one's own voice over religious edicts—have a mass cultural appeal not seen to this degree since the last fin-de-siècle. The anxiety about the feminization of spiritual or religious life is not limited solely to an anxiety about New Age culture, however. While in this project I focus on the fear of the New Age woman as a marker of ubiquitous irrational, marginal spiritual beliefs, it should be made clear that an apprehension about women's current involvement in religion generally mirrors a similar concern in the nineteenth century that Douglas documents. Many critics feel that women have feminized even mainstream religions to such an extent that religion in contemporary America is preached and worshipped almost exclusively by women. As religion critic Kenneth Woodward has noted, "Like the suburbs in a John Updike novel, the weekday world of American religion is a world without men" (10). Just as nineteenth-century women influenced mass culture as well as mainstream religion and sermons in the pulpits, thus supposedly fostering their decline, so too does the rise in female clergy and church attendants in recent times supposedly disenfranchise men. We can trace a historical trajectory of women's supposed negative influence on all things spiritual and religious in America.[4]

By examining critiques of New Age culture, I show just how critics perceive women's participation in New Age culture. These critiques constitute a "reaction formation" in relation to New Age culture. By perpetuating conservative gender ideologies and disregarding exactly how women engage in the New Age, this "formation" of critiques has so influenced how New Age culture is perceived that many believe the New Age to be solely negative. While not all of these critiques are entirely false, they have been dominant enough that other possible readings of gender and New Age culture have been invisible. This is not to say that women's participation in New Age culture is entirely liberatory. In fact, New Age women often perpetuate many of the worst gender stereotypes that feminism has worked to eradicate. Still, New Age women have been the leaders and producers of a movement that while often antithetical to feminism still gives white women certain kinds of authority. What critics overlook is how for the large numbers of women practicing certain spiritual beliefs, New Age practices may be a vehicle for identity formation and spiritual power; that is, they are a strengthening, not a weakening, agent.

From my reading of diverse New Age critics, three main critiques surface over and over again: the New Age causes a rise in narcissism and individualism; the New Age is a marketing ploy rather than an "authentic" spiritual experience; the New Age increases a susceptibility to irrationality and hysteria. Critics use their indictment of the New Age on these three charges—narcissism, consumption, and hysteria—to imply that New Age spirituality is fraudulent. After briefly defining the New Age and placing it in a rough historical context, I trace these three prevalent critiques of the New Age and show how they are gendered. This chapter looks at how critics have appropriated the image of the female New Ager in various contexts and also asks: just what is it that these women articulate that critics find so alarming, titillating, and indicative of our cultural decline?

A Short History of the New Age

Just as Douglas argues that by 1875 women had turned "female virtues" into larger societal behavioral norms, by 1975 female virtues were once again turning a country marked by war and civil unrest into the Dawning of Aquarius. Of the nineteenth century, Douglas argues, "America lost its male-dominated theological tradition without gaining a comprehensive feminism or an adequately modernized religious sensibility" (13). I would argue that most critics fear the "feminization" of America now for similar reasons: because a New Age sensibility is identified as a feminized sensibility, critics fear that once those values circulate as the cultural norm, they will corrupt rational, ethical, and religious thought. But what exactly is this threat, and where did it get started?

Some say the United States is in the midst of a "spiritual revival" or another "Great Awakening," as religious historians call periods of extensive spiritual crisis and reorientation. The first and second American Great Awakenings, dated roughly from the early eighteenth century (1730–1740) and early to mid-nineteenth century (1800–1865), respectively, were times when religious experimentation rose and preaching proliferated (Butler, Wacker, and Balmer 172). Mark Noll notes provocatively how the Awakenings had different gendered outcomes—in the first Awakening, "conversion for women was more likely to free from inherent corruption," and yet by the second Awakening, the "same evangelical religion that was revolutionary . . . contributed significantly to the stiff boundaries of the nineteenth century's separate spheres" (178). While declaring Awakenings is a speculative business—are we in the third? the fourth?—most scholars agree that we have been in another Awakening in which many Americans identify as "spiritual, but not religious," as Robert Fuller describes it (5).[5] Though church and synagogue attendance may be down currently in the United States, spiritual belief is high. Studies show that "more than 90 percent of Americans profess a belief in God," and a surprising number believe in the supernatural generally (Woodward). A 2001 Gallup poll stated that those who believe in the "paranormal, the occult, and 'out-of-this-world' experiences" rose from the past decade ("Americans' Belief in Psychic and Paranormal Phenomena Is Up Over Last Decade").[6] In a 2005 update to the Gallup poll, the numbers only rose, with "three in four Americans" believing in "the paranormal" ("Three in Four Americans Believe in Paranormal"). In 2009, a Pew survey summed it up best by saying, "The religious beliefs and practices of Americans do not fit neatly into conventional categories," with a lot of "mixing" of "diverse traditions" (Pew Research Center):

> Many say they attend worship services of more than one faith or denomination. . . . Many also blend Christianity with Eastern or New Age beliefs such as reincarnation, astrology and the presence of spiritual energy in physical objects. And sizeable minorities of all major U.S. religious groups say they have experienced supernatural phenomena, such as being in touch with the dead or with ghosts. (Pew Research Center)

There is a difference between those who identify themselves by their New Age beliefs and those who subscribe to some New Age beliefs but do not claim them as the basis for an identity. Given that belief in the supernatural is so prevalent, what in particular constitutes the New Age?

The New Age is usually defined as an umbrella term for diverse spiritual, social, and political beliefs and practices that attempt to promote personal and societal change through spiritual transformation. The contemporary New Age movement's first spokesperson is often considered to be Ram Dass, and Marilyn Ferguson's book *The Aquarian Conspiracy* (1980) has been "accepted more than any other single book as a consensus statement of the New age perspective" (Melton, Clark, and Kelly 169). Most also acknowledge, however, how difficult it is to define the New Age at all—like trying to define pornography, "you know it when you see it." Nonetheless, a description follows, because however difficult it may be to define different aspects of New Age culture, there are underlying commonalities. Generally, New Age culture marks a move from spiritual "dwelling to seeking," as scholar Robert Wuthnow calls it, that is, a move from being firmly rooted within *one* religious tradition to exploring *multiple* practices from many traditions (6). This multiplicity of New Age practices ranges from the specific to the general: some New Agers engage in particular practices such as channeling, Wicca, shamanism, and self-help, while others simply hold certain beliefs such as acknowledging that the earth is our "Mother" and that her resources are limited, or sensing that a larger societal turn toward technology and materialistic consumption ends in spiritual decline. Typically, New Agers hold four foundational beliefs: (1) a belief that a thin line exists between the material world and the world beyond (which is why such practices as channeling or past-life regression are so popular within the New Age); (2) a belief in holism, that is, as opposed to "dualism or reductionism," a sense that all things are interrelated, not separate, and that one action can affect the whole; (3) a belief in the "evolution of consciousness," that is, that we are evolving toward a higher consciousness that can be accelerated by seeking out psychological, spiritual, or physical healing; and (4) a belief in "the psychologization of religion and sacralization of psychology," or that your mind is what is holy and creates your environment, in turn (Hanegraaff 114, 115).

It is generally agreed upon that such New Age beliefs in the United States are historically based in five traditions: the "alternative religious tradition in the west (Swedenborgianism, Kabbalah, gnosticism, mystical traditions, etc.); Eastern religious concepts (karma, auras, chakras, etc.); the American metaphysical movement (Spiritualism, Theosophy, the Arcane School, etc.); the occult (goddess cults, witchcraft and paganism, Satanism, magic, astrology, etc.); and the Transcendentalists (Emerson, Thoreau, Alcott, Margaret Fuller, etc.)" (York 33). J. Gordon Melton cites the combination of Eastern religion and transpersonal psychology as the "key elements needed to create the distinctive synthesis" of the New Age (Basil 36). The New Age is not so "new" but a recirculation of older movements already present in the United States, as many critics have noted. Because New Age culture pulls from various traditions, religious scholars in particular are wary of giving credence to a movement seemingly comprised of spiritual dilettantes.[7] Dabbling, or taking little bits from here and there, is what theologian Huston Smith calls the "cafeteria approach to spirituality" (Snell 42). Though Smith and others sneer at such practices, the ability to consume multiple spiritual practices is what allows New Agers to create a spirituality tailored to their needs.

Women in particular seem drawn to New Age culture. The sociological data so far suggest that women are "more likely than men to believe in and participate in New Age movements" (Mears and Ellison 293), and that "women are more likely than men to be attracted to the holistic milieu and subjective wellbeing culture" (Heelas and Woodhead 98). A *Body Mind Spirit* magazine questionnaire found that 73 percent of those who self-defined as New Age adherents were female (Jorstad 175).[8] At the Omega Institute, one of the biggest New Age centers in the United States, cofounder Elizabeth Lesser said, "We do 300 to 400 workshops a year, and 75 percent of our students are women" (qtd. in Evans 123). Scholar Michael Brown, in his study on channeling (communicating with spirits in the past or future), notes that at "channeling sessions, women often outnumber men by a factor of three to one or more" (95). While men have also participated greatly in New Age culture, particularly in creating the "men's movement" that was influenced by Robert Bly's *Iron John*, New Age culture as a whole remains overwhelmingly female. What is interesting about this is that women not only account for the majority of participants but also the majority of leaders. As scholar Stuart Rose points out, "The number of influential female teachers in the New Age movement appears to be on the ascendancy, increasing seven-fold between 1977 and 1994" (330). While it is not exceptional to find coed subcultures in which women are statistically dominant in the United States, it is still unusual to find women occupying the primary positions of leadership in coed subcultures. In virtually every New Age practice, for every famous man, such as channeler Jack Purcell, there are two equally famous women, such as channelers Jane Roberts or J. Z. Knight. In New Age culture, women are not relegated to one subscribed position but occupy multiple positions from producer to consumer.[9] The New Age movement has given women the opportunity to figure publicly as spiritual authorities in a way that has not been seen since the last fin-de-siècle.

New Age culture is also profoundly white. "White people will often say they are 'spiritual' but not religious," notes Christian Lander, author and blogger of *Stuff White People Like*, a parody of white identity. One of Lander's first blog entries claims that white people like "religions that their parents don't belong to." That Lander mocks whites for spiritual seeking is not surprising, since post-1960s spiritual seeking is often seen as a privilege, especially for those committed more to individual nirvana rather than to group salvation. Elisabeth Lasch-Quinn, in her explanatory book title *Race Experts: How Racial Etiquette, Sensitivity Training, and New Age Therapy Hijacked the Civil Rights Revolution*, suggests that New Age culture is not just harmlessly and predictably "white" but perniciously so: "The solution to social problems like racial tensions, class exploitation, and warfare is a kind of wholesale therapy program" (138). For her and other cultural critics, the New Age agenda hijacked progressive race politics and solved that demand with feel-good aphorisms. Because this critique is presented as the definitive one of the politics of New Age culture—and not just the race-based one—it supposedly "explains" race without analyzing the racial formation of the culture. New Age culture is produced and consumed almost exclusively by white women and men who play out racial dynamics that depend on white privilege and ideas of primitivism and essentialism; these dynamics also intersect with complex notions of identity, nation, and the public sphere. If Lasch-Quinn has one thing right, then New Age culture really does begin in the 1960s, and that is not accidental.

Although New Age pulls from historically disparate sources—from Transcendentalism to the countercultural movements of the 1970s—it was really the 1960s that birthed the American New Age movement as we now know it. First, the leftist political and drug counterculture of the 1960s provided a springboard for many to experiment with spirituality. Second, the repeal of the Asian Immigration Act in 1965 caused an influx of Asian religious practitioners, which made Eastern practices more accessible. Eastern philosophies were particularly appealing to leftists: "Many who felt that racism, exploitation, oppression and other basic ills characterized American society turned to the Oriental philosophies and religions that form so much a part of New Age thinking," notes scholar Mitchell Pacwa (Di Veroli B4). However, even as the New Age was emerging, political critiques were already being levied against it for being passive, apolitical "navel-gazing." The New Age movement in the 1960s was not associated with overt political action or with any of the many political countercultures of the time and was already splintering off from what was perceived to be "activism in the world" (Hanegraaff 11). It was soon generally accepted that "the youth movement à la Reich [Charles Reich's *The Greening of America*], the human potential movement à la Esalen [the "mother church" of the New Age movement], and the humanistic psychology movement were all of a piece—euphoric, naïve, and depoliticized visions of a hastening upper middle class millennium" (Anderson 233). In the midst of the many flourishing civil rights movements—racial equality, gay pride, women's rights—New Age culture seemed willfully and woefully unaware of broader power imbalances. Rather than organize protesters, New Agers declared a coming shift in consciousness; rather than work for structural change, New Agers declared that structures were outmoded and new paradigms would hasten this New Age of consciousness. This critique of being apolitical still dogs New Age culture today.

However, if the political movements of the Left found the New Age too tame and apolitical, then mainstream religions found it too liberal and individualistic. The 1960s saw not only the growth of political movements but also the growth of "conservative Protestantism"; New Age culture was critiqued by both of these groups.[10] For mainstream religion, New Age culture was associated with the counterculture and became polarized against God-fearing, family-values citizenship. Yet there were those who did not see the New Age as countercultural at all, such as Abbie Hoffman, who said in 1987, "If I close my eyes and think of New Age consciousness, I see yuppies," and those who, like the Protestant mainstream, saw the New Age as blasphemous (Long 80). Regardless of how it was viewed, the New Age had become a movement in its own right. In 1987, the Harmonic Convergence alone had thousands of attendees.[11]

In the 1960s and 1970s, increasing numbers of women critiqued patriarchal religious institutions and sought spiritual solace outside of those institutions. In the 1980s, a wave of spiritually oriented and New Age books, workshops, and seminars burst forth to meet that demand. Best-selling books, films, television shows, and corporate workshops all reflected New Age sensibilities. By the 1990s, not only was the New Age already "so visible that it is invisible," but it had also become strongly associated with women (Jones 48). As Nina Wisniewski, New Age workshop leader and teacher, says, "A lot of women who come [to New Age workshops] have a longing to connect with an inner self" (Evans 178). Female New Age authors—Marianne Williamson, Shirley MacLaine, Sarah Ban Breathnach, Rosemary Altea, Caroline Myss, Betty Eade, and others—consistently topped the best-seller list in the 1990s, often by writing books dealing with women's issues.[12] New Age authors frequently use their life story as a model of spiritual progress to inspire their largely female readership—if they have been able to go from victimhood to realizing their potential through spirituality, then the reader can hopefully do the same. For example, author Rosemary Altea, the famous channeler of an Indian spirit guide, chronicles how during her abusive relationship with a man she found the strength to leave her partner after discovering her psychic powers. Author Caroline Myss also tells her life story as a model of moving from being victimized and reveling in "woundology" to discovering her powers as a "medical intuitive," or someone who can telepathically diagnose the diseases of others. "We are not meant to stay wounded," says Myss, and the rest of her book shows how to leave wounds behind to gain personal and physical power (15). With so many spiritual "makeover stories," it is easy to see why women, often struggling as single or working moms, underpaid workers, or abused spouses, find them so appealing.

Perhaps the most famous woman to use her spiritual "makeover story" to promote spirituality and its particular relationship to women has been Oprah Winfrey.[13] While many New Age practices such as channeling or the use of crystals are part of particular New Age subcultures, Oprah has taken general New Age philosophies and translated them to the mainstream. Oprah not only promotes New Age values on her talk show but also injects spirituality into her products through movies such as *Tuesdays with Morrie*; her *O, The Oprah Magazine*, which is filled with New Age writers such as Suze Orman, Dr. Phil McGraw, and Mark Epstein; her "Book Clubs"; her inspirational seminars; and her Oprah Winfrey Network (OWN). Oprah has created a genre that draws on self-help, new spirituality (female centered, less concerned with original sin), and New Age techniques such as Deepak Chopra's health care regimes and Gary Zukav's metaphysical theories of the multisensory body. In other words, Oprah has given both permission and products to an audience that was already consuming similar materials, though without the Oprah rubric. When Oprah came out with "Change Your Life TV" to revitalize her talk show by including more direct spiritual segments such as "Remembering Your Spirit," the critics hated it, calling it the "church of O" (Taylor 44). But over 7 million Americans continue to watch her every day (Anburajan). When Oprah was asked, "What is it about you that people connect to?" she answered, "The idea of being every woman" (Clemetson 44). Like so many popular New Age books and workshops for women, Oprah has made women (regardless of their race or class background) feel like they too can change the damaging circumstances of their life and claim "responsibility" through spiritual practices (Clemetson 44).

While many critics had predicted—perhaps wishfully—the death or decline of New Age culture, it seemed as if the spiritual renaissance in the United States was just getting bigger, though often with new names like "spiritual" or "seeking" or "metaphysical." Even the "Material Girl's" turn away from the material proved to be another signal that spiritual seeking was hitting a new high. In the late 1990s, Madonna, the pop cultural style and music icon for many women, moved from selling sex to touting spiritual nirvana on her album *Ray of Light*. In a typical New Age quest, Madonna pieced together practices from several religious traditions (yoga, the study of Sanskrit, and the Kabbalah) and combined them with self-help to finally, as she put it, "become aware of people's divine nature" (Powers). When Madonna said, "I'm slowly revealing who I am," she verbalized many women's description of their spiritual autobiography (Powers). For Madonna, her quest was a *self*-quest of spiritual discovery, and for many critics, as we shall see, that marks precisely what is ailing American religious culture.

The "New Narcissism": Individualism in New Age Culture

In his oft-cited definition of religious experience, William James describes it as "the feelings, acts and experiences of individual men in their solitude . . . in relation to whatever they may consider the divine" (31). While James's definition of religious experience is foundational for understanding American religion, the gender of his subject is noteworthy—individualism is often permissible if gendered masculine. While the New Age is critiqued for being narcissistic, this can be read as code for a fear of women's approach to religion: when men have an individual religious experience, it is considered profound, and when women have an individual religious experience, it is often considered narcissistic. Because the lingua franca of the New Age can be summed up in the phrase "self-spirituality," women are presumed to be in trouble spiritually (Heelas 18). This section documents how critics see women's turn inward toward the spiritual not as a valid spiritual expression à la James but as a form of infantile narcissism, and how they regard this turn as fostering a break in national communal bonds.

Robert Bellah's sociological study, the foundational and widely quoted *Habits of the Heart*, argues that a rise in individualism is destroying American culture. Tellingly, one of his primary examples is a woman named Sheila, who names her faith after herself. "Sheilaism" has been cited so often by critics that it has become "a synonym for American religious shallowness and autism" (*The Culture of Religious Combining* 18).[14] In contrast to "Sheilaism," Bellah urges that we "remember that we did not create ourselves, that we owe what we are to the communities that formed us" (295). Bellah's call that we "remember that we did not create ourselves" marks his fear that "self-creation" will corrupt America. While several scholars have challenged Bellah's neglect of gender issues, few critics have examined why one of the most cited examples of this lamentable individualism is a woman. Critic Dorothy Grimes notes that "the most disquieting omissions" of Bellah's study are "1) the silence about the women's movement in particular and feminism in general, and 2) the absence of a clearly stated set of assumptions about language and culture" (19). I want to move beyond these critiques to investigate a further neglected area: the fundamental fear of women's turn toward individualism, a turn that is foundational to New Age culture.

In Bellah's description of his interview with Sheila, he says that she "actually named her religion (she calls it her 'faith') after herself. This suggests the logical possibility of over 220 million American religions, one for each of us" (221). Bellah's bias comes through in his incredulous use of the word "actually" and his disingenuous projection of her act onto the not-so-logical possibility of 220 million American religions: Bellah thinks that to name your "faith" after yourself is misguided and narcissistic. Bellah's fear is that if all Americans were to partake in loopy self-naming, then we would have no "community" at all—only individuals practicing their own "faith." Bellah goes on to describe Sheila in more detail: "Sheila Larson is a young nurse who has received a good deal of therapy and who describes her faith as 'Sheilaism'" (221). Sheila says:

> I believe in God. I'm not a religious fanatic. I can't remember the last time I went to church. My faith has carried me a long way. It's Sheilaism. Just my own little voice. . . . It's just try to love yourself and be gentle with yourself. You know, I guess, take care of each other. I think He would want us to take care of each other. (221)

Notably, here Bellah interrupts Sheila's description of her faith by adding dismissively, "Sheila's faith has some tenets beyond belief in God, though not many" (221). As a prominent scholar wielding the authority in the text, Bellah asks his readers to not only scoff at Sheila's naïveté—after all, what kind of faith is made up of simply loving one-self?—but to also understand Sheilaism as the worst case of how rising individualism splinters the nation. Bellah notes that Sheila's belief is "significantly representative" of an American turn toward individualism and away from community, and thus a national symbol of the kind of solipsism and undeveloped religious sensibility that leads to cultural fragmentation (221).

But what does Sheila have to say? Through her words, we under-stand that she, like William James, has a private experiential sense of God. As she says, "I can't remember the last time I went to church." Bellah, however, ignores the tentativeness of Sheila's claim that she has faith in "just my own little voice." Sheila's use of "little voice" is instruc-tive and suggests that her self-faith is a qualified self-love, not unbridled narcissism (221). Bellah also dismisses how Sheila may be able to find her "voice" only *outside of* mainstream religion. Furthermore, when Sheila says that one should "love and be gentle with yourself," this desire has gender implications when having a self, as well as having self-esteem, has been challenging for many women, especially in religious contexts that have encouraged female submission. But Sheila does not stop with just self-love: her faith tells her that we must "take care of each other"—which, as a nurse, she spends the bulk of her time doing—for "He would want us to" (221). Here she returns to a morality that is firmly grounded in community, and ultimately in an external sense of God—thus the reli-gion of "herself" is tempered by the final authority of a God figure, interestingly a masculine one.

Though Bellah sees Sheila articulating a "religious individualism" that neglects the "public realm," Sheila navigates the gender complexities of transforming her alienation from established religion into finding God within, while still serving in the public realm, both vocationally and through her assertion that "God wants us to take care of others" (248). Sheila's clear need to "do good" not just privately but publicly is neglected by Bellah's focus on her need to find God within. Sheila is not alone in trying to reconceptualize God. As scholar Wade Clark Roof notes, people have replaced a "distant, formal figure of God with a less judgmental, more comforting, supportive, nurturing, and perhaps a lot more feminine" God, one that is "personal, intimate, authentic for themselves" (qtd. in Evans 123). Rather than appreciating Sheila's drive to seize spiritual truths on her own terms without clerical expertise, Bellah sums up Sheila's inner faith as a "language of individualism, the private American language of self-understanding, [which] limits the ways in which people think" (290). Ultimately, Bellah draws on a lineage of women finding God inside to make his point about rising individualism: "How did we get from the point where Anne Hutchinson, a seventeenth-century precursor of Sheila Larson's, could be run out of the Massachusetts Bay Colony to a situation where Anne Hutchinson is close to the norm?" (221). While Bellah obviously does not want heretics killed—his book is about strengthening democracy, not eradicating it—there is still the trace of a lament that the kind of heretical spiritual seeking that once was culturally condemned is now almost celebrated. Bellah asks what so many other critics also want to know—why are so many women trying to find their spirituality within?

While in his study Bellah acknowledges that he did not find "vast numbers of a selfish, narcissistic 'Me generation' in America," his concern remains that the "language of individualism might undermine civic commitment" (290, xvii). I would argue, instead, that the newly formed language of women's so-called "individual" self-questing is more about creating an identity for women within a repressive theological terrain than about abandoning citizenship. Furthermore, I would argue that the articulation of a fear of "individualism" is more about a fear of women's spiritual quest as a form of gender assertion than about a reality of rampant narcissism.

"Self-questing" is one of the most critiqued aspects of New Age culture. For white middle-class Americans, turning inward through therapy, spiritual retreats, and private rituals has become the norm. Scholar Wendy Simonds notes in her work on self-help, a subgenre of New Age culture that rose dramatically in the 1970s, that the "consensus of various critics" is that self-help is a marker of "the self-indulgence of post-Freudian Western capitalism," and that "self-centeredness has come to define our age" (4). Numerous books, ranging from Christopher Lasch's

The Culture of Narcissism to Charles Reich's *The Greening of America*, document strong feelings, both negative and positive, about self-exploration, particularly as it arose in the 1960s and 1970s in relation to the countercultural movement. Furthermore, popular psychological works of the same period by Eric Fromm, Carl Rogers, Rollo May, and Abraham Maslow "all effectively criticized the stifling and restrictive effects of self-denial; all had reserved their highest moral approval for those aspects of the self that are 'authentic'—unblocked, spontaneous, well-nourished" (Yankelovich 245). For many New Agers, this quest for authenticity is a spiritual journey, though, as Christopher Lasch has noted pejoratively, New Agers "equate salvation with feeling good" rather than with a "return to the real thing." We can only assume that Lasch's "real thing" is religion proper and not an individual spiritual journey ("Soul of a New Age" 180).

However, it is not just Sheila who will not return to the "real thing" but also other women like her who find God in the authentic expression of self, as the aforementioned psychologists note. In Alan Wolfe's study, a Mrs. Tompkins, who "views herself as a religious person," says, "I think everyone inside has their own persona of God . . . you don't have to accept anybody's dogma whole. Live with the concept of God as you perceive it" (51). Though most believers whom Wolfe studied would not take the next step, which is to practice and promote several spiritual beliefs at once and even to subscribe to a kind of pantheism, they do subscribe to a "laissez-faire economics" of belief like Mrs. Tompkins (Wolfe 63).[15] This "tolerance" is important to note—when a New Age woman employs a number of spiritual technologies, it sparks the fear of a rise in irrationalism and a decline in piety. In fact, as the Gallup poll indicated, her behavior may be practiced by more Americans than is generally acknowledged, though it is not loudly proclaimed.

However, most critics continue to view New Age questing as not just individualistic but blatantly narcissistic. Critic Mel Faber sees "narcissistic inflation, the longing to go about in the belief that one is somehow magical, wonderful, unique, radiating special qualities and energies, as opposed to being simply another regular person in the world," as one of the worst signs of New Age culture (8). Perhaps not surprisingly, conservative cultural critic Christopher Lasch says that the end of "The American Adam" as a type marked the beginning of the narcissistic type (*The Culture of Narcissism* 8). While "the American Adam" (the rugged, masculine hero in the wilderness) is a type that feminist scholars such as Nina Baym, Judith Fetterley, and others have already taken to task, his counterpart, known as "the American Eve," is theologically relevant to a historical fear of women's narcissism. She has the spiritual curiosity, supposedly born out of narcissism, which destroys paradise and initiates sin in the Garden. When Lasch notes that in contrast to "discipline" or "submission" to a "body of [religious] texts," the New Age seeker reduces religion to therapy, he articulates a paradigm in which feminized values— what Lasch would call self-indulgent talk about emotions, or whimsical and self-gratifying spiritual seeking—are pale shadows of true spiritual life ("Soul of a New Age" 82, 180).

It is not just cultural critics and scholars who are skeptical about the New Age. Most feminists also find "the revolution within," as Gloria Steinem's self-help book is called, equally troubling. While the early feminist movement's "the personal is political" was one example of how personal questing became synonymous with countercultural activity, most feminist critics today are profoundly skeptical about the New Age, both because it has no public politics and because its origins are founded in an untenable liberalism. As Marxist feminist critic Dana Cloud argues, "The liberal ideal depends on a meritocracy that presumes liberal agency, consciousness, and rationality" (113). Some critics go a step farther and argue that the emergence of self-help is a signal of an "advanced liberal democratic society" in which "citizens are psychologically 'healthy' inasmuch as they are governable, predictable, calculable, classifiable, self-conscious, responsible, self-regulating and self-determined . . . this is the social subject of a liberal governance" (Rimke 63).[16] In this model, "the self-conscious" and "self-regulating" spirituality of the New Age is simply the illusion of self-control. Ideology permits this "illusion" in order to make one even more subject to state control. In other words, the threat of individualism is not that it destroys a good religious community, but that it is the sum product of the state. In this paradigm, New Age women are simply duped subjects.[17]

But what are the reasons that New Age women look within? There is a powerful allure to define spirituality on one's own terms. Inner authority has long been a difficult struggle for many women. However, New Age culture, with its "sacralisation of the self," urges women to see themselves as a holy source of wisdom rather than look to an external authority (Aupers and Houtman 205). A recent psychological study on women and individualism discovered that increases on the "individualism index" in "self focus (narcissism)" and "ego strength . . . may have helped women respond to radical changes in women's roles during the late 1960s and 1970s" (Roberts and Helson 641). In his interviews with New Agers, Jon Bloch found that "locating the self as final authority" is a way to both establish a "countercultural" spirituality and to "protest rigid social control" (33). As Sylvia, one of Bloch's interviewees, says, "The inner voice is my best teacher" (33). In repeated narratives, women articulate a sense of relief that spiritual wisdom does not have to emanate from a church or synagogue but can be found within: while "to some Americans, the phrase 'born divine' fairly shimmers with blasphemy, to some, it sounds like New Age cant; and to others, it sounds intuitively like a welcome truth" (Cope 104). For many women, feeling that one is "born divine" has been theologically impossible with religious institutions' denigration of women, and thus indeed a "welcome truth."

New Age women look within not just for their own growth but to share the experience of individual seeking. Women turn within in order to then turn out. In that way, women participate in communities that may defy the norms of traditional religious community. Critics, however, do not conceive of these New Age communities as "authentic" spiritual communities. When I asked Robert Bellah if watching *Oprah* constituted a community, he said, "No, people can just turn the TV off." Bellah's understanding of community may be restricted to traditional church/ synagogue membership that he conflates with true spirituality. A Gallup poll asserted recently that congregation membership does not guarantee spiritual commitment, and that there may be a "possible disconnect between faith and practice for some Americans" ("Does Congregation Membership?"). Community and spiritual growth are complex: women involved in *Oprah*, for example, not only feel a connection to her beyond the talk show, but they participate in "Oprah's Book Club" and form both actual and virtual groups based on Oprah's model of female connection. Viewers watch *Oprah* religiously—she has devoted fans who talk about her show in spiritual terms; like "real" communities, female viewers learn and grow together. As scholar Adam Possamai claims, "New Agers are indeed religious individualists, but they exchange their cultural and material products in both a cultic milieu and in everyday life. They perform this change by 'affinity' networking" (38). Thus New Agers frequently belong to several different communities—often ones created by figures or gurus, centered around a common health practice such as macrobiotics, or concentrated in individual home altar use, which is supplemented by attending a Wiccan group or even mainstream religious services. Critics overlook the complexity of the "seeking" paradigm that, while drawing on multiple practices and beliefs, is integrated and communal in new ways. To counteract this view that New Agers have no sense of community, Bloch calls the New Age movement a "fluid social movement" (23). Bloch says that while a "fluid social movement" is "weak in the way of formal organization or political agendas, it nonetheless promotes an alternative set of values or lifestyle options—such as engaging in spiritual activities with a mini-

mum of dogma or hierarchy, and pronouncing so doing as acts of dis-
sension" (23). Bloch concludes that "an emphasis on self-autonomy
does not preclude a sense of social solidarity, or an active promotion of
shared interests" (23).

But two questions about New Age culture remain for critics. Religious scholars ask: Does this participation involve sacrifice and discipline? And feminists and/or activists ask: Does this turn inward ever turn
outward to real organizing? Critics conceive New Age culture as taking
women away from either "more authentic" religious communities or
from "more relevant" feminist politics. As Wendy Kaminer has decried,
the New Age "has helped create a self-appointed spiritual elite of middle-
class Americans who are disengaged politically" (117). While I could
point to how some New Age women articulate a kind of activist politics,
from Marianne Williamson's edict to volunteer and become involved in
fair distribution of resources by petitioning the U.S. government to
Wiccan actions to protect the environment, I think these questions are
the wrong ones to ask. Though I have sympathy with these questions
and critiques, they seek evidence on their own terms, and thus "discipline" and "activism" have particular meanings that do not allow for
other uses of New Age culture to emerge. Some of the primary reasons
that New Age women look within, which include the allure of defining
spirituality on one's own terms and the desire to participate in nontradi-
tional communities, have been glossed over. In fact, for New Age
women, discovering the spiritual self and joining in groups to do so may
be more political and community focused than anyone had imagined.

The Gender of New Age Consumption

However, even as the presence of a strong women's community in New
Age culture may go unobserved, the most public face of the New Age—
that of "conspicuous consumption"—does not. "The common assumption among academics is that the internalized authority which is such a
pronounced feature of New Age understanding is used to consume,"
notes Paul Heelas (*Spiritualities of Life* 3). Director Michael Tolkin has
lambasted the empty pathos of rich, white, consuming, New-Agey types
in his satirical film *The New Age* (1994). When the two lead characters,
Katherine and Peter Witner (played by Judy Davis and Peter Weller),
lose their jobs and are in a New Age support group, they turn for
answers to Jean, one of two enigmatic, powerful New Age gurus in the
film. Guru Jean asks them what they are afraid of, to which Peter

responds "poverty" and Katherine responds "work." Then Jean asks, "If the two of you could do anything right now, go anywhere, where would you go, what would you do?":

> Katherine: Shopping. Oh, my God! What did I just say?
> Peter (*laughing*): What!
> Katherine (*amazed*): We'd go shopping.
> Peter (*still laughing*): That's right. That's what we're good at. Shopping and talking.
> Jean: There's your answer. You know, in Chinese the word for *crisis* is the same as the word for *opportunity*.
> Peter: Now, if I ask him to explain that, is he going to tell me to live with the question?
> Katherine: No, no, I know what he means. It's so—it's so clear, it's brilliant. He wants us to open a store. Isn't that right? Shopping and talking? A store. (Tolkin 189)

Later in the conversation, Peter asks, "What kind of store?" and Jean does indeed respond, "*Live* with the question" (Tolkin 190). The absurdity of Tolkin's dialogue, which viciously satirizes the interplay between consumerism and New Age aphorisms, indicates just how vacuous and spiritually inept the Witners are—they cannot "live" with anything, especially themselves. Their "spiritual epiphany" is to continue the shallow patterns already so familiar to them by going shopping. Tolkin makes the point that other critics make—in New Age culture "spirituality" translates into increased consumerism. Christopher Lasch goes a step further in repudiating the New Age: "Its blatant commercialization prompts the suspicion of large-scale religious fraud" ("Soul of a New Age" 79).

By the 1990s, all things New Age, from crystals to American Indian crafts to Gregorian chants, could be purchased anywhere. As one New Age entrepreneur says, "It's so mainstream . . . you can see [these products] in a mall" (Phillips 99). New Age products span the range from a $5 amethyst pendant to a $500 angel workshop. In 1996, *Forbes* estimated that "close to $2 billion goes every year to thousands of aromatherapists, channelers, macrobiotic-food vendors and assorted massagers of mind and body" (Lee 86). There is a booming business for those who want to cash in on New Age products. As Douglas McDonald, editor at Amazon.com says, "Religion and spirituality is one of the top categories at Amazon.com in unit sales" (Marty 879). Bear & Co.'s "Medicine Cards," based on American Indian animal folklore, are the "hottest product in our line," says publicist Jody Winters, with worldwide sales of over 1 million copies (Garrett 39). Bumper stickers, Goddess icons, crystals, recorded books, and spiritual documentaries are available not only at New Age bookstores but also frequently at major bookstores and other mass-market venues. Even mainstream commercials include yoga, and major beverage companies use New Age "health" marketing to increase sales.

Who, then, buys these products? The "typical profile" of a New Age customer "is a white, upscale female, age 35–65, who may have been raised within a Judeo-Christian tradition who is in search of more spirituality or alternative spirituality and a continuum of mind, body, and spirit," states Jerry Clow, owner of a large, independent New Age publishing house (Jones 45). Furthermore, New Age consumption patterns seem to be largely middle to upper middle class: a 1988 poll documents, "91 percent of *New Age Journal*'s subscribers are college educated, with an averaged household income of nearly $42,000 and a median age of 39.5" (Wilson 37).[18] By and large, white women are the largest consumers of New Age products, as workshop and book sales indicate, and their consumption patterns have spread beyond a particular niche and into the mainstream. In a recent study, 89 percent of alternative medicines were purchased by women (Easthope and Rayner 167). According to Amy Hertz, an editor at HarperCollins San Francisco's "spiritual division," "Open up any women's magazine—and they're all kind of closet New Age magazines" (Jones 47). At *O, The Oprah Magazine*, which had the "most successful launch in the history of magazine publishing," editors say, "Women are looking for meaning in their lives . . . it's the right message at the right time" (Gonser 26). It is no coincidence that *O*, which as the editors suggest is "about looking inside yourself," is bought by over 2 million women (Kelly).

In New Age culture, money has been seen as both benevolent and harmful. Marilyn Ferguson's *The Aquarian Conspiracy*, a central book in New Age culture, encourages readers to turn away from material goods and advocates practices such as "voluntary simplicity" (living simply with few material goods). On the other hand, Rhonda Byrne's best seller, *The Secret*, sees money as having benevolent energy, and the author tells readers how to invoke more money by visualizing it. In spite of these mixed messages, the New Age lesson is that if you change your orientation to money, money will come to you. As Paul Heelas explains, "Prosperity teachings can thus be located in terms of that central trajectory of the cultural history of the self in the West: the development of the notion that something lies within; that it can be tapped and improved; and that it can then enable the person to operate more successfully in obtaining what the world has to offer" (*New Age Movement* 108). This sense of endless self-improvement and work combines money and spirituality in the ever-present "American Dream," though Lisa Aldred calls it "spiritual rationalizations for wealth" and social inequity ("Money Is Just Spiritual Energy" 72). Cloaking finance in the language of the spiritual has a particular allure for women—it gives women the power to have money, but with a tempered, spiritual gloss. Earning and managing money becomes not only a woman's right but a virtue. Handling finances is a powerful self-esteem enhancer, when many women have not been trained or given access to money strategies. Suze Orman, financial expert, combines New Age spirituality with financial advice to teach women, in particular, how to change their orientation to money. While many women benefit from understanding their finances, the average questing New Ager is often depicted as a woman who ravenously purchases material objects.

David Brooks derides just such material consumption in his book *Bobos in Paradise: The New Upper Class and How They Got There.* Brooks describes Bobos, or bourgeois bohemians, as the mostly white "educated class" in fin-de-siècle America that has a foot in both the bourgeois and bohemian worlds (rather than being part of either exclusively, as was common in the 1950s to 1970s). Brooks's Bobos fit the demographic profile of New Age consumer. Most importantly, in Brooks's chapter on spirituality, the Bobo is gendered female, though in the rest of his book, Brooks does not either mention gender or single out the female Bobo. This female Bobo imagines heaven as the accumulation of material goods. While Brooks extends Bellah's study on the negative effects of individualism, known as "Sheilaism," he depicts the spiritual female consumer through "Boboism."[19] The picture from these two studies, spanning roughly forty years of upper-middle-class white American spiritual life, is reducible to two images: the first of a woman, Sheila, who is mocked for seeking God in a sloppy theological manner, and the second of a woman, a female Bobo, whose vision of spiritual paradise is conspicuous consumption.

Bobos keep spiritual depression at bay by drawing on bohemianism. Only Bobo bohemianism is reduced to purchasing goods with hippie aesthetics but a yuppie price tag. In Bobo morality, there is no contradiction between spiritual seeking and accumulating wealth. Heaven is the perfect home full of antimaterial material goods. Brooks describes Bobo spirituality:

> Picture a saintly Bobo woman pausing on her Montana hilltop at dusk, with thoughts of her law practice or mutual funds or teaching load far away. . . . As she approaches the house [her second home], she can hear the soundtrack of a Merchant-Ivory

film wafting up to greet her; the melodies echo off the walls of
the outbuildings that now serve as guest cottages. The biggest
thing they had to do when they moved in to this place was to
triple the size of all the windows. . . . The living room is large
but spare. The furniture is rustic but comfortable. There are
three of those massive curl-up chairs, each the size of a comfy
Volkswagen. . . . The Bobo glances at the wooden ladles she has
been collecting. She is taken by their slender curves, and prizes
them more than any of the other objects she has harvested
during her counter-connoisseur browsings. . . . Her favorite
statue is of the Bodhisattva, the spiritual entity who achieved
enlightenment but delays entry into Nirvana in order to help
others get there. (253)

After the long description of the Bobo's survey of her material goods, she
sees the Angel of Death who tells her that though she has just died "she
gets to exist forever amidst all this glorious materiality . . . in a New Age
eternity" (254). While this Bobo is ostensibly on a spiritual retreat, her
peace comes not from inner seeking but from the security of her material
aesthetic.

Bobo spirituality is not spiritual but material. Here, smooth wooden
spoons, large chairs, extensive lighting from windows, and spare decora-
tions all signal upper-class simplicity, or the ability to have fewer items of
high quality rather than many of lower quality. Attaining "spiritual
enlightenment" requires moving up in the class hierarchy and purchasing
the goods of said class. This is a bleak view of spiritual life indeed—there
is no space for any authentic inward or communal spiritual experience,
only the lust to consume. The only direct mention of an actual spiritual
orientation is the gesture to the bodhisattva statue, a female deity who
practices self-sacrifice for others. This gesture is the crowning touch on
Bobo satire. It also indicates Brooks's belief that while the female Bobo
can shop to meet her spiritual needs, she cannot make sacrifices for
others, a request often made of women through motherhood, career, or
social expectation. Instead, the female Bobo is a pure consumer: she has
the authority to accumulate wealth and display her wealth to those
around her.[20] Heaven is a woman whose soul is cathected to her material
goods—she is inseparable from her aesthetic desires.

The ability of the female Bobo to turn "Eden into money" is precisely what alarms critics (Brooks 251). Scholar Mark Edmundson
describes the malaise he believes comes from "purchasing" spiritual
truths: "Devotees of easy transcendence—the self-help programs, the
spiritual journeys, the New Age philosophies—move so rapidly from

one to another, as though on an endless carousel . . . it suggests the despair that often underlies the current quest for self-renovation" (83). This "endless carousel" is spiritual capitalism, and for most critics religion must be wholly segregated from the marketplace. As Jeremy Carrette and Richard King argue, "God is dead and has been resurrected as capital" (1). By this logic, expressing spiritual seeking by amassing consumer goods and exchanging money for spiritual goods is blasphemous. From Buddha to Christ to Mohammed, spiritual enlightenment narratives require abandoning material pleasures, as well as undergoing rigorous spiritual trials. Typically, a lack of comfort is essential for spiritual progress. Or, at the very least, it includes what Catherine Jurca calls "sentimental dispossession" or "the affective dislocation by which white middle class suburbanites begin to see themselves as spiritually and culturally impoverished by prosperity" (7). But as Michael Brown points out, New Age seekers "reflect the new religious consumerism of our time, [and] pursue advice and treatment to address constantly shifting needs" (173). Therefore, certain New Age practices look "more like a boutique in the shopping mall of the New Age" than any conventional spirituality because they "mirror so perfectly the society in which [they] have arisen" (173). For most critics, "purchasing" spiritual goods is the opposite of finding religion privately or through a more "rigorous" means, such as the study of theology.

Consequently, most critics are horrified by the commodification of spiritual life, whether Suze Orman's best-selling *The Courage to Be Rich*, the promise of enlightenment through the spiritual objects that proliferate in New Age catalogs and stores, or the purchase of sanctioned New Age experiences through workshops and travel. Scholar Dana Cloud argues that New Age culture "dislocates political movements of the late 1960s into a track of personal lifestyle work and conspicuous consumption" (133). In the most cynical assessment, "New Age" is simply a predictable retreat of the professional managerial class away from the boredom of money and whiteness into the thrills of soul seeking in other ethnicities and religions, a kind of spiritual imperialism. Scholar Andrew Ross suggests that the New Age may be just another invention of capitalism and is therefore wholly contained within it: "Perhaps there is nothing more to be observed here than the old Marxist lesson that a dominant culture has the power to engender an opposition in its own image" (532). Consuming New Age objects appears to be countercultural when it is not. As Kimberly Lau warns, we have succumbed to a kind of "false consciousness" about the New Age: "Despite the fact that the commodified discourses which constitute the public sphere of alternative health sound and feel and seem political, consumption is not political action. Believing it to be so is perhaps the greatest risk of modernity" (140).

I would argue that the fear of New Age consumption being a "risk" to "modernity" is similar to what critics Rita Felski and Andreas Huyssen have noted about how nineteenth-century critics viewed women's consumption habits. Felski writes that "the consumer was frequently represented as a woman" who began to shop in newly created department stores: "The emergence of a culture of consumption helped to shape new forms of subjectivity for women, whose intimate needs, desires, and perceptions of self were mediated by public representations of commodities and the gratifications they promised" (61). When women participate in structures of commodification, they are not simply duped capitalist pawns but participants in complex systems of meaning and longing. However, most critics see consumption as ruining orthodox religion, an aesthetic that includes "good politics" and hard religion. Again, this divide is strikingly similar to how nineteenth-century critics viewed crowds and "the mass" as the engulfing, ravishing, feminine. As Andreas Huyssen notes, "The gendering of mass culture as feminine and inferior has its primary historical place in the late nineteenth century, even though the underlying dichotomy did not lose its power until quite recently" (62). In relation to New Age culture, this dichotomy between the "high and the low" has not lost its power at all. Rather, the New Age feminine has been wholly mapped onto mass culture, which relies on the "exclusion of women from high culture and its institutions" (Huyssen 62).

Because women are still excluded from the upper levels of religious institutions in the United States, many purchase spiritual goods to meet their needs. According to scholar Paula Nesbitt, the most prestigious and gratifying positions go to men in the clergy, even while women do much of the ministry and are attending divinity schools in record numbers. A recent study indicated that "even though 60 percent of American churchgoers are women, the clergy remains overwhelmingly male" (Bowers). When access to religious institutions (read as high culture in contrast to mass culture) remains challenging, women participate in religious and spiritual mass culture, which is immediate, accessible, and fulfilling. For many women, the freedom to choose and/or purchase spiritual practices is a source of power, not despair. By now, many theorists such as Jennifer Scanlon, John Fiske, and Erika Rappaport have suggested that consumption is multilayered and gendered: indeed, in New Age culture women's relationship to spiritual commodities represents a complex power negotiation between the private and public sphere.

In New Age culture, women consume goods for "home shaman-ism," or the ability to actualize their own mystical spiritual practice. This power to consume New Age goods that can be used for home altars (like the Bobo's bodhisattva) or ritual has not been investigated. For many women, adopting spiritual goods is one of the easiest ways to have a spir-itual practice, especially when many women work outside of the home, work the "second shift" in the home, and perhaps cannot afford to take on "rigorous" spiritual training because of a shortage of time and/or money. By using animal medicine cards, angel cards, boxes of runes, crystal packs, colorful wands, or tarot cards, a woman can quickly draw on spiritual guidance, as does Beverly Barre, age forty-seven, whose daily ritual follows:

> Each morning in her Phoenix home, Barre practices yoga, medi-tating before a small altar adorned with a crystal, a cross, and a small Buddha. These items, she says, represent "the power" and "the energy" from which all things come. Her daily ritual includes drawing from a small deck three cards that feature an angel on one side and the words that will predict her day on the other side. . . . She purifies her home by using the American Indian practice of burning sage. (Perkes 54)

All of these items give women a sense that they can pull, say, an animal medicine card on any given day and believe that an animal spirit may come to them in a dream or through the body of an actual animal and deliver spiritual wisdom. I would argue that it is no mistake that one publisher said, "New Age has become very similar to the self-help move-ment: people are looking for more how-to spirituality, rather than for spiritual teachers who have reached some enlightened state" (Garrett and Kinsella 39). In that way, women use these items to fulfill their own spir-itual needs rather than turn to an external authority for answers. If some-thing is missing in their spiritual lives, then they can purchase a new spiritual tool (such as a box of runes) to augment their home rituals.

White women are also the largest consumers of New Age books, which serve as a kind of informal liturgy for conducting a service in the privacy of their own home for a congregation of one—herself. Books play a central role in women's participation in New Age culture—they are easily purchased and more affordable than many therapeutic treat-ments, and female authors dominate a market of self-help titles. Further-more, books are used in various ways, other than just being read quietly alone in the home. Wendy Kaminer vilifies these texts that "shine with moral vanity" (129).[21] What bothers Kaminer is the "complacency and

childlike passivity encouraged by these books" and the "habits of unreason they encourage" (127). Indeed, Kaminer is right in that they privilege
"personal truths and personal testimony over logic and verifiable fact"
(127). While more sympathetic to New Age culture, ultimately Edmundson suggests that books such as *The Celestine Prophecy* and Thomas
Moore's *Care of the Soul* are "visions of the therapeutic sublime [which]
so lack the true element of resistance to their vaunting hopes that they
stand as little more than spiritual travel guides for those who never
intend to leave home" (102). The critique that books are merely "travel
guides" has gendered implications, however.

New Age women use books as "spiritual travel guides" when they
cannot leave home because of familial obligations.[22] "Spiritual travel
guides" are valuable for women in particular who have historically not
been able to take more "traditional" spiritual journeys. Typically, spiritual journeys have an archetypal trajectory: young man leaves home,
experiences spiritual trials, and may return to begin a family and/or
become a deity. In *The Feminine Face of God*, Sherry Anderson and
Patricia Hopkins document how in androcentric religious traditions
"home-leaving" means to "sever relationships" when beginning a spiritual quest (46). In numerous interviews with women, Anderson and
Hopkins found that because of familial responsibilities, few women
could embark on a radical journey and leave their kin, and thus the traditional spiritual apprenticeship had to be reconceived. They found that
unlike "virtually every male spiritual seeker from the Buddha to the
knights of the Holy Grail" who did leave home, the women they spoke
with had made "their connection with the sacred before they ever left
home" (49). New Age books and objects provide an equal-opportunity
resource for spiritual growth—they are relatively affordable compared to
an actual trip, and they promise guidelines for initiation into the power
of healing and even "ministry."

But the use of New Age objects is not just for individual self-help; it
is also for building community. Sociologists Mears and Ellison found
that purchasers of New Age materials form "social or familial ties to
other New Age consumers" and thus have a community in part through
reading and sharing similar books, CDs, and so on (308). As on numerous Web sites, such as best-selling author Lynn Andrews's site, women
and men form a virtual community by e-mailing and discussing her
books, workbooks, and classes. This is similar to the Oprah Book Club,
where women form a community by joining book groups: they read the
Oprah selections; they use the questions in the back of their books to
guide their discussion; they tune in to Oprah's show to watch a discussion of the book with the author; and they follow up online for further

topical chats. Oprah's Book Club, like other New Age Web sites and programs in New Age bookstores, creates a vast informational network. Writer Marilyn Johnson suggests that "half a million reading groups link a sisterhood of women" who feel that their book club is "the fire we gather around . . . like the fire in *The Clan of the Cave Bear*" (32). Some have even suggested that this explosion in women's book clubs is akin to the feminist movement's earlier consciousness-raising (CR) groups. Consumerism not only gives women purchasing power but allows them to build communities through shared experience, such as readings, as well as educate themselves into a kind of "priesthood" where they can initiate their own religious services.

In one of the only studies on the actual use of space in New Age bookstores, Nurit Zaidman argues that New Age bookstores are not just capitalist enterprises but spiritual zones (371). In his study of New Age bookstores in New Zealand and Israel, he discovered that not only did the bookstore serve as an actual spiritual space even as it was a commodified one, but that booksellers also viewed their role as facilitator of spiritual questing rather than just a capitalist convenience (372). Store owners would even go so far as to accept lower profits in order to maintain the spiritual community of the store. Zaidman suggests that contrary to all of the other scholarship that discusses the "unlimited commercialization" of the New Age, at New Age bookstores store owners steer customers toward items to enhance spiritual growth rather than just put cash in the till (371). Zaidman's study is critical. Unfortunately, gender is not a major category of analysis in examining consumer patterns (perhaps I should say ironically, since repeatedly we have seen how the New Age consumer is synonymous for "woman"). Because these consumption patterns related to New Age and alternative spiritualities are underresearched, we cannot grasp the pragmatic, strategic, everyday spiritual realities of women who appear to be consuming but may actually be spiritually searching.

Irrationality and Hysteria in the New Age

Even as women pay for products and services to serve their own ends, critics continue to feel that New Age consumers have lost their minds to quack products, gurus, and even diseases. New Age culture is often regarded as consummately irrational. Critics decry that it is a "rejection of the rationalistic base of modern society" (Lippy 211) and a "denigration of rationalism" (Kaminer 129). Susan Jacoby, in *The Age of American Unreason,* calls irrationality "junk thought" and says it

"greatly expanded its reach during the seventies, as onetime social protesters retreated into narcissistic New Age and self-help movements"
(217). According to Wendy Kaminer, "Recovery movement gurus,
experts on angels, and other aficionados of New Age, as well as adherents of mainstream religions, traffic in 'feeling realities.' They exhort us
ultimately to rely on our hearts" and to "ignore reason" (6). Critics fret
that New Age beliefs will drag American culture back into the "Dark
Ages," where mysticism and feeling reign over science. Indeed, New
Agers are skeptical of Western knowledge and privilege "feeling" over
knowing. New Age narratives often narrate spiritual self-discovery as a
movement from the "head" to the "heart." But the accusation of being
overly emotional, hysterical, and/or irrational is one of the oldest forms
of misogyny, and one that has been extensively critiqued by feminist
scholars. Few critics have scrutinized the gendered valence of judgments
against the "irrational." Without seeing the latent misogyny of such critiques, one might believe that these accusations against New Age beliefs
are value-neutral and founded on science and reason instead of being
slightly hysterical reactions to a feared feminized culture. In this section,
I survey how this fear operates in three different depictions of New Age
irrationality.

One critic of the New Age who is surprisingly unaware of her
gender bias is feminist Elaine Showalter. In *Hystories: Hysterical Epidemics and Modern Media*, Showalter sets out to save American culture
from hysterical maladies. She feels that various syndromes and disorders
such as chronic fatigue syndrome, multiple personality disorder, and
recovered memory syndrome destroy rational liberal democracy.
Notably, these diseases are almost exclusively female maladies. The threat
of a "ruined democracy" is projected onto white middle-class women,
who use emotional rhetoric because of a lack of access to actual power.
White middle-to-upper-class women get these maladies for reasons that
have not been researched thoroughly yet: some women need covert out-
lets to express their needs when they are exhausted. However, Showalter
is afraid that these diseases, which she sees as founded on hysteria, might
"reverse" feminism: "Feminists have an ethical as well as an intellectual
responsibility to ask tough questions about the current narratives of illness, trauma, accusation, and conspiracy" (13). Ironically, Showalter does
not suggest that feminists have a responsibility to ask why so many
women are getting sick in the first place.

Instead, Showalter indirectly blames women for leading the culture
into irrationality. By not placing her subject matter within a larger conversation about subculture, ideology, and gender, Showalter is left simply
to say, "If we can begin to understand, accept, pity, and forgive ourselves

for the psychological dynamics of hysteria, perhaps we can begin to work together to break the crucible and avert the coming hysterical plague" (207). Showalter falls prey to the very hysteria she rejects. Rather than seeing how these diseases are ideologically constructed, she reverts to a humanist psychological model (the one she ostensibly critiques) to "solve" this "problem" of hysteria. Her argument implies that women are "ruining" any gains made by feminism: "the hysterical epidemics of the 1990s have already gone on too long, and they continue to do damage: in distracting us from the real problems and crises of modern society, in undermining a respect for evidence and truth, and in helping support an atmosphere of conspiracy and suspicion" (206). Showalter has the sense that *something* is happening "out there" in mass culture that is sullying the "real" work of hard science and that threatens to atomize government and culture if we ignore it.

Another medium that explores the issues of New Age irrationality, hysteria, and disease—the issues that so alarm critics such as Showalter—is the film *Safe* (1995), directed by Todd Haynes. *Safe* depicts the life of Carol White, a suburban Los Angeles housewife who gets environmental illness (EI). With EI, one's body develops allergic reactions and sensitivities to the multiple chemicals and pollutants that exist in daily life, from common household cleaners to pesticides and car emissions.[23] EI is exactly the kind of disease that Showalter believes women and men—mainly women—make up. Like many who get EI, Carol initially has no idea what is happening to her body: she is mystified and frightened by her sudden nosebleeds, asthma, and fainting as her body slowly breaks down from toxicity. And as Carol gets sicker, her friends, doctors, and husband exhibit responses ranging from wariness to disbelief. Eventually, Carol abandons conventional medicine—which has only suggested she is crazy—and chooses to attend a New Age center, Wrenwood, where, for better or worse, people finally believe her.

Carol is a classic example of a hysteric—she cannot speak or act, and so her body must. At the beginning of *Safe*, Carol's friends have a conversation about a New Age book that indicates a thematic current of the film—lack of agency. One friend says, "I just eventually found the whole twelve-step thing was like another form of addiction." Another friend says, "That's exactly what this book is saying—it's about how to own your own life. What he's saying is that we don't really own our own life. We're taught what to do, what to think, but emotionally we're not really in charge." Indeed, Carol and her friends do not seem emotionally in charge but, rather, emotionally empty. If any characters interact at all in the first part of the film, it is in disjointed, halting speech. Unable to express herself verbally, Carol's body does the talking: as Carol gets sicker, her body rejects the banal, rich husband; the large, empty house; the subservient, Latina maid; and, ultimately, the twentieth-century urban culture that spawned all of the toxins that are killing her. As Carol loses control of her body, she seems to gain control of her self. When she asks "Who am I?" it is clear that the question has crossed her mind for the first time. While the "self" Carol discovers may not be her own construction, at least there is an inquiry where there had been none.

Whether or not Carol's disease is real is at the heart of critics' questions about the authenticity of these seemingly irrational maladies. And what appears to be the solution to Carol's problems, her discovery of New Age glory at Wrenwood, may be her downfall. Haynes's film satirizes the head of Wrenwood, Peter Dunning, a gay man with chronic fatigue syndrome, EI, and AIDS. Peter preaches about loving one's immune system back into health, and, in the worst New Age fashion, he believes that we are ultimately responsible for our illnesses. As film critic Chuck Stephens points out, "As this fuzzy-wuzzy guru cajoles his followers into an endgame of self-blame . . . Haynes adopts an apparently straight-forward observational mode that does nothing to contradict him, searching beyond the satire to explore the desperate need for control and punishment that slowly courses through millennial America's aging veins" (79). Peter tells Carol things she has clearly never heard: "We can look in each other's eyes and see personal transformation and growth—why? We've left the judgmental self behind—all the judging and shaming." These are strong words for a woman who is terribly sick, does not understand why, and has virtually no support system. While so many critics castigate New Age platitudes such as these, Haynes rides the fence on how meaningful these "truths" may be and whether they make Carol well emotionally, even as her body gets sicker.

By the end of the film, Carol seems to have lost her body, even if she has gained herself. After Claire, a Wrenwood counselor, tells Carol that when she had EI "every day I would sit in my room and look in the mirror and say, 'Claire, I love you, I really love you,'" Carol mouths these same words to herself in the mirror at the film's end. Over the course of the film, the cinematography mirrors Carol's experience of her life: at the beginning of the film, the frame situates her in static poses within a wide screen. She literally takes up little space and seems devoid of any personality. Slowly, as her disease worsens, the camera comes closer and closer like a skeptical investigator, until the end of the film when a close-up of Carol's face fills the screen. As the camera closes in on Carol, now at her unhealthiest and living in a porcelain dome "safe house," we see her face with a lesion growing on her forehead. Yet Carol says, "I love you, I really love you." While most critics could scoff at self-love as a physical healing practice, it is unclear where Haynes and the viewer should be positioned. The viewer feels uneasy whether or not to take Carol seriously when she mouths the words "I really love you" in an effort to save herself. When Claire says that when she had EI "everything got taken away in the material world and what was left was me," critics would respond that "what was left" after falling prey to a hysterical malady was a skewed sense of narcissism called "me," not any kind of authentic self. Haynes is ambivalent about whether or not Carol has an awakening. This ambiguity makes the film intriguing rather than purely didactic. Haynes says he was drawn to ask of New Age philosophies, "What is it about these philosophies that make the sufferer of incurable illnesses feel more at peace? Why do we choose culpability over chaos?" (Stephens 80). Those who are choosing "culpability" are often women and/or people who are vulnerable and sick with EI, AIDS, and other incurable diseases. Few have ascertained that those most likely to blame themselves (women and the marginalized) are the very ones doing so and trying desperately to replace bad thoughts with good ones.

Most critics of New Age culture do not believe that maladies such as EI exist in the first place, and they argue that even if treatment were needed, it should be scientific and medical, not emotional and spiritual. The emphasis on the emotional healing of physical or spiritual ailments disturbs many critics and is not "healing" but rank narcissism. Critic Mel Faber dismissively characterizes New Age "pathologies" as hysterical, narcissistic reactions to problems and breaks them down into two main misguided notions, which are

> first, the overarching presence of *infantile omnipotence*, the ego-centric, unconscious belief in one's unlimited power as those powers are derived (and internalized) from the omnipotent caregiver of life's first years (the phenomenology here is the *baby's, not* the caregiver's); [and] second, the urge to *fuse regressively* with the environment, to attach oneself to the surrounding world (universe) in a way that denies . . . the ever-present sense of *separation* which the chronologically mature individual must cope with during the course of his days on the planet. (7, emphases in original)

Faber's analysis suggests that some form of self-obsession, if not insanity, underlies New Age diseases. Not surprisingly, he places the blame for such diseases on mothers. Faber claims that mothers do not help their children to separate from them effectively, and thus they create weak-willed and self-obsessed children who are susceptible to every kind of irrationality (26). Ultimately, then, New Age women are twice blamed: first, for giving credence to irrational beliefs to such a degree that anything from contracting bizarre and unfounded diseases to visiting a shaman begins to seem "normal"; and, second, for being the bad mothers who fostered such irrational tendencies in the first place.

Though critics accuse New Age women of narcissism, rampant consumerism, and hysteria, such behavior may have an underlying gendered logic. What some see as hysterical, others call liberatory. As one New Age woman said about why she sought alternative medicine, "When I had breast cancer 17 years ago, I was very passive and gave the doctors all the authority." Now attending a "wellness week" workshop at the Omega Institute, a New Age center, she says, "It's wonderful to have something you can do to get better. That is empowerment" (Wallis 71). For many, her practices of yoga, meditation, and eating organic food are no longer considered "irrational" but beneficial. However, in the 1960s, practicing yoga, meditating, or consuming organic food was considered countercultural and often a cause for alarm. In fact, when sitcom star and "thigh master" pioneer Suzanne Somers decided to seek out homeopathic treatments for her breast cancer and forego chemotherapy and radiation, there was a huge backlash.[24] People wrote numerous letters, in shock that Somers would choose such an unconventional treatment and take her health in her own hands, without using Western medicine. Repeatedly in New Age narratives, when women try to heal themselves in some way, critics mock their attempts as irrational. Surprisingly, critics do not recognize how Western medicine has sometimes been detrimental to women. It was not so long ago, for instance, that breast cancer was a severely underresearched form of cancer. It is not surprising that some women would rather learn techniques to heal themselves than leave their healing to an external authority, no matter how qualified.

However, critics deem New Age women kooky. When the *New York Times* published a piece on Roxanne Louise, a hypnotherapist, Reiki master, and director of Unlimited Potential (her own "healing" company), letters to the editor contained complaints that reporters should not waste column space on such irrational and unfounded "healers." But many New Age beliefs are based on a renewed interest in "intuition," or on an individual's belief that she or he has the answers internally. For some women, especially those with abusive pasts, using "intuition" may be a provocative tool after having little agency. Louise, in her Reiki practice, uses a pendulum to divine where she should work on a person's body, and that information, along with her own ability to "read" body energy fields, tells her how to heal her clients. Contrary to the New Age stereotype, she, like many New Age women, has some skepticism about her work: "Am I necessarily right? Maybe yes, maybe no. I may be hallucinating the whole thing. But if someone has a problem, and I help remove it, then what? Nobody can tell you what the truth is. We have models of reality. Everybody has a different view" (Kannapell 4). Interestingly, Louise articulates a "quasi-feminist" view of knowledge that it is located and situated, not universal. Rather than use feminist terms, Louise draws on New Age paradigms—even while it has been feminists who have critiqued Western medicine for often using women's bodies in the name of science, medicine, and truth. Louise tries to assert her own authority for healing when little authority has been given her.

Furthermore, critics have neglected the trajectory of New Age women's spiritual autobiography, which often moves from extreme trauma and abuse to spiritual liberation. In the story of Louise, the reporter makes no connection to her current New Age practices when she narrates "a miserable 14–year marriage to a man she describes as a raging alcoholic" (Kannapell 4). Once Louise says about her new life as a New Age healer and teacher, "I make things happen, I don't wait for life to happen," it is not surprising that New Age beliefs buttress her (Kannapell 4). Louise looks for practices that validate her inner spiritual sensibilities as well as make her spiritually powerful in order to ward off past trauma. These ostensibly irrational, hysterical practices often provide New Age women with tools for finding agency in the midst of either personal trauma or the cultural trauma of confronting Western medicine.

The Culture Impotent: Conclusions about the Fear of the New Age Feminine

Women in New Age culture experience many of the rituals, healing methods, and self-improvement techniques not just as spiritual self-exploration but also as a validation of themselves as women. While New Age practices such as Goddess worship explicitly embrace the feminine as divine and often have an explicitly feminist political stance, other New Age practices are still implicitly feminist. New Age practices encourage women to look for spiritual life within the self rather than finding it in an external patriarchal authority; to consume spirituality outside of mainstream religion by purchasing books, attending workshops, and doing lay training in any number of New Age practices, from channeling to performing energy work; and to heal the female body by making it as healthy as possible through diet, massage, and crystal healing, as well as by embracing alternative medicine.

In numerous books and workshops, female New Age authors such as Shakti Gawain, Clarissa Pinkola Estes, and Louise Hay emphasize "power" constantly—becoming a female warrior, taking control of one's life, and even drawing on a more essentialized "feminine" power. Steven Sutcliffe claims that "the typical actor in 'New Age' is a religious individualist, mixing and matching cultural resources in an animated spiritual quest. Standing in sharp contrast to traditional participatory roles in Anglo-American religion such as 'member,' 'communicant,' 'congregant,' or 'convert,' we can call this actor a 'seeker'" (200). The fear of the feminization of American culture is a fear not just of stereotyped "women's values" but a fear of an articulation of a new powerful spiritual sensibility, especially one of "seeking." Indeed, many New Age claims that women make are quasi-feminist claims, although New Age culture does not articulate feminism's sweeping gender-focused platforms that have made so many systemic legal, political, and social changes. Interestingly, while there is no more a single "feminism" than a single "New Age culture," there are definite similarities among women in feminism and in New Age culture, though most feminist academics would be loath to admit it. As long as the analytical emphasis continues to be on establishing the difference between these two communities and rejecting what is seen as solipsistic or irrational within the New Age (channeling, aliens, past-life regression), then what is common to both discourses will remain invisible—that is, the quest for gender "self-actualization."

Other critics continue to fear that as in nineteenth-century America when "religion was given over to women, in its content and in its membership," American spirituality may once again have been "given over to women," which is seen as a negative, volatile change (LeBeau 131). Perhaps historian Gary Wills best articulates this fear of what may happen to American spirituality now that many women have left traditional religions:

> With women no longer presiding, along with their ministers, over their "own" realm of religion, morality, and higher culture, religion faces a difficult choice: It must try to maintain the old sphere without its principal ally and patron [women], or it must follow those patrons (mothers and culture consumers) into the secular world. (277)

For many critics, the outcome of the "realm of religion" is wholly dependent upon "women"; a gendered logic persists that where women go spiritually, there too goes the nation. But many women currently—

"mothers and culture consumers"—find a middle ground between being aligned with a "minister" and entering the "secular world." New Age practices allow women to have an inner authority that bridges the world of established religion and the marketplace, blurring the boundaries between the two in a freeing way. Even as critics warn that these practices will lead to national decline, New Age women find them provocative and satisfying. And if, as critic Guillermo Gomez-Pena notes, "Radical politics was to the '80s and early '90s what 'radical spirituality' is to the twenty-first century," then the intersection of New Age spirituality, gender, and culture will need to be recognized as a site of white female empowerment (25). While many dismiss these New Age women, practitioners find their reconstituted spirituality regenerative as they continue to carve out new identities understood by few.

2

"The Indian Way Is What's *Inside*"

Gender and the Appropriation of American Indian Religion in New Age Culture

> Playing Indian has become a national American pastime.
> —*Kathryn W. Shanley*

At an "American Indian rituals" weekend at a nearby retreat center attended almost entirely by women, I sat across the dinner table from two other white women, whom I will call Sara and Kate.[1] As we were eating, I asked them, "What brought you to this weekend?" Sara said, "I've always been interested in gardening and vegetarian food, and it just seems like the Native way of life is very close to the earth and incorporates the things I believe in." Kate nodded and remarked that after participating in a sweat lodge (a sacred Indian ritual), "I began reading Lynn Andrews's books. I just love her stories of these powerful old Native women." Sara replied, "Don't you just feel the need to be eldered?" As I watched Sara and Kate emphatically nod their heads "yes," that they needed to be "eldered" or mentored by an older, wiser woman, I realized with both surprise and reservation that this nearly all-female weekend might have less to do with American Indians than it has to do with gender.

For women like Sara and Kate, "Native rituals" were less about gaining knowledge of American Indian culture than about experiencing personal power as women and bonding with other white women. Was it possible, then, that pursuing all things Indian was actually a means to a different end—a transformed gender identity? And did this "gender empowerment" matter when the whole retreat was starting to look like a textbook case of racial appropriation? Indeed, when I asked Kate who had led her sweat lodge and if there were any Native people present, she did not know on either score. Whatever fantasies of gender empowerment Kate and Sara might share—fantasies of "healing Mother Earth," rejecting "patriarchal" meat consumption, learning about "powerful old Native women" and being "eldered"—they existed alongside unacknowledged racial appropriation. That is, while putatively honoring American Indian traditions, such retreats can all too easily become a place to honor oneself—the white woman improved, with a new ethnic flavor.

Kate and Sara, of course, are not alone in their fetishization of American Indian culture. The celebration of "Indian ways" gained momentum in the late 1960s. As American New Age culture emerged, white artists such as Carlos Castaneda, who wrote about his Yaqui teacher, began to document their Native experiences in popular spiritual autobiographies. As whites chronicled all they had gained from American Indian wisdom, they also gained monetarily from these hugely successful books, workshops, and travel adventures based on their descriptions of "the Indian" as "communitarian, environmentally wise, [and] spiritually insightful" (Philip Deloria 174). Indian writer Sherman Alexie calls this "the romantic myth of the spiritual Indian," where all Indians are expected to embody an impossible and annoying *Dances with Wolves* or *Pocahontas* stereotype (qtd. in Safransky). In an attempt to take on such characteristics themselves—to explore their inner Indian—whites bought various pieces of Native paraphernalia, items such as dream catchers, stylized paintings of noble Indians, and carpets with Indian patterns. As scholar S. Elizabeth Bird notes, "In the 1990s, as never before, Indians were chic. . . . New Age culture appropriated Indian religious practices, clothing, music, and myths, while Indian-inspired art and design became all the rage" (76).

Such consumption of Indian practices by whites has not gone uncontested. Several Indian tribes declared warfare on "Shake and Bake shamans" or "plastic medicine people," whom they accuse of claiming Indian blood, taking Indian rituals, and spreading lies about Indian culture (Aldred, "Plastic Shamans and Astroturf Sun Dances" 331).[2] This spiritual and material appropriation of Indian beliefs and practices has been seen by some tribes as a form of spiritual genocide. Typically, appropriators are accused of stealing—stealing a community's resources, stealing the right to perform rituals, stealing the profits from these rituals and objects, and, ultimately, stealing the very right to control what is and is not stealing (Ziff and Rao 24). Often theorists who are concerned about appropriation "describe a community of insiders and outsiders" that is "incontestable" (Ziff and Rao 3). This "incontestability" of whether one is an "insider" or an "outsider" of a community affects the racial logic of appropriation: if you are "in" the community, then you can take from it, and if you are "out" of the community, then taking is stealing. This dynamic, however, depends on a stable cultural identity based in "ethnic or racial authenticity," which has been debunked by theorists such as James Clifford, Walter Benn Michaels, and others. As scholar Eric Lott points out, "A dismantling of binary racial categories in favor of multiply determined and positioned subjects has begun to trouble the notion of 'racial' representation itself" (8). Thus while I agree that whites abuse Indian religions for their own benefit, we must critique their investments without invoking an untenable and politically suspect idea of ethnic authenticity.

By assuming a direct and unequivocal relationship between appropriator and appropriated, those indicting others for appropriation erase the ways in which a given act of "appropriation" is mediated, and thus changed, by other social factors. This chapter will examine how inserting gender into the appropriation model does and does not transform it. The standard appropriation paradigm "invisibilizes" how race and gender are interconnected through the shared experience of oppression, though the experiences are by no means synonymous. These perceived affective bonds between oppressions, for all of their moral deficiencies and miscalculations, indicate how oppressed peoples can experience alliances and lines of affiliation, though these lines are tangled and not neatly bound together.

So far, the relationship between gender and the appropriation of contemporary American Indian culture has gone largely untheorized. When it has been examined, New Age white women's use of American Indian practices has been dismissed as entirely appropriative. In fact, in 1984, the American Indian Movement (AIM), known as the radical arm of Indian activism, blacklisted the two white authors I will be discussing, Lynn Andrews and Mary Summer Rain, for appropriating Indian religion. Scholars as well as Indian activists abhor Lynn Andrews and her "1990s snake-oil empire," as critic Micaela Di Leonardo calls it (37).[3] While Andrews, who is from Beverly Hills, California, has been called the "Beverly Hills Shaman" by some, others have called her the "Beverly Hills Witch" for her "commercial exploitation of indigenous spiritual traditions" (Aldred, "Plastic Shamans and Astroturf Sun Dances" 331). According to Di Leonardo, Andrews is an example of "dreadful women's self-help literature . . . which admonish[es] women not to challenge the outer world, but to get in touch with the goddess within, through learning from one or more types of female noble savage—of the 'correct' race/ethnicity, of course" (36). While Di Leonardo makes a crucial point about race fetishization, she also perpetuates the dismissal of Andrews on the grounds of racial appropriation, and yet she does not explain exactly how that appropriation operates nor examine the gendered valences of racial longing.

In one of the few analyses of Andrews's work, scholar Laura Donaldson sets out to explore how gender and race operate together, since "non-Native women increasingly employ Indian traditions to escape the patriarchal biases of monotheistic religions and to become empowered, as well as individuated" (677). Ultimately, Donaldson argues that Andrews's appropriation can only be understood as commodity fetishism leading to "postmodern neocolonialism" (681). Appropriation is "pure conquest" and gender is simply a means to an end—imperialism. Scholar Shari Huhndorf also argues that for Andrews, "going native—in this case through cross-cultural gender identification—participates in the process of conquest even as it denies its complicity" (184). Huhndorf compares one of Andrews's texts, *Medicine Woman*, to Mary Rowlandson's *The Sovereignty and Goodness of God*, an infamous eighteenth-century captivity narrative, and argues that Andrews creates a "New Age" captivity narrative that uses "spiritual knowledge" as "the last domain of conquest" (179). While I absolutely agree that white authors such as Andrews and Summer Rain "go Native" in ways that shore up white privilege, I want to examine those very structures that enable a racial transition and to understand how those structures build a New Age women's community founded in gender and race essentialism.

This chapter explores how two of the most influential white New Age women writing on Indian culture, Lynn Andrews and Mary Summer Rain, use "Indianness" to create a fantasy of gender authority. Both authors describe their experience of being a student to a female Indian shaman as a training in "feminine power." They move from feeling aimless and ineffective to feeling strong through the fantasy that Indians, Indian women in particular, have power.[4] Though this belief that female American Indians are particularly strong is not essentially Indian, Andrews and Summer Rain still attribute it to Indian culture through "imperialist nostalgia," or what Renato Rosaldo calls "a pose of 'innocent yearning' [employed] both to capture people's imaginations and to conceal its complicity with often brutal domination" (18). Despite the fact that their whiteness makes them "outsiders" to Indian culture, both authors create practices and beliefs that justify their transition to insider status. Over the course of their work, both white authors even claim to "be" Indian. Because of this, Andrews and Summer Rain have been perceived as the worst kind of appropriators, and their enormous popularity has been cited as proof of how whites steal Indian culture and get away with it. Both authors have been asked repeatedly through boycotts, magazine articles, and letters to their Web sites to stop stealing Indian practices. In spite of these demands, their book sales continue to climb.

I want to eliminate the false and unhelpful dichotomy of whether or not they are appropriators. Instead, this chapter takes as foundational the imperialism undergirding their desires for Indian culture, even as it examines how these authors use race to get to gender, and vice versa. These moves of cross-racial identification, which have had such a long and fraught history in the United States, are built on similar notions of how race and gender work, notions that say as much about gender as about race. Let me be perfectly clear: this is not an apology for the work of Andrews or Summer Rain but an exploration of how their "possessive investment in whiteness," to use George Lipsitz's well-known phrase, works hand in hand with their longing for female power at this particular historical moment. Within Andrews's and Summer Rain's work there exists not only a complicated longing for a certain gender identity but also an impulse for an alliance between women and Indians. Though this desire for an alliance is failed—Indians continue to reject both authors— Andrews and Summer Rain persist in describing a vision, albeit a flawed one, of social transformation. Somehow race allows them a gender identity that seemingly cannot be had through other means. Their sleight of hand in talking about race and gender—using one to stand in for the other—is essential to understanding the mechanisms of appropriation.

Sisterhood Is Powerful: From Gender to Race and Back Again in the Works of Lynn Andrews

Lynn Andrews is known as the "'female Carlos Castaneda'" and has been astonishingly successful as well as widely condemned (Bruchac). Di Leonardo notes, "[Andrews] is so popular that chain bookstores have whole shelves labeled for her" ("Gender, Culture, and Political Economy" 37). But her books are "so outlandish in their pretensions as to make Castaneda seem a model of propriety by comparison," notes Ward Churchill (189). Indeed, the line between truth and fiction in Andrews's work is as fuzzy as the line between an autobiography and a self-help workbook: not only does Andrews write the "truth" like fiction, but constant rumors also circulate that her stories are, in fact, fiction. Accusations abound that Andrews associates with other notorious appropriators of Native material, such as David Carson and Hyemeyohsts Storm. Still, Andrews continues to have devoted followers: her books are best sellers; she makes the rounds on the "New Age" circuit; her school has a curriculum, yearly gatherings, and an extensive Web site; and Andrews has even started to publish on "non-Native" topics such as menopause and relationships in her book *Love and Power*. In Andrews's New Age dynasty, she articulates her central purpose persistently—to teach the "ancient ways of woman" in order to heal "Mother Earth."

In her eighteen wildly popular books, her workbooks, and her school, "The Lynn Andrews Center for Sacred Arts and Training," (known as LACSAT), she documents her apprenticeship with two American Indian women, Agnes Whistling Elk and Ruby Plenty Chiefs. Using the genre of what one critic calls "visionary autobiography," Andrews structures her plots around several key lessons in her shamanic training:

> First, [Agnes Whistling Elk] wanted to make me physically strong. . . . Second, she placed me in situations where I learned to balance the maleness and femaleness within me. . . . Third, Agnes also taught me about making an act of power or an act of beauty in the world. . . . Last, Agnes made it clear to me, through paranormal events, my travels in Canada, and work in dreaming, that a person must be lifted out of her mechanical existence long enough so that real change and transformation has a chance to occur. (*Star Woman* 4)

Each book, which depicts an element of her training, functions on several different levels: as travel and adventure writing in exotic and dangerous locations, as anthropological exploration into the romanticized wisdom and knowledge of Native cultures, and as a true story with which her mostly white, middle-class, female readers can identify, and which they can replicate in the "home shamanism" of Andrews's companion workbooks.

But why are her works so popular, and who is buying them? Their popularity comes as much from their focus on the empowerment of women as from their description of American Indian practices. "An interest in feminine wisdom is on the rise," according to publishers, and women are longing for books by women authors "who have already embarked on a spiritual quest," says editor Amy Hertz (Winston 26). Hertz goes on to note, "A woman's spiritual journey may look different because we are different" (Winston 26). And Andrews accentuates that gender difference: the stories of her apprenticeship are stories of *female* power. It is not just that she is growing stronger spiritually, but that she is growing stronger as a woman. Whistling Elk tells her, "In writing the story of your experience, you have given some women a tool for going beyond. Women need that. If a woman makes an act of power, she's created something like a work of art" (*Flight of the Seventh Moon* 22).

Andrews's act of explicitly identifying as a woman makes her implicitly identify as Indian. She believes that this identification gives her the right to Indian practices. However, she does not appropriate Indian practices proper but instead inverts Indian practices to gain gender authority. The practices she describes are not actually Indian. She just names them as such to give them a fetish power. The historical and cultural reality of American Indians and their practices is less important to Andrews than constructing a mythical tradition of Indian female power. Historically, Indian women have most often been reduced to two stereotypes: the "Indian princess," like Pocahontas, who is the female counterpart to the "Noble Savage"; or the "Indian Squaw," the lustful and inhuman savage "who has sex indiscriminately with whites and Indians alike" (Bird 80). While obviously American Indian women's roles have been and continue to be infinitely more complex than these white stereotypes, Andrews still reduces Native women through "romantic racialism" to a grown-up "Pocahontas" stereotype (Fredrickson 101). Since she recognizes that American Indian women have been discriminated against, she imagines that "positive images" will remedy a racist situation. What Andrews constructs, then, is an older, mischievous, female "noble savage" who, like Pocahontas, "wants" to show Andrews the way to "true power," which is the power of women.

Understanding the oppression of women and Indians as analogous to each other forms the foundation of Andrews's racial logic: if women and Indians are yoked together by both experiencing oppression, then they have a "right" to one another's experience, teachings, and even identity.[5] Throughout her books, Andrews not only articulates this belief herself but also uses the voice of her primary Indian teacher, Agnes Whistling Elk, to back her up. As Whistling Elk argues: "I said long ago that native people stand in the place of the woman on mother earth. They are under siege, just like feminine consciousness" (*Windhorse Woman* 195). By feeling oppressed as a woman, Andrews believes she understands the oppression of Indians: she reasons that because women and American Indians both experience oppression, they must, therefore, be fundamentally alike.

Constant comparisons are made between women and Indians: they both experience oppression, they both have ancient wisdom, and they both have the power to heal a wounded earth. Andrews maintains that while women have "made enormous strides," "now we're moving into a time of much deeper spirituality," which "revolves around exploring the Goddess, Native American traditions, shamanic trainings, all kinds of spirituality that relate to Mother Earth and the firstness of woman," and that "men in power" are "creating a force field that would pull us [women] down at every moment" (*Dark Sister* xvi). Simultaneously, as Whistling Elk says, "The world sees the Indians as a conquered people. . . . Our real power is hidden" (*Flight of the Seventh Moon* 25). Both women and Indians are "under siege," and "native people, like woman, symbolically represent the regenerating principle of our mother the earth. They understand and should be keepers of the primal power of this planet" (*Windhorse Woman* 195). Gender and race, for Andrews, have an essential connectedness through what is "ancient" and "primal": "It is as if for centuries we [white women] have moved like chromosomal mutations isolated from the gene pools of the originally sacred, our primal female nature stolen from us, from the world pool, just as though it never existed" (*Jaguar Woman* 165).

Andrews discusses gender using a logic that is homologous to the logic of racial authenticity. She slides between gender and race because she perceives these terms to be synonymous. By retrieving a gender essence within a context in which the recovery of racial essence is always already assumed to be a worthwhile project, she can collapse the two projects into a single quest for the primal nature. Women can reclaim their "primal nature" and inner essence by following certain rituals. Whistling Elk reminds Andrews frequently that she is learning nothing new in her shamanic training but "remembering what you already knew" (*Jaguar Woman* 195). They (Andrews's white, middle-class, female audience) must "return" to that which is "originally sacred," and yet the paradox is that one cannot "return" to it because it is always already there as their true "nature," which has been "stolen" and must simply be comprehended to be regained. By going a step farther and utilizing "scientific" language such as "chromosomal mutations" and "gene pools," Andrews establishes the primacy of a racialized "pool" from which women were born and must return. Andrews, then, is always already Indian. She attempts to retrieve what has been stolen just as Indians also reclaim what has been stolen (land, grave sites, artifacts): in this case, Andrews uses her own "primal" nature as the equalizing justification for practices that restore the "gene pool."

The analogy between Indians and women is so strong that eventually Andrews takes out the mediating term of "women" and "becomes" Indian. By assuming an Indian identity, there is an implicit analogy between gender and race that is always at work, though not always visible on the surface of the text. This analogy reaches an apotheosis of racial identification such that she no longer makes it explicit. Andrews also gains acceptance through her initiation into the "Sisterhood of the

Shields," a secret society of shamanic women of color of which Andrews is the only white member. Most of Andrews's adventures are with this "Sisterhood," which is supposedly a "real" group of women, though Andrews has offered no further proof that they exist in "real" time, except to say that "We work together to this day" (Hughes). The Sisterhood has chosen to train Andrews in "tribal ways" so that she can go out and teach them to white people, and also hopefully transform white culture for the better. Through her initiation into the Sisterhood, Andrews again blurs the division between gender and race. While she acknowledges that she is allowed into the Sisterhood because of her gender, once she understands their teachings and rituals as a member of the Sisterhood, she in effect "becomes" a woman of color.

Not surprisingly, tensions arise from her cross-racial identification. Andrews is at once a fetishizer of women of color, and then also "one of them," related by oppression, "gene pool," and spiritual practices. We see this doubleness of her positioning on one of her quests for the "Sisterhood." When Andrews travels to South America, she sees it first as "other": "The energy of the Yucatan felt naked, as if thousands of years of life had worn away the usual veils a country wears to protect itself. It seemed as if the Yucatan stood nude before me. Her jungle and rain and foliage weren't hiding from me" (*Jaguar Woman* 38). The Yucatan metamorphoses into the body of a woman of color, which Andrews, as colonialist voyeur, watches undress. Her fantasy is that the woman of color wants to reveal her body to her because she is the pleased lover and appreciator. But Andrews also wants to be that body. The Yucatan, both literally and figuratively, "browns" Andrews's own body as she strips white culture to reveal what she has always been: Indian.[6] As Andrews passes into "brown" countries, she depicts scenes in which she passes as Indian. At the same time, she is still recognized by most people of color in her books as distinctly white and "first world." Because of racial privilege, Andrews is able to assume identities others cannot put on and take off as readily.

This desire to "go Native," or cross from white to Indian, is also depicted on the front and back covers of Andrews's workbook, *Teachings around the Sacred Wheel*. The front cover art is by Susan Boulet, a famous New Age artist of mystical female and Native figures, and shows a figure composed of halves: it is half woman, half man, half moon, half owl, and half lion, though fully Indian. "She" holds a feather that signifies both the eagle feather, a sacred Indian symbol protected by the U.S. government, and also a quill for writing and thus Andrews's tool for empowerment. There are two heads—the anima and animus—representing the male and female, though the images are intentionally blurry to

Figure 2.1. Cover image from Lynn Andrews, *Teachings around the Sacred Wheel: Finding the Soul of Dreamtime.* San Francisco: HarperCollins, 1990.

depict a "beautiful androgyny." Interestingly, the male image has been placed within the heart of the female, signaling a desire to "soften" maleness through the heart or emotions. The image reflects Andrews's quest to unite the dualisms of white/Indian, male/female, and even animal/human in one body: her body. On the back cover is a picture of Andrews herself looking like a "white ethnic." Standing in front of large rocks symbolizing not only nature but the stereotypical nature of the "Indianness" of the Southwest, she has a curly white Afro, woven clothing, Native jewelry, and a deep tan. Thus Andrews is more than the "bridge between two worlds, the primal mind and the white consciousness": she is the embodiment of Indianness in the twenty-first century (*Star Woman*, back cover).

Through the "Sisterhood of the Shields," Andrews learns "Native" practices, which are actually lessons in gender authority. When Whistling Elk shows Andrews how to make her own medicine shield, all of the directions are understood in terms of archetypal Womanness: "You become conscious of your sex—your vagina. That will get you to the south. The south shield is the mother or mothering shield" (*Flight of the Seventh Moon* 89). Andrews's world looks more like a separatist utopia than a coed Indian culture transmitting tribal rituals: her teachers, members of the Sisterhood of the Shields, primarily teach women lessons in female empowerment. Whistling Elk says, "Look, Lynn, we all come into this earth walk to heal our femaleness" (*Jaguar Woman* 29). Teachers emphasize repairing personal wounds from the patriarchy and transforming a wounded Mother Earth. Zoila, Andrews's South American teacher, notes, "The earth is female, as I am sure Agnes has instructed you. A woman translates her energy in the form of the ecstatic Rainbow Mother or the nurturing Great Mother" (*Jaguar Woman* 48). The balance of each woman and the planet depends on the use of the "primal" or the equally mysterious and romantic "ancient ways" wherein the world once offered a powerful place for women that they can return to by practicing "ancient" rituals.

By performing certain rituals, readers of Andrews's books can follow her spiritual teachings and experience the same transformation. Readers who purchase companion workbooks, such as *Teachings around the Sacred Wheel*, are led through meditations, exercises, journaling, and ceremonies for their explicit shamanic training. In an exercise called "Medicine Woman in Crystal," Andrews tells readers to find a "very, very special" crystal, perform a particular meditation to visualize their medicine woman in the crystal, and carry the crystal with them in a red pouch or "power bundle." Andrews says, "I want you to know this medicine woman living within yourself and make contact with her. She has always been with you, from the day you were born. It's just that you have not understood that this energy force is within you" (118). Andrews's goal in the workbook is to help readers manifest "feminine consciousness" and by buying the list of "what you will need"—including a drum, rattle, chimes, smudge stick, and crystals—and following her instructions, one can become aware of the "primal energies of the earth as female" with a Native flavor.

Here, Andrews uses "Indianness" to access gender. She finds woman power in Native culture, but it is a representation of Native culture that she herself has created. Andrews is deeply invested in her lessons and practices, which promote woman power and are sprinkled with Indian symbols, language, and lore, though she never discusses Indian history, politics, or particular tribes and beliefs. The American Indian aspects seem to serve mainly as a window dressing to make female empowerment more mysterious and appealing: Andrews has manufactured her own brand of New Age "feminism."

Andrews's fantasy gender system, which she says comes from Indian culture, has two beliefs about gender: that "Woman" is greater than man, and that men and women need to integrate their masculinity and femininity to be whole. Andrews claims that "Woman" is the source of power: women are superior to men, have ancient wisdom that must be reclaimed and celebrated, and will heal a wounded Mother Earth. In the preface to *Medicine Woman*, the first in her series, she describes one of the first instruction scenes between her Indian shaman, Agnes Whistling Elk, and herself. In overwrought language, Andrews details the "yellow moon" rising, and the coyotes "singing a mournful song" as she sits in front of a fire with the "old Indian woman" whose face is "creased like that of an apple doll" (preface):

> "Woman is the ultimate," she said. "Mother earth belongs to woman, not man. She carries the void." These were her words to me before I became her apprentice. She is a *heyoka* medicine woman. I was destined to follow in her path for seven years. This book is a record of my journey into her strange and beautiful realm—a celebration of the power of woman—as she made me see that power. (preface)

Whistling Elk's "apple doll" face, her "high cheekbones," her "long braids," and her "medicine wheel necklace" conjure up a mythic Woman herself: not a "real" American Indian who straddles two worlds, as many contemporary American Indians do, but a fantasy woman who lives in a rarefied world of continuous contact with the source of woman power (preface).[7] As scholar Kathryn W. Shanley notes, "American Indian communities struggle to regain the power to determine their communal futures through economic, governmental, social, educational, and kinship refigurations, and all the while many of the 'Indian' voices most popular in mainstream America reinscribe nineteenth-century romantic images of

Figure 2.2. Back photograph of Lynn Andrews from *Teachings around the Sacred Wheel: Finding the Soul of Dreamtime*. San Francisco: Harper-Collins, 1990.

Noble Savages" (677). Indeed, Andrews critiques the contemporary material world by holding up the romantic image of the Indian woman as salvific. "Mother Earth" here "belongs" not to those who are "advanced" but to those who "celebrate the power of woman." As Whistling Elk says, "The sisterhood is not a club, Lynn. . . . It's not a sorority or a bridge party. . . . We assume power" (*Jaguar Woman* 77). By attributing these gender beliefs to "ancient" Indian culture, Andrews reaps the double reward of "assuming power" to become both a powerful woman and eventually a powerful "Indian."

The second gender belief that Andrews attributes to Indian culture is that men and women need to integrate their masculine and feminine sides. This belief is a "nonseparatist" extension of "difference feminism": though Woman is superior and the genders are understood as essentially different, integration of masculinity and femininity is necessary for wholeness, an important goal in New Age culture. As Whistling Elk says, "Lynn, it is good that you have held council with your ancestor father within you" (*Star Woman* 114). However, while Andrews ostensibly desires "divine androgyny," her narratives more often demonstrate how she uses masculinity to claim a more aggressive power or to trick evil characters who are almost always male. When men appear in Andrews's books (which is seldom), they are portrayed as either an evil influence or as being able to be contained in some way because they are paranormal manifestations such as ghosts, androgynous men who have a highly developed feminine side, or men of color, who are feminized in some way. Stereotypically aggressive white males—particularly Andrews's ex-husband, who makes several appearances—are shown as malevolent characters who must be dominated. Whistling Elk says, "Men do not know how to live. Women must teach them that. But first women have to take their own power and heal themselves" (*Jaguar Woman* 29).

Though all of the focus in Andrews's books is on building a matriarchal utopia where men are superfluous, there is an anxiety about lesbian relationships that is never overtly stated. Interestingly, while Andrews depicts intense female love and bonding, it seems that lesbian desire must be repressed for the possibility of a heterosexual desire that is rarely realized. As Whistling Elk notes, "When you are a goddess, then you can mate with your god successfully, and only then" (*Jaguar Woman* 29). Consequently, heterosexual coupling is rare: most of the women are single, and only a few women of color have successful heterosexual relationships, which is not surprising since in Andrews's schema women of color are usually more spiritually evolved. It is easier to create a spiritual union with men by appreciating the "masculine" in "divine androgyny" than to create a material union in the flesh. Andrews's school, LACSAT, emphasizes this "male/female balance": "The first year of study will include the La Ultima Madre Heyoka teaching of energy, an in-depth exploration and examination of the four kinds of female energy within both man and woman" (Lynn Andrews's Web site). In their four years of training, Andrews states that students will be "approaching the world in a chosen state of feminine awareness," and "becoming your opposite energy," as well as "performing a shamanic play," and learning "Spirit Retrieval" (Lynn Andrews's Web site). With a diploma from LACSAT, one should be well trained in teaching gender empowerment and possess a thoroughly integrated gender self. Ultimately, there is no contradiction between the desire for women to be superior to men and the desire for women to integrate their masculinity and femininity: they both work toward the same ends—an Amazonian utopia where women teach men how to repair the world they have ruined.

Andrews's primary obsession is with the perceived power and strength of women of color. While it is clear from the introduction to her first book, *Medicine Woman*, that Andrews already had the cultural and monetary capital to act "powerfully" in the world, she "could not" until she realized her spiritual power. Here, spiritual "mining" is less about Indian culture and more about utilizing those cultural tropes to have a feminism without feminism. This dilemma is at the center of New Age culture: while the culture itself is largely by, for, and about women, white women in particular, it negotiates women's authority not through feminism but through whatever is perceived to hold spiritual power. However, Andrews's narratives frequently articulate feminist concerns like the victimized status of women, the "second shift" women perform in taking care of housework and child care, and the difficulties men and women encounter when trying to have equal, healthy relationships. For Andrews, female power is not realized within a U.S. feminist context but exists outside of white Western capitalism and bourgeois family structures. For example, in *Jaguar Woman*, her teacher Zoila says to Andrews:

> Your culture accepts only the great nurturing matriarch, the type of woman who grows the corn and raises the children. These women love routine, get married, raise their children, and generally have a much easier time than their rainbow sisters. While the Rainbow Mothers are frustrated, unfulfilled, and perhaps alcoholics because of the expectations of others, the Great Mothers are the pillars of society. (49)

Through the voice of Zoila, Andrews privileges "ancient" societies where "Rainbow Mothers" like her might survive. Like many classic second-wave feminist narratives by Betty Friedan, Gloria Steinem, Marilyn French, and Doris Lessing, where white women discover their dissatisfaction with the purely domestic experience of being a mother and wife, Andrews says that she was not cut out to be a "Great Nurturing Mother" (King 74). Andrews states, "I knew that there was some kind of destiny in my life which I was wasting, so I got a divorce" (King 74). Andrews never understands this struggle within a larger framework of hundreds of other women going through a similar experience at a similar time—instead, her experience is about her own individual spiritual destiny.

Though Andrews struggles with the foundational issues of feminism—such as discrimination against women, pay equity, and marriage equality—she never mentions feminism but filters her struggles through her vision of ancient female culture. For instance, when Whistling Elk teaches Andrews about making her shield, she says, "When you go to work in a system that is basically patrilineal and patriarchal in its approach, your tendency, whether you are conscious of it or not, is to pick up the male shield. Now this can become very complicated, because your male shield may be part of your Nurturing Mother structure" (*Jaguar Woman* 28). Once more the tension is between the difference feminism of the "Nurturing Mother" and the "male shield," or the patriarchal approach, which privileges the "male shield" over the female.

Andrews attacks patriarchy through a discussion of shields; the way to resist patriarchy is to navigate the "ancient" ways, not to blame current U.S. structures of power. Andrews's critique of gender relations exists between worlds. It is unrecognizable to feminists who might not understand the spiritual packaging; yet for most New Age women, the feminist content would be less appealing if not understood through "Indianness." At the same time, her romantic teachings on Indian culture obscure gender relations even within Native culture, which are multifaceted and not solely about prelapsarian female power.

Andrews creates an analogy between race and gender to claim the right to use Indian practices whose power, authenticity, and identity are generated out of the experience of oppression. Simultaneously, she violates the Native standard of appropriation by teaching Native rituals and passing on inaccurate information about Native cultures. Through "romantic racialism," Andrews elides differences in race and gender in order to empower herself, and by analogizing gender and race, she reifies the practices of an authentic racial Other while enabling herself as a gendered subject to move freely through various zones of culture: "In *Star Woman*, her journey will be guided by Arion, a magnificent white stallion she will ride into the world of illuminating visions . . . where she enters the most frightening and difficult place of all . . . the dark side of her own spirit" (back cover). The white stallion rides into the dark side of the "primal," and the dark side of Andrews herself that needs to be "healed" in some way. Whiteness penetrates a darkness that is both outside of Andrews and within her, in the spiritual sense. While the "dark side" here refers to the Jungian concept of the "shadow," which is ostensibly not racialized, it connotes the darkness that is Andrews's "tainted" racial identity.

By performing rituals and acts, like riding a stallion bareback into the darkness where she can imagine herself as a powerful Indian, Andrews believes she can possess racial authenticity. Whistling Elk tells her, "There are some people who will fight against your message, but it is so necessary that it be heard that you must try. You are a white woman from a glamorous city, and they will find it hard to believe" (*Flight of the Seventh Moon* 3). Yet the "white woman from a glamorous city" can also maintain the authenticity of her oppression and experience as a woman. Ironically, though she dismisses "her" white culture repeatedly, she can only participate in Indianness because of the gender oppression she has suffered from it.

Suffering as a woman is not enough to make Andrews fully Indian. She says, "Some of the native people don't understand what we are doing. They think I'm trying to hurt them, and I love them so much.

They don't see the love I have for them or the reason I am writing" (*Windhorse Woman* 195). Andrews is confused because she "feels" like one of them: in her fantasy of gender authority, she imagines that she has the blessing of Indians to practice, believe, and teach rituals that "stress the ancient powers of woman" (*Star Woman* 6). Andrews believes that her racial performance can sidestep a long history of imperialism, where "pretending to be Indian or believing that it is possible to 'know' what it means to be 'Indian' is within the purview of most Americans" (Shanley 679). But Andrews's work is conceived as "just another rip-off in a long history of cultural struggle" (Mankiller-Mendoza). On the Lynn Andrews Web site forum, a recent debate was instigated by a letter from American Indian Lclair Mankiller-Mendoza, who wrote, "Among The People we see Lynn Andrews and her fabrications as a joke—but a cruel joke—for her fantasy novels give a totally distorted view of living Native today." On the one hand, Andrews separates gender power rituals from "authentic" Indian rituals. She practices "portable spirituality," claims that "no one owns the truth," and says that anyone can practice these rituals for "the shaman in all of us" (*Teachings around the Sacred Wheel* introduction). Andrews tries to bank on Universalism. As Whistling Elk asserts, "You write about the beauty of balance. I am Indian, but what I have taught you is about a universal truth not traditional Indian medicine. A truth that has no cultural boundaries" (*Windhorse Woman* 195). On the other hand, Andrews has been accused of making up her Cree teacher, Whistling Elk, altogether. According to informal research done by Cree people, no one by such a name has ever existed in their tribe or area (Bruchac). Thus her fantasy of becoming an Indian woman is, in the end, truly a fantasy.

The Gendered Possibilities of Paranormal Memory: Mary Summer Rain and Indian Identity

While Andrews states repeatedly that women and Indians are the "same" because they are linked by oppression, Mary Summer Rain never makes this link explicit. Andrews moves between the analogy of race and gender oppression and the assumption that she is Indian. There is an unspoken transition between moments when she makes explicit the analogy between women and Indians and moments when she assumes the analogy. Summer Rain is all assumption—she enacts what Andrews articulates. Summer Rain's connection between women and Indians is implicit from the start; the analogy of gender and race never comes to the surface of the text. Instead, what surfaces is her desire for Indian female ancestry, which she establishes through the use of the paranormal. By looking at how Summer Rain goes back into the past in order to be an Indian woman in the present, we can see marks on the surface of text left by the disappeared foundation of race and gender.

Like Andrews, Summer Rain feels called to share the teachings of her teacher, the blind American Indian woman, No-Eyes, whose story appears in her first book, *Spirit Song: The Introduction of No-Eyes.* Like Whistling Elk, No-Eyes is a stereotypical fantasy of a wise Indian woman with long braids, leathered brown skin, and even "Tonto Speak"—a white racist fantasy of how Indians speak (Aldred "Plastic Shamans and Astroturf Sun Dances" 332). As Summer Rain's second teacher, Brian Many Heart, predicts, "The literary success will be finalized by the *tandem* efforts of [No-Eyes'] living life and your tender writing style" (*Dreamwalker* 63). Beginning with the No-Eyes series, the first volume of which was published in 1985, Summer Rain is the author of over eighteen books, including nonfiction, fiction, children's books, and audio recordings of her material. According to Ken Eagle Feather at Hampton Roads Publishing Company, where Summer Rain's books are published, she is hugely popular and "has sold over 1 million of her books altogether."[8]

Both her wide-ranging commentary on a number of New Age subjects, from children's spirituality to communication with aliens, and her spiritual "clearinghouse," the Mountain Brotherhood, which answers correspondence from her readers, contribute to her popularity. Unlike Andrews, Summer Rain refuses to make public appearances. As Eagle Feather says, "She refuses to do signings, readings, or interviews. If she did them, she would be rich." However, over the course of her writings, Summer Rain has moved in and out of seclusion and self-promotion. In letters she insists repeatedly that spirituality should not be sold; because she refuses to "teach" Native practices, she has resisted coming forward. Instead, Summer Rain exists in what she calls the "shadowland," literally and figuratively: she is invisible, yet she presents herself with authority through continual assertions that she is an Indian visionary.

For Summer Rain, lessons in the paranormal are lessons in gender authority—they give her the experience of going into the past to retrieve what is most powerful, that is, the identity of an Indian woman. As her spiritual training progresses with her teacher No-Eyes, Summer Rain is "given" first the tools to recover memory and then the memories themselves through the use of the paranormal or "psychical phenomena" (*Spirit Song* 168). Her training in the paranormal includes learning extrasensory perception (ESP, an umbrella term that covers telepathy and clairvoyance), which enables her to "obtain information at a distance by paranormal means," and, through precognition and retrocognition, to gather information about future and past events (Campbell and Brennan 168). With these new powers, Summer Rain can travel back to the past. When No-Eyes "feel sorry for Summer" that she missed "a beautiful way of living and believing," No-Eyes does not have to "feel sorry" for long because she has taught Summer Rain how to move telepathically back in time (*Spirit Song* 37).

Within moments, No-Eyes and Summer Rain are visiting the "glorious days before the White Man" (*Spirit Song* 128). Summer Rain describes her psychic experience of seeing Indian life as it was: "I witnessed a marriage lodge. And was moved by the tender love and respect I found therein. I was one of the People. And it was a beautiful way of being. It was a way of life that made the Great Spirit glad He created Man" (*Spirit Song* 128). Summer Rain's vision of this idyllic life is disrupted when No-Eyes shows how "White Man come to People's land" and committed genocide (*Spirit Song* 129). Soon Summer Rain is in tears from empathizing with Indian pain; however, we find out that those tears are, in fact, for her own pain as an Indian woman. Though Summer Rain has missed the "days before the White Man," once the paranormal allows her to experience them she claims "I was one of the People" (*Spirit Song* 129). Before coming back to the present moment, No-Eyes tells Summer Rain that she " 'have Medicine Woman in her . . . I Medicine Woman. I know these things. One day you have many come to Summer's land. They come to learn ol' ways. Summer and man teach. Summer not forget old ways. Summer not forget song of Shaman' " (*Spirit Song* 129). Suddenly, the differences between a twenty-first century white woman and a seventeenth-century Indian medicine woman are elided. Within a paragraph, Summer Rain goes from having never experienced Indian life to having enough "Medicine Woman" to teach others. No-Eyes insists that "Summer not forget old ways" (*Spirit Song* 130). Summer Rain is called by her teacher to teach what is not forgotten but just dormant (just as Andrews's teacher, Agnes Whistling Elk, insists that what women "learn" they have always known, and simply need to remember).

Summer Rain scripts a situation where she has no agency in claiming whiteness or Indianness but must simply follow her teacher's request: she has been chosen for shamanic training and will become the heir apparent of a medicine woman line. Summer Rain takes the step from romanticizing and feeling the pain of Indians to embodying the pain herself. No-Eyes expresses concern that people will be "drawn to Indian stuff an' culture. But then they gonna go off on wrong path with their new knowledge." Summer Rain responds:

People who have their carryover Indian souls awakened will
always want to be Indian. They'll want to seek out Indian teachers and do Indian ways—like Medicine Wheel and Pipe ceremonies . . . because they're trying to grasp onto the exterior
Indian ways instead of bringing the *inner* Indian ways to their
hearts. They're walking the Without Trail before the Within
Path has been journeyed through. . . . The Indian way is what's
inside. (*Earthway* 425, emphasis added)

By feeling Indian on the inside, feelings that have been accessed through
the paranormal, Summer Rain can claim the power she seeks, the power
of an Indian heart that must not justify itself through Indian practices.
Thus memory determines identity for Summer Rain. Her concept of
memory is not static but is one of continuing revelation over time. Not
surprisingly, Summer Rain is accused of appropriation because her
memory appears to be manufactured through the paranormal and, therefore, nonexistent in real time. However, Summer Rain's paradigm recognizes the paranormal as viable and "continuing" memory as legitimate.

Summer Rain wants to become an Indian woman to such a degree
that she constructs a racial logic justifying that transition. Through
retrocognition and clairvoyance, Summer Rain accesses what she calls the
"Akashic Records," or God's large book of history and prophecy, to
understand past and future (*Daybreak* 81). By drawing on the authority
of "God's book of history," Summer Rain has created the ultimate
authority on her identity—God. Summer Rain declares what has been
revealed to her through spirit guides, psychic revelations, her teacher,
No-Eyes, and even God:

I am a descendant (both physically and spiritually) from the
Spirit Clan of the Anasazi. I was known as See-qu-aa-nu
(Sequanu) of the Anasazi People in the year 650 A.D. It is from
this life that much of my personal information has been recalled.
The Spirit Clan was one comprised of the visionaries. . . . Their
purpose was to collaborate with the extraterrestrials in seques-
tering the articles of wisdom from the ensuing invaders they
foresaw coming upon the land. The following two lifetimes were
spent as a member of the Shoshone tribe which was comprised
of those Anasazi who left the original compound when the
others left to return home. No-Eyes confirmed this, as did Brian
Many Heart. It would appear that the recording on my ancestors
was tampered with. But I care not for this indiscretion for the

sake of 'propriety,' for I'm comfortable to walk the Shadowland and not force the issue. (*Daybreak* 82)

Summer Rain's genealogical claims are impossible to verify. On the one hand, she validates the paranormal as the legitimate source of her identity. On the other hand, she asserts that she lives in the "Shadowland" and has no interest in claiming to be Indian in the present. Her racial logic buckles under its inconsistencies. Though race is Summer Rain's foundational term, she destabilizes it in a way that gives her power and agency: through "paranormal" memory, her identity becomes increasingly intricate and convoluted as she moves from white to Indian.

Summer Rain establishes conceptual structures that allow her to cross racial boundaries instead of asserting the impermeability of boundaries or the inevitable continuity of boundaries over time. The racialized past becomes a point of exchange rather than setting up racial difference for the present. In a later book she says, "AIM blacklists my writings and those others like me on the sole basis of ethnicity" (*Fireside* 101). She critiques racial analysis that does not privilege spiritual essence, and yet she conserves racial essence and gives herself access to it by going into the past. She has both access and purity. Summer Rain claims that "most lost historical data can be recaptured" through "carry-over memories": "Past civilizations should no longer present mysteries to us, for within the many facets of our spirits we each carry the imprinted memories of many lives lived" (*Daybreak* 102). Eventually, Summer Rain uses "spiritual memory recall," also known as channeling, to write several books, among them *Ancient Echoes*. Written in honor of "her" people, the Anasazi, who lived from 100 to 1300 A.D., Summer Rain channels chants, prayers, and songs from that time period in their voice, spirit, and even language. Summer Rain's transformation is complete: through the paranormal, she gains the ultimate power of being a female Indian visionary who can summon up the voice of her past for healing the present.

For Summer Rain, authentic Indianness means being the descendant and inheritor of a visionary female lineage. Though appropriation theorists and American Indians define blood as a determinant of race, Summer Rain makes her own claims to Indian authenticity—the only problem is that they cannot be verified. Summer Rain opens her first book in the No-Eyes series with an account that illuminates her desire for power and her racial logic. She establishes her female Indian heritage by narrating the ancestral history of Walks-in-Woods or She-Who-Sees, whom we eventually find out is Summer Rain's grandmother.

Summer Rain begins her story in 1805, when She-Who-Sees is born and grows up as a Shoshone visionary. The main point of this account is She-Who-Sees' vision of the disintegration of her people, and her people's resistance to that vision: "Of all She-Who-Sees' visions of the future, one terrified her the most. She envisioned her bloodline thinning and thinning into total obscurity. . . . Where were the strong, high cheek-bones? Where were the firm chins and hair the color of raven wings?" (*Spirit Song* 11). After She-Who-Sees dies at the age of 102, the "People-of-the-Land," as Summer Rain calls Indians, "deny their heritage": "They all sought the good life, and that just wasn't possible for an Indian. As the old woman became farther and farther removed from her ensuing generations, it became unthinkable for the People to even remotely consider admitting that they were of Indian descent. Sadly enough, they had successfully convinced even themselves" (*Spirit Song* 13). The narrator's own status vis-à-vis Indian culture is questionable: if we presume Summer Rain to be the narrator, though the opening sections do not include a first-person narrator and appear fictional, then she has become the arbiter of "real" versus "fake" Indians.

The reader knows that Summer Rain is white, and yet she narrates the story as if she were the "good" Indian who has the right to judge Indian subjectivity. At one point in the story, she contrasts the birth of She-Who-Sees, who predicts the demise of her people, next to Saca-jawea's guidance of Lewis and Clark, to show how one Indian tries to lead her people to recognize their heritage, while the other leads white men into Indian territories, thus leaving them vulnerable to ongoing exploitation.[9] This slippage between Summer Rain's autobiographical voice and the voice of the narrator of the beginning "histories" is a formal example of the tension in her racial logic. Summer Rain shifts between placing herself firmly within Indian culture and drifting on the margins as a white supporter. In fact, throughout the No-Eyes series, it is difficult for the reader to keep track of Summer Rain's changing identity.

Ironically, Summer Rain, who is accused of rampant Indian appro-priation, constructs a sympathetic character, She-Who-Sees, who fears white blood thinning Native blood. Since Summer Rain eventually declares that this visionary is her actual great-great grandmother, she locates herself within the bloodline that has been "thinning" but of which Summer Rain is the rightful inheritor. Summer Rain says: She-Who-Sees "was my ancestral grandmother and I am Summer Rain. I won't forget you, old grandmother" (*Spirit Song* 13). According to her story, Summer Rain is the true ancestral grandchild: in contrast to earlier full-blooded but "misled" Indians, Summer Rain does not want the "good life" and proudly claims her Indian heritage, as full-bloods did not. Summer Rain notes that previous descendants of She-Who-Sees could not "consider admitting" they were of Indian descent, and they had even gone so far as to psychically "convince" themselves that they were otherwise. Here, Summer Rain creates a new story of racial identity: one can forget that one is Indian but then realize it and become Indian once more. This story allows her to be "born again." She is lost and then found as Indian, but with all of the privileges of whiteness. This double bind is doubly desirable: Summer Rain writes herself as Indian.

With each successive book, Summer Rain orients herself ever more toward the spiritual world, where her Indian identity is secure, and away from the material one, where it is not. Her decisions are increasingly based on what spirits instruct her to do. Throughout the No-Eyes series, the sense of "being called," chosen, or spoken to by ancestors, Indian teachers both dead and alive, aliens, spirit guides, and different plants and animals of the forest overrides Summer Rain's own agency. After Summer Rain finishes telling the story of She-Who-Sees, she says, "I heard this pitiful story several years ago"; the "story" cannot be found in "accurate records" and might just be an "Indian legend" (*Spirit Song* 13). But because Summer Rain was "haunted" by the story in her daily life and dreams, it insists on being told. The story *tells* Summer Rain what to do: by now the story has gone from history to fiction to legend to ghost story.

Being commanded by spirits is central to Summer Rain's racial logic: she has absolutely no agency in asserting her Indianness but simply does what spirit guides tell her. For example, after hearing the "ghost story of She-Who-Sees," Summer Rain says, "I found myself purchasing all manner of Indian items and filling my home with pottery and weavings . . . it felt like coming home" (*Spirit Song* 13). Her use of the passive is instructive, as it is throughout: phrases such as "it [the story] sporadically interrupted my daily thoughts" and would "weave hauntingly in and out of my dreams" or "I found myself purchasing . . ." point to a higher authority that has called her to this identity, not something sought after for personal gratification. The compulsion to purchase "all manner of Indian items" is not based on material greed. Rather, Great Spirit "led" her to buy Indian blankets. Similarly, since the truth of her identity—that Summer Rain is She-Who-Sees' great-granddaughter—"was revealed only under strict conditions" and not something she "clamored" after, it allows her to rest securely in a tradition that recognizes Indian women over time (*Spirit Song* 13). Summer Rain enacts the gender unconscious of her work: though gender is not ostensibly central to her cosmology, she is empowered to teach, write, speak to ghosts, and practice a whole range of paranormal phenomena because her rightful place in a female Indian lineage is asserted.[10] In *Dreamwalker*, the third volume of the No-Eyes series, when asked how Summer Rain names herself, she says, "I have been known as Summer Rain, Sequanu and She-Who-Sees, who was formerly Walks-in-Woods" (*Spirit Song* 40). Thus she identifies herself by her family name through the female line. By saying "I have been known as," Summer Rain indicates that she is at once a descendant and an actual embodiment of her powerful female ancestry.

On the one hand, Summer Rain insists that she is following the path of her Indian shaman, and that she cannot help but be "Indian in her heart." On the other hand, her use of external Indian signifiers, such as dress, language, actions, and self-presentation, belies her quest for purity. At several moments Summer Rain discusses the importance of having Indian symbols around her: "Jan had recently hung Indian mandalas and paintings around the place and I felt very much at home. The ethnic decor had no negative effects on my tender sensitivities. Instead, it made me feel darn good inside" (*Phantoms Afoot* 55). Summer Rain describes in detail the numerous Indian objects in her various houses, as well as the Indian gifts received from her readers. But perhaps Summer Rain's most important artistic choice in marking herself as "Indian" is her use of Carole Bourdo's Indian art for her book jacket covers.

Bourdo, like Andrews's artist Susan Boulet, is recognized for specializing in American Indian subjects, called "Indian kitsch" by some. "Indian kitsch" is usually understood as stereotypical, sentimentalized Indian portraits with extreme color palettes that are marketed to whites in particular. For example, on the front cover of *Dreamwalker*, there is a drawing of a mysterious hybrid—half-Indian, half-animal—creature with large haunting eyes, all painted in bright hues. On the back cover, Summer Rain is dressed in full Indian regalia, wearing a woven poncho and moccasins with her long black hair flowing down as she holds what appears to be a Lakota peace pipe. This book art, which graces at least eleven book covers, is so beloved both by Summer Rain and her readers that it is now inseparable from the content of her books. Readers can even buy a series of china collector plates of the book covers with the signatures of the artist and the author in gold. Interestingly, Bourdo's racial identity (she is white) is as changeable as the author's: "Carole Bourdo's native heart was recognized and honored when her Native American Naming Ceremony was performed by Chief Earl Old Person on the land of her People of the Blackfeet Reservation in May of 1989" (*Spirit Song* 159). Bourdo's "native heart" (like Summer Rain's "native soul") is necessary to validate Bourdo's white artwork as Indian. Notably, Bourdo's paintings almost exclusively depict images of Indian

Figure 2.3. Cover image from Mary Summer Rain, *Soul Sounds: Mourning the Tears of Truth*. Norfolk, VA: Hampton, 1992.

women and mirror the fantasy that both she and Summer Rain have of becoming the image of their own creation—a beautiful, mournful Native woman who is a leader of her people. For Summer Rain, the trappings of Indianness are the trappings of female power.

Summer Rain can also further claim an Indian identity by refusing to teach Indian rituals. Her power is in her Indian blood. In her journal *Bittersweet*, she discusses AIM's boycotting of her by saying: "I'm not a teacher. I don't go out and teach lessons or ceremonies. I don't speak of native ways. I don't conduct seminars. I'm not anything other than a person who wrote of her personal experiences. . . . According to AIM I need a Council Elder's express permission to write of my life and what I've learned from its experiences" (139). When No-Eyes asks "Summer gonna tell 'bout sacred Indian lessons?" Summer Rain's reply is that she will not teach Indian ritual. Summer Rain recognizes that she may be accused of appropriation even before she has been publicly charged with it. In order to avoid this, she refuses to teach and refuses to claim "Indian organization membership":

> No-Eyes? I'm wondering, though, if those with true Indian car-ryover souls wouldn't inherently recognize and respect the real-ity of their current ethnic difference. I mean, I know I've lived before as Shoshoni and Anasazi, but I don't go into reservations or try to gain any Indian organization memberships because of that. My heart and mind are Indian and that's enough. You can't expect to be taken seriously by Indians when you're not cur-rently Indian. (*Earthway* 425)

Immediately after Summer Rain makes this speech, that her "heart and mind are Indian and that's enough," her teacher No-Eyes says that Summer "do got Indian blood in them veins—it not be a lot, but it still be there anyways" (*Earthway* 425). One moment Summer Rain insists on racial purity but another moment she invents a way to give herself access to authenticity: she creates a liminal space between inauthentic white experience and current Indian culture. She sets up racial bound-aries in order to transgress them—she maintains distinctions to keep her-self outside of the Indian community. In her current life, she is white and therefore "outside," yet because of her past paranormal experience, she has racial authenticity. When Summer Rain says, "I think those non-Indians with the true Indian memories will just naturally know their place. . . . They'll comprise both Indian and non-Indian aspects—they shouldn't need to shoulder their way back into present-day Indian soci-ety. I think that would be all wrong," she strategically theorizes a way into Indian culture, but into an Indian culture of the "past," where the real power lies (*Earthway* 426).

Rather than teach, Summer Rain asserts her power as a female spiritual leader in other ways. Through her writing, her extensive correspondence with her readers (which has been turned into several books), and, most significantly, as an Indian shaman, Summer Rain embodies the Indian teachings she has learned. She assumes the power, experience, and knowledge of an Indian visionary by displaying specialized knowledge about Indian life to her reader. And with each book, No-Eyes calls on Summer Rain to perform greater acts of spiritual power. For example, No-Eyes asks Summer Rain to help guide spirits between worlds or those "who are unfortunately caught between dimensions . . . and the most beautiful and emotionally-moving experience one could have is being actively instrumental in freeing a confused and lost soul" (*Phantoms Afoot* 1). Summer Rain sets off into the spirit world, with her then-husband Bill, to help these lost souls into the next dimension. Upon encountering a group of Native female ghosts who are dead from small-pox and whose husbands died fighting white men, Summer Rain says, "I come from the Great Spirit. Summer Rain comes with much magic in the form of sacred words. The power words will show you the way" (*Phantoms Afoot* 83). By using "power words" to speak to dead Native women, Summer Rain has achieved the ultimate spiritual power—she can literally send souls into the next world. This is a power that even teaching rituals would not equal. Whether Summer Rain gives up anything by not teaching rituals is questionable. However, Summer Rain insists on making a crucial distinction between her beliefs and "others" who appropriate Indian culture by teaching Indian ritual.

Over time, as Summer Rain identifies more and more as Indian, and as others also see her as Indian, accusations of appropriation mount. Though Summer Rain's Indian ancestry is questionable and the veracity of No-Eyes is dubious, the back cover of *Earthway* states, "Spiritual writer Mary Summer Rain, an American woman of Shoshoni descent, was the last apprentice to the renowned Chippewa visionary, No-Eyes." Yet Summer Rain discredits her readers for focusing on her Indianness:

I have also been concerned because many of my correspondents tend to zero in on the ethnic aspect of my teachings. This is a mistake. Although my teacher was Native American, the wisdom she gained over the many years of her life went far beyond Native American tradition. Accordingly, I do not mean to misrepresent the knowledge I share with you here as being solely based on Native American teachings. Much of No-Eyes' wisdom grew out of her childhood among the Chippewa in Minnesota . . . the ultimate knowledge she shared with me came from many other sources. If you are in search of purely traditional Native American teachings, I suggest you turn to a Native teacher or the history books. (*Earthway* xiv)

She notes that she did not come to teach Native traditions but to point to the "nobility" of the Indian race, to the "importance and beauty of the Native Way," and to "awaken all to listen to the voices of the Native wise ones" (*Earthway* xiv).

However, Summer Rain understands fully the outcome of appropriative acts. She states that she could never claim Indian blood: "I could also envision full-bloods being more than a little upset with these whites trying to learn their sacred ways and ceremonies. That would just never do! There were age-old traditions to maintain here. Certain lines cannot be crossed" (*Earthway* 475). Later in her career, Summer Rain chooses not to use Bourdo's Indian artwork on her books because she wants "the spiritual message to be universal and not give the impression that it is connected to any kind of ethnic slant" (*Fireside* 56). She even considers changing the "ethnic aspect" of her name but decides that that would be a bad business decision (*Fireside* 56). Finally, she redefines racism and insists that "Passive racism is keeping one's *own* ethnic culture separate, and aggressive racism is negativity or aggression toward *another*, different ethnic culture"; furthermore, the "focus of personal identity is erroneously determined by geographic culture rather than the primary species of the self, which is a human being" (*Fireside* 98, 99, emphases added). This startling final transformation, from Summer Rain declaring "I was her last student, so to me the war shield was passed" (*Earthway* 423), to writing New Age philosophy and dressing in plain cotton clothing without any Indian regalia, is not so mystifying when the goal is gender empowerment. As her publicist Ken Eagle Feather says, she has to "become her own woman"—now that she has established herself as powerful, perhaps the Indian signifiers are no longer needed.

"Feeling Indian": The Gender of Appropriation

Although Lynn Andrews does not claim Indian blood, she feels that she has a right to Indian practices; though Mary Summer Rain claims Indian blood, she feels that Indian practices are sacred and should not be freely distributed. Each is aware of and defines appropriation differently. However, both "feel" Indian through the common bond of oppression.

Andrews and Summer Rain, to a greater or lesser degree, articulate three main beliefs about gender that they attribute to Indian culture: first, that "Woman" is essentially different and better than man; second, that men and women need to integrate their masculine and feminine sides; and third, that in the spiritual realm, souls have no gender. Here gender assuages the anxiety of cross-racial identification: either they want to feel empowered as women and imagine that Indian culture provides such a space, thus using race as a means to solving the problem of gender, or they want to be Indian but cannot be, and so they collapse the distinct identities of Woman and Native by "feeling" Indian through the common bond of experiencing oppression.

Andrews and Summer Rain illuminate the various ways in which race is conceived in New Age culture and how Indianness is the legitimating force used to shore up claims about both race and gender. Though both authors believe that their "romantic racialism" is a tribute to Indians, it is entirely offensive. Scholar Nancy Shoemaker remarks that more often than not "those who [have] portrayed Indians as superior to Euro-Americans" have done "so in ways that made Indians appear inferior," usually by invoking an "anti-modern" sentiment of Indians as superior because they are "simpler, less civilized, less intellectual, more natural" (224). Both authors believe with millennial fervor that there will be a coming "time of the Indian," where the abuse of Indians will be recognized and righted and that Indians and women will save the world.

These strategies for empowerment are used in different ways by each author, but they have one thing in common—both are a means to the same end, authority. While both subscribe to the idea that blood is a determinant of race, Andrews uses her gender to justify her practice of Indian ritual and to claim a kind of Indianness herself. Summer Rain, on the other hand, uses the paranormal to "discover" her Indian blood and legitimate her right to a female Indian heritage. While they use Indian culture in offensive and faulty ways, their impulse for transformation, both personal and cultural, is bound up with the forms in which it is expressed. Each author tries to make claims about her own subject position by drawing on a "cult of sympathy" from her largely white female audience. Rather than assenting to feminist scholar Cynthia Kasee's view that "feminists engaged in religious imperialism towards Native faiths are dupes" of a patriarchal "divide-and-conquer strategy," I argue that these women use Indian culture to create a community of New Age women rather than to explore Indian cultures proper (87).

Scholar Shari Huhndorf gestures toward what *is* central to this project when she says, "Though important, the question of whether

Andrews's notions do in fact challenge patriarchy is not central to my concerns here. It is worth noting, however, that her extreme gender essentialism would doubtless give many feminists pause" (187). Andrews and Summer Rain revive "extreme gender essentialism" (the very kind that women's and gender studies scholars hoped was dead) by drawing on the "strong tradition of Native women" to instruct white women how to gain basic feminist goals: empowerment, freedom to choose, a right to vocation, and equality with men (though for them that usually means superiority to men). So far, gender, as a central component of their cross-racial identification, has only been understood as a justification for their gross racial appropriation. I would like to suggest that for better or for worse, this "difference feminism" is not only alive and well in New Age culture but is kept alive partly through racist appropriation. In other words, one kind of essentialism (racial) helps them understand another kind (gender), and the two work in tandem to create a subculture, where as white women take away racial authority from Indian women, they "gain" gender authority. But why does it matter when one form of power obviously comes at the expense of another? To understand appropriation, we need to grasp how certain gender satisfactions are built into the use and abuse of Native rituals such that gender identity is inseparable from the construction of whiteness.

The use of the paranormal by Andrews and Summer Rain is one of the most powerful examples of how race and gender both work together and are at odds with each other in New Age culture. Traditionally, the paranormal is not a part of memory, which is usually assumed to be a recollection of real events in real time. However, for Andrews and Summer Rain, accessing the paranormal means they have a limitless memory: it includes that which did not happen in this lifetime but in multiple past and future lifetimes as well, and it also means that one can time travel to experience what has happened previously. For example, Andrews learns from dreams and paranormal experiences, such as telepathy, past-life recollection, and time travel, how she came to be a part of the Sisterhood of the Shields, and thereby understands her place in this circle of indigenous women of color. Interestingly, Andrews does not claim a Native heritage through these experiences, yet she believes she is called on to pass on Native rituals necessary for transforming the current earth crisis. Summer Rain, in contrast, claims Native blood through her paranormal memories, but she refuses to pass on Native rituals. Both authors shore up their respective racial identities and choices about transmitting Indian culture through their use of the paranormal. "Paranormal memory," in this case, affirms either the right to be a white student in a lineage of Native teachings or the right as a white person to a Native bloodline.[11] But the paranormal is used as much to assume gender as racial power. Through paranormal experiences, both authors rescue people from the dead as well as kill evil intruders. In effect, their powers are limitless: they read minds, heal bodies, save souls, and generally become Goddess-like.

With large followings and almost twenty books to each of their names, Andrews and Summer Rain indicate the complex intersection of gender, race, and appropriation between the white female New Age culture and the American Indian one. As the primary consumers of New Age texts, workshops, and rituals, white women recognize a racialized "Other" most glaringly in terms of Indian spirituality, though for these women the discourse perceives Indians not as "Other" but, in fact, as same. Race here functions as a double mirror for white women: it reflects a desired subject position through a constructed fantasy of Indianness, and it reflects, though unwittingly, the construction of a gendered culture, New Age culture, through the articulation of philosophies and through habits of consumption and production. Given the heavy participation of white New Age women in Indian practices (though "inauthentic" and suspect ones), I argue that unless we examine how desire for Indian culture operates in these relationships, we cannot understand what is at stake, finally, in "stealing."

3

Gender on a Plate

The Calibration of Identity in American Macrobiotics

Macrobiotics, an approach to food unfamiliar to most Americans now, was once seen as a countercultural diet that threatened the nation. Known as "the most popular of the countercultural eating regimes," macrobiotics promised followers a new life if they subscribed to the primarily vegetarian, seasonal, whole foods regime based on the Asian philosophy of yin and yang (Levenstein 182). However, critics of macrobiotics responded to it with alarm: as Dr. Fred Stare warned in a 1971 article entitled "The Diet That's Killing Our Kids," macrobiotics will "destroy the health of its young disciples," and so parents should "speak out against that phony religion before your child leaves home for campus or commune" (70).[1] For many, this kind of critique of macrobiotics just added to its radical glamour: by eating macrobiotic meals, followers could taste the "exotic East," purge their systems of toxic late-capitalist food, experience spiritual or even physical highs, and even rebel against mainstream culture, all at the same time. Why stop? Even drug guru Timothy Leary said that it was "the only kind" of food "that enables one to hallucinate" (Stare 76).

Currently, in the twenty-first century, the countercultural status that macrobiotics had in the 1960s, along with food co-ops, back-to-the-land movements, and health food restaurants, has waned. What was once a threatening political statement has now become a political privilege—not only is it expensive to buy "healthy" organic food, but it is also a lifestyle marker of the baby boom generation. In this shifting historical terrain, the most prominent critiques of diets do not come from a right-wing backlash against countercultural practices but from feminist scholars who have critiqued the diet industry, beauty culture, and unhealthy body ideals as particularly fruitful points of inquiry into understanding the oppression of women. As feminist theorists such as Hilda Bruch, Joan Jacobs Brumberg, Kim Chernin, and Susie Orbach point out, "Most women in Western cultures" are unhappy with their bodies—an unhappiness that stems from the relentless societal pressures that determine women's appearance (Grogan 25).[2] Because many women have internalized assumptions about the "ideal" female body, they diet or binge and purge to attain that unattainable image (Grogan 25). "Diet culture" is so powerful that dieting continues to flourish despite feminist criticism that it is a puritanical, prescriptive, and guilt-inducing patriarchal tool. In other words, "women's subordination is locked into food" (Cline 3).

Looked at through this lens, macrobiotics becomes simply a diet, in the narrowest sense of the word: another rigid set of rules to monitor and limit women's eating habits. Though macrobiotics is more concerned with inner health than external beauty and thinness, it can still be viewed as a way to control, rather than liberate, women's eating patterns. Like traditional diets, it categorizes food into better and worse options; it requires a radical dietary change to an almost no-fat, no-meat diet; it demands a schedule of eating times and encourages low portions; and, like many fad diets, its products—in this case organic and Japanese—can be costly. Furthermore, macrobiotics thrives on some of the same obsessive energies that eating disorders do—whether with the goal of health or beauty, diets promise that controlling one's food will control one's life. The latest concern is orthorexia—an eating disorder in which sufferers become mentally ill through an obsession with health food.[3] Some macrobiotic practitioners may have underlying eating disorders; in such cases, the intense focus on the eating and preparation of food can exacerbate an already existing condition. Moreover, the macrobiotic emphasis on free will and choice in all matters of eating puts tremendous pressure on practitioners to always "do the right thing" and choose brown rice instead of a chocolate sundae.

Macrobiotics has been censured from many different angles—it resembles traditional diets that have been critiqued, its countercultural practices can appear suspect, "bizarre," and "cultish," and it also subscribes to extremely conservative gender ideologies (which I will discuss later) (Belasco 164). The question emerges: what is macrobiotics' enduring appeal? In spite of the aforementioned critiques, macrobiotics continues to have "millions" of followers (Hirsch). Macrobiotic stars such as Madonna and Gwyneth Paltrow add glamour to the diet. The stupendous growth of health-food stores, small and large, has meant that the once difficult-to-find food is now ubiquitous. Although macrobiotics attacks feminism for alienating Western women from their superior role as keepers of the family, many practitioners, especially women, have been drawn to the diet. While there have been a handful of academic studies on macrobiotics, few have accounted for its particular appeal. In spite of macrobiotics' take on gender, which at first glance is conservative and rigid, part of macrobiotics' ongoing popularity is that it actually offers a more fluid gender identity.[4]

Though macrobiotics is often criticized for its essentialist or static views of gender, I argue that, rather than being entirely manipulated by their diet, macrobiotic practitioners use their diet to manipulate their gender through their spiritual belief in the principles of yin and yang. Typically, yin and yang, which play a part in a variety of religious and secular traditions, are seen as complementary opposites; but macrobiotics does something unusual by applying these principles to food. In macrobiotics, yin symbolizes what is female, weak, and passive, and yang symbolizes what is male, hot, and aggressive. This principle of opposites is the foundation for understanding gender in macrobiotics. This view of the fundamental difference between the genders represents a crude understanding at best, which creates a false binary of gender essentialism.[5]

However, in everyday life rituals such as food consumption, macrobiotic practitioners do not simply subscribe to a theoretical understanding of gender but adjust the intake of yin and yang to change their gender in a daily way. They fiddle with the yin-ness and yang-ness of food like a gender-adjusting knob. With each turn of the knob, one can become more yang or less yin. Therefore, understanding yin and yang as simply different terms for masculine and feminine misunderstands the material application of these terms. Through food, one can manipulate how spiritual essences manifest themselves in the body—for example, on any given day, by eating more or less fish, which is yang, one can be more or less aggressive, controlling, assertive, and powerful. In this way, the satisfaction of macrobiotics comes not from trying to fit one's body into an unattainable gender ideal, as in most traditional diets, but from creating a sense of control over one's gender. By examining macrobiotic principles of yin and yang, diagnosis of disease, food and cooking practices, and chewing and excretion rituals, to name a few, I argue that macrobiotics' allure comes largely from providing a way for practitioners to adjust their gender through a spiritual belief system.

A Short Macrobiotic History

Macrobiotics, a dietary and spiritual philosophy that claims to cure illness and promote health, began with Japanese writer George Ohsawa (originally named Yukizaku Sakurazawa, 1893–1966). In 1908, after

Ohsawa was diagnosed with tuberculosis, he began experimenting with a dietary system he learned from a Japanese healer, Sagen Ishizuka. Through this diet, Ohsawa cured himself of tuberculosis (*Essential Ohsawa* 4). Ohsawa modified the diet—the yin/yang philosophy is his addition—and in the 1940s, he traveled to the West to introduce macrobiotics (*Essential Ohsawa* 213). Ohsawa taught that if one eats whole grains, vegetables, beans, and sea vegetables, and eliminates sugar, meat, dairy, alcohol, and caffeine, then one could attain both good health and spiritual enlightenment.[6] Because he theorized that food affects everything from the systemic (e.g., societal oppression or governmental policies) to the individual (e.g., quality of daily life), macrobiotics can be compared to other revolutionary systems of thought, such as Marxism or feminism. In macrobiotics, food is the single term, like class or gender, that constructs an ideology so profound that it "interpellates subjects" into "a dream from which we cannot wake," as Louis Althusser might say (158). Food precedes and creates every thought, speech, feeling, and act for macrobiotic practitioners: the old saying, "You are what you eat," becomes literally true. Consequently, people have flocked to the diet to become "what they eat"—pure, and, therefore, healthy. Those who are already healthy turn to macrobiotics to improve their life, and those who are sick and have found Western medicine inadequate to cure them hope that macrobiotics will transform them.

Macrobiotics is most simply defined as a whole foods diet, planned according to the seasons, that is built on beans, grains, and vegetables. While the diet was particularly strict from its origins until the 1980s—meals often consisted of a bowl of brown rice and miso soup—it has adapted to include both a wider range of foods and a wider variety of recipes beyond the standard Japanese ones. Practitioners who follow a "standard macrobiotic diet" ratio will eat 50 percent whole cereal grains (including brown rice, barley, millet, etc.), 20 percent vegetables (which should be locally grown, organic, and especially include leafy greens such as kale and round and root vegetables such as carrots and daikon), 5 to 10 percent beans and sea vegetables, 5 to 10 percent soups, and 5 to 15 percent fish and other occasional foods such as nuts or naturally sweet desserts (*Guide to Standard Macrobiotic Diet* 18). Food is cooked with little to no spice, which is difficult for many. It takes a long time to prepare because one is not allowed to use microwaves or grills, and naturally one cannot use pre-prepared foods such as takeout or frozen dinners. With the flourishing of health food diets in the United States in the past forty years, macrobiotics is no longer an odd "exception" but in company with several diets that are low in fat and high in carbohydrates with few, if any, animal proteins, including vegan, McDougall, Pritikin, and

Ornish. Still, macrobiotics distinguishes itself in several ways: it is not just a diet but a lifestyle, with philosophies on reincarnation, world peace, home decoration, dreams, God, marriage, and so on; it retains its Japanese origins not only through the frequent use of Japanese food products but especially through the foundational yin and yang philosophy; and, unlike most diets, it promises radical health transformations, such as becoming cancer-free or eliminating depression. Typically, those new to macrobiotics focus less on the larger philosophical issues and instead try to stick to a strict form of the diet for immediate, tangible benefits. Cooking a fairly strict macrobiotic diet is nearly a full-time job. In the long run, while many begin the diet with high hopes, few are able to follow through, not only because of the time commitment but also because eating out in restaurants is virtually impossible. In this way, macrobiotics is truly a "slow-food" diet, one that is out of sync with the ever-increasing speed of globalization.

Macrobiotics initially came into vogue in the United States in the mid 1960s (Fields 263). As the Beats popularized Zen Buddhism, macrobiotics became the natural dietary extension of this spiritual quest. As the desire for Eastern philosophies rose, so did the desire for macrobiotics. Ohsawa's two major disciples, Michio Kushi and Herman Aihara, came to the United States and established the two most extensive macrobiotic teaching, learning, and retreat centers in the world.[7] While there are variations on the macrobiotic diet taught by teachers around the world, all of whom have their own particular "spin" on the essential practices, most teachers are trained by either Kushi or Aihara who, while having some differences in their practices, share a philosophy that is fundamentally the same: food cures all ills. As Kushi and Aihara began spreading the macrobiotic gospel (Kushi on the East Coast and Aihara on the West Coast), seekers began purifying their diets by rejecting the meat and potatoes associated with mainstream culture. Seekers also wanted to purify themselves from white middle-class values even while honoring the exotic, fantasizing about the East, and choosing expensive Japanese food products that were underwritten by class privilege. Early practitioners eliminated all of the foods their parents were eating, such as "meat, sugar, dairy, white flour, canned foods, and artificial additives" (Colbin 65). Just as Zen practitioners in the 1960s used Buddhism to critique Christianity and the West, macrobiotic practitioners used food to critique advancing capitalism and Western decadence while unabashedly longing for the East as an exotic spiritual epicenter.

Practitioners believe that turning back to the food and culture of "ancient peoples" is the only hope for survival, since Western culture, medicine, and technology have brought the world to apocalypse.

Western culture caused these problems, and Eastern culture will fix them. If you live the ideal macrobiotic life, then you live in a pastoral Eastern utopia by harvesting the land, eating what you grow, supporting a large family, living simply, and participating in a community.[8] The most basic act of eating rice means eating an entire fantasy of Eastern and utopian values, since food and nation are "so commingled in popular discourses" (Bell and Valentine 168). White middle-class men and women filtered Asian philosophy through a Western lens and found a spiritual home in the "exotic" or "foreign."[9] As macrobiotic theorist Alex Jack notes, "In addition to overcoming prejudice and discrimination, Oriental teachings helped us develop complementary opposite qualities within ourselves . . . macrobiotic teachings from Japan tend to focus on self-development and the inner life, enabling us to become more artistic, spiritual and intuitive" ("Macrobiotics and America's Destiny").[10] This Orientalist sensibility is still apparent in macrobiotics today: from fetishizing the superiority of Japanese food products to worshipping the "better truths" of Taoist religious principles and from exoticizing Asian house design (feng shui) to longing for the pastoral rooted in Oriental wisdom, all things Asian get marked as the locus of primal truths.

Gender and the Philosophy of Yin and Yang

Much in macrobiotics is overtly essentialist, not just in racial terms but in gendered ones as well. Some macrobiotic beliefs, such as the belief that women are superior cooks, mirror conventional mainstream beliefs about women and food. "Foodwork" has been "women's work" ever "since the advent of industrialization," notes Janet Flammang (25). Many Americans still believe some version of "a woman's place is in the kitchen," and as sociologist Sally Cline notes, even after the rise of feminism, "the most important thing is not how 'healthy' the family meal should be but that the woman should be in charge of its organization" (111). Furthermore, "these women felt that families whose diets did not include a regular consumption of proper meals were not proper families" (Cline 108). A meal still is not a family meal unless it is hot, contains meat, has fresh—not frozen or canned—vegetables, and is, by and large, prepared by a woman (Cline 107). Thus macrobiotic theories about women's roles play into already existing American beliefs that encourage women to do the bulk of domestic labor and food preparation, even if also working outside of the home.

If Westerners tend to believe that women should be in charge of food preparation, then macrobiotics sees not only all aspects of food in

gender terms but all aspects of life—everything, from types of vegetables and cooking techniques to facial hair and nuclear energy, is classified as either yin or yang. In Asian philosophy, yin and yang are defined
as opposite but complementary forces: yin is composed of feminine,
cool, upward spiraling energy, and yang is composed of hot, downward,
forceful energy. Good health is defined by a balance of yin and yang.
When one eats yang foods, one takes on their yang characteristics.
Kushi says that "a large volume of extreme yang foods—such as meat,
eggs, cheese, and poultry . . . produces a more aggressive and offensive
attitude [yang qualities] . . . and a large volume of extreme yin foods—
such as milk, fruits, hot spices, and alcohol—produces fear and exclusiv-
ity [yin qualities]" (*The Book of Macrobiotics* 130). When at every turn
one must decide yin or yang, the life of a macrobiotic practitioner
becomes primarily diagnostic. Every mouthful chewed and every meal
ingested will inspire multiple readings. If one is emotionally excessive or
hysterical, especially in a stereotypically "feminine" way, then perhaps
one ate too much sugar or yin food. If one is rigid and angry, then perhaps one ate too much yang food, such as meat or eggs. Practitioners are
close readers of their body as text.

To achieve a healthful balance, one must use yin foods to even out
yang foods, and vice versa. As food expert and macrobiotic proponent
Annemarie Colbin notes, "By knowing which foods are the opposites of
others, you can quickly undo any simple health problems that arise from
excessive reliance on one category" (66). For example, in order to avoid
an "aggressive" yang attitude brought on by eating meat, you might eat a
mountain of grated raw radish to balance the harmful and gendered
effects of this extreme yang product. In contrast, if you want to feel particularly strong, aggressive, or yang, then you might eat fish stew or sea-
weed salad. Not surprisingly, practitioners often talk about the
ever-shifting yin-ness and yang-ness of their personalities, because in
macrobiotics, you can create your personality through food:

> In order to be more sensitive and aesthetic, eat mostly vegetable-
> quality food, including raw salad . . . to be social and busi-
> nesslike . . . include grains and beans, cooked in a standard way,
> in a wider variety of methods with the addition of a small
> volume of animal food . . . to be violent and warlike, eat more
> animal food and sugar, with a variety of food prepared in a dis-
> orderly manner. (*The Book of Macrobiotics* 234)

When there were rumors at the Kushi Institute that one man ate eggs (a
taboo animal protein), which accounted for his harsh, uptight, rigid

demeanor, he was taunted for being "too yang." If balance is desired, then one should cook a perfect selection of yin and yang vegetables, grains, and beans, prepare the food in a yin and yang manner, arrange contrasting yin and yang foods on a plate, and chew carefully for better yin digestion. At that moment, this single plate of food could have perfect gender harmony.

Cooking your way into a desired gender enables practitioners to perform private acts that affect their public gendered selves. In fact, preparation methods transform the gendered personalities of food that has qualities such as a "dominant personality," which "may include a stronger flavor . . . a more pronounced color, and more limitations as to how it can be prepared and what other foods it can be prepared with. *Compliant foods* are usually milder in flavor and color, softer, [and] more yielding to a wider range of preparation styles" (Gagne 49, emphasis added). In this stereotypical analysis, *compliant foods* are gendered female and give way to masculine foods. However, cooking changes the gender of the food. For example, to make kinpira, a famous burdock and carrot cleansing dish, one must cut the vegetables in small yin shapes in order to sauté them in a yang manner, and then must consume the dish with other ones balanced for complementarity. Even cooking methods are categorized into a feminine/masculine or yin/yang schema in macrobiotics: "The most feminine cooking methods [are] steaming and boiling [which] impart a mild flavor to meats . . . the more masculine methods, often preferred because they bring out the strong flavors of meat, [are] grilling, broiling, frying, and roasting" (Gagne 131). Grilling a yin celery stalk changes the structure and quality of the celery's gender from passive to strong. The celery retains its inner yin-ness while displaying a new yang power; the once-quiet celery becomes strong (in flavor). In macrobiotics, practitioners can change the gender of celery just as they can change the gender of a human.

Those who have not yet started macrobiotic diets are usually diagnosed as sick from the two foods at extreme ends of the gender spectrum—meat, which is too yang, and sugar, which is too yin. Men are meat. Historically, meat consumption has been tied to masculinity. Macrobiotic philosophers agree that "beef eating makes for violent and aggressive tendencies." By eliminating meat, along with most animal products, one will achieve a superior spiritual sensibility and not have, as Kushi suggests, "strong cow-like bodies, big in structure, but low in intelligence" (*One Peaceful World* 48). The spiritual goal for all people, and men especially, should be to reclaim the "passivity" that comes from "a 'vegetable' way of living" (Adams 94). Some feminists could not agree more—from *The Sexual Politics of Meat* to ecofeminism, they have linked carnivorism to aggressive masculinist behavior: excessive anger, strength, power, rape, speciesism, and world domination. In nineteenth-century American health-reform movements, the pure, feminine body was the implicit ideal achieved by hydropathy, fasting, and other dietary and health manipulations (Albanese *Nature Religions in America* 125). The "yang-ness" or aggressivity of meat eating is so abhorrent, particularly with its connection to pornography and the abuse of women, that vegetarian feminist Carol Adams insists that "meat eating is the reinscription of male power at every meal. . . . If meat is a symbol of male dominance, then the presence of meat proclaims the disempowering of women" (187).

Macrobiotics, however, is not a purely vegetarian diet. Even so, Kushi believes that beef eating blocks the energy flow from heaven, as many religions that have promoted vegetarianism believe. Excessive meat consumption "tends to limit our perception to the immediate environment and inhibit our awareness and receptivity to the unlimited scope of infinite time and space" (*The Book of Macrobiotics* 129). Eating meat prevents one from having clear spiritual impulses.[11] If a macrobiotic practitioner were to eat meat, then he or she would dull his or her sensitivity to the spiritual world while simultaneously inviting certain negative gender characteristics into his or her body. The only way to recover gender health is to compensate for the extreme (meat in this case) and apply other food remedies to feminize the yang intake.[12] Because consumption "is at the same time a form of self-identification and of communication," food choices communicate a desire to fine-tune oneself to the spirit world (Mintz 13). Bodies are vessels through which energy from heaven ("heaven's force") and energy from earth ("earth's force") travel. If the vessel is clogged, then no spiritual energy flows.

If men are meat then, conversely, women are sugar. While men are usually diagnosed initially as "extreme yang," women are often diagnosed as "extreme yin." Macrobiotics says that when out of balance, we crave the very thing that makes us sick. Being too yin, women therefore crave even more yin and eat enormous amounts of sugar (which is highly yin), which then makes them susceptible to disease. Unwittingly, women consume what destroys them. Whereas men frequently die from yang diseases such as heart attacks or particular cancers, women fade away from chronic fatigue syndrome, fibromyalgia, and breast cancer—diseases of nurturing others, while neglecting oneself. In that way, women play a part in their own demise—they make themselves so yin that they become unable to take action. Eliminating all refined white sugar (one of the main causes of yin diseases) is a frequent directive for women beginning macrobiotics. In macrobiotics, "taking action" means having a "big dream," a dream beyond "space and time," as Kushi calls it (*The Book of Macrobiotics* 201). According to macrobiotic gender theory, a woman's ultimate dream may be for a happy family; in practice, many women take the idea of the "big dream" and channel it into careers such as macrobiotic lecturers, cooks, and teachers.[13]

Eliminating sugar in order to "take action," however, is tortuous. From candy bingeing scenes in movies such as *Stella Dallas* to mass-media images of purging, women are shown as being unable to control their appetites, particularly when it comes to sugar. Macrobiotics claims that most women are oblivious to their self-induced sugar suicide. Women's mental diseases are classified as predominately yin, brought on by consuming excessive sugar. While feminists would diagnose many of these illnesses as stemming from gender oppression, macrobiotics diagnoses women's illnesses as stemming from food.[14] As sugar wears women out, it even affects the unconscious: "Too much sugar creates floating, misty, disconnected dreams that are easily forgotten and that make us tired upon waking" (*The Book of Macrobiotics* 200). On an unconscious and a conscious level, sugar is enslavement.[15] However, women can take control of this situation as soon as they eat yang foods that prevent them from withering away. Food is spiritual power that rescues women from one disorienting gender universe to indoctrinate them into another one of supposed gender freedom. Food gives women ritualistic control over the spirit world. Rather than being enslaved by old food choices, women have agency not only in the material world but in the spiritual one as well. Power has a double valence—power in this world and the next.

While gender is more often conceived as a material concern rather than a spiritual or religious one, in macrobiotics, the two are united: gender is a manifestation of spiritual well-being. Balanced yin and yang heals not just physical but spiritual health. Kushi emphasizes the spiritual: "Understanding yin/yang is not just for diet, but for freedom. At least 70 percent of our friends think the biological application of yin and yang is enough . . . and these people are fools" (*Macrobiotic Seminars of Michio Kushi* 21). In the spiritual realm, yin and yang are products of *ki* (energy or life force). In the macrobiotic "Twelve Laws of Change," the first law explains yin and yang by saying, "One infinity changes itself into complementary and antagonistic tendencies, yin and yang, in a process of endless transformation" (*The Teachings of Michio Kushi* 152).[16] Yin and yang are always infused with holy energy because they spring from the holiest single source, "one infinity." Furthermore, practitioners believe that yin and yang not only "arise endlessly" but also transform constantly (*The Teachings of Michio Kushi* 152). As distinct energies—yang is energetically downward moving, and yin is energetically upward moving—they attract and repel one another, and eventually they turn into one another in a cycle. Since men and women are yin and yang, they too transform constantly. "All things are ephemeral, constantly changing their proportion of yin and yang energies; yin changes into yang, yang changes into yin" (*The Teachings of Michio Kushi* 152). Nothing is ever "neutral" or static, but fluid.

Although I argue that macrobiotics can at moments offer a fluid and porous relationship to gender, it also relies on beliefs that are overtly essentialist, and sometimes misogynist. Macrobiotic practitioners subscribe to some form of gender difference, ranging from the more to the less extreme. If you believe in yin and yang, then on a theoretical level you must believe that women and men are essentially different. As Ohsawa suggests in his argument for an extreme form of gender essentialism, women are more yin and should stay that way:

> If a Japanese man discovers hair on the legs of a woman, it makes his flesh crawl. Hair on a woman's arms is even more ominous— the arms being more Yin than the legs. This is a sign that the woman is afflicted with the most fatal and decadent malady of all—the loss of her sexuality. A woman with hair on her arms and legs is considered no longer a woman. She has lost her femininity. (*You Are All Sanpaku* 121)

In this misogynist diatribe, if a woman appears too yang, then she has rejected her "natural" yin role and is "no longer a woman." Ohsawa's insistence that female sexuality is only recognizable when it is stereotypically "feminine" is both aggressively sexist and implicitly homophobic. From his perspective, woman must not only be appropriately yin and display no signs of yang (hair in particular), but she must be properly heterosexual to follow the law of the attraction of "opposites." In macrobiotics, the loss of sexuality is "fatal" not simply because it denies a man pleasure but because it kills the biological family, conceived as the microcosm of the world. For heterosexual mating to lead to procreation, men and women must not disrupt the "antagonistic complimentary opposites" which they embody (*Macrobiotic Seminars of Michio Kushi* 68). In contrast, "the modern world" misunderstands yin and yang principles to such a degree that they treat the sexes similarly through such practices as coeducation, argues Kushi. Thus the sexes "are becoming more alike and the attraction between them is growing less" (*Macrobiotic Seminars of Michio Kushi* 69). Sexual attraction depends on gender polarity.

Macrobiotics also has essentialist gender beliefs when it comes to a woman's place: many macrobiotic theorists believe that women belong in the home. They argue that a macrobiotic woman has power because the family is in her hands: she can create or destroy the health of the family and the quality of their dreams, an important macrobiotic focus. Kushi explains:

> The trouble with our society is that woman has forgotten the endurance and patience that enable her the final victor (*sic*) . . . she wants to win in man's world of competition (*sic*). Because of this, families are decomposing faster and faster. Women do not need to struggle to win; at the moment of birth, they have won. Unless we restore this understanding, human happiness will never return. ("What Is Love?" 48)[17]

The theory that women "control" family life through the kitchen is reminiscent of the nineteenth-century domestic ideology of the "angel in the house." In macrobiotics, women keep the family together through food production and consumption. A family who eats whole foods together stays together. As Kushi says, "Love, for a man, means 'I will eat your food.' For a woman, love means, 'I will follow your dream'" ("What Is Love?" 50). As in the most patriarchal familial relations, the woman exchanges her private domestic work for the financial safety that his public career provides. The ideal macrobiotic family is the nuclear family. In fact, macrobiotic theorists have commented on how the "demise" of the nuclear family and the lack of regular family meals have caused many world problems. To help a family cohere, a woman should channel her power through food: "A good wife then, will (1) cook well, and (2) never complain. . . . However, there are two things that a woman should complain about. First, if her husband's dream is too small; and second, if he eats out too often" ("What Is Love?" 49). Though there are only "two things" a woman should complain about, she is actually the cause of the problems in the first place—it is the quality of the food that creates dreams and makes a person want to eat out. Ultimately, then, there is great pressure on women to cook well (i.e., strictly macrobiotic), to control the blood quality of the entire family.

Though macrobiotics limits woman's role, it simultaneously values that which has been devalued by its association with women—the production and consumption of food. Historically, cooking has been the domain of women and the kitchen their sanctuary (*Food and Gender* 4). In macrobiotics, not only is cooking a "moral process," but the kitchen is elevated even further to a shrine or temple, and cooks are priests (Lupton 2). Because food "is a reflection of the cook's condition and judgment," one must be as purified as possible (*Aveline Kushi's Complete Guide to*

Macrobiotic Cooking 11). Indeed, in order to prepare foods with the right gender proportions, one must be in a peaceful gender state. Cooking is so important that practitioners believe that when they cook they place themselves in an "evolutionary order of eating" (*Macrobiotic Cooking for Everyone* 80). This order is

> based on billions of years of biological development, culminating in the appearance of cereal grains in the vegetable world and man in the world of animals . . . we seek to encompass this entire evolutionary process in the range of foods that we cook, from the most primitive, single-celled enzymes and bacteria . . . to the most highly developed cereal grains. (*Macrobiotic Cooking for Everyone* 80)

Cooking completes an evolutionary process, from "caveman" to "macro man." Not surprisingly, discussions about cooking take on a primitive aura, harkening back to stereotypes of "hunter/gatherer cultures" where women cooked around the fire. If a woman cooks badly, then she might destroy this human evolutionary chain, thereby destroying traditional yin/yang gender paradigms. Praise and blame are ready at hand for women who complete this vital task.

By placing traditional women's work first through supporting food preparation and the nuclear family, macrobiotic practitioners believe that apocalyptic trends in ecology, politics, and health can be reversed. For example, Dr. Martha Cottrell argues that the power women have is their "essential" nurturing power. However, technological invasions and the accumulation of "male" diseases are eroding that power, and "the female needs to be protected as well as the young so that nurturing can take place until the next generation can get along on its own" (*Women's Health Guide* 38).[18] She argues, "Traditionally, the female has been the one that has received fertilization, given birth, and nurtured the next generation. And now we see that we are allowing this to happen in the test tube. We are giving over this power that is female to technology" (*Women's Health Guide* 39). Here, "civilization" and technology are coded male. In order to repair this damage, we must elevate the status of woman as mother. Mothers gain power in macrobiotics by determining the health of their children through the food ingested during pregnancy. Mothers even determine the quality of a child's "gender," that is, the quality and strength of a baby's yin-ness or yang-ness. When a child is born, its yin or yang status is as important as its gender: "At birth, the boy is yin, the girl yang" (Kushi "What Is Love?" 48). Whether praised or blamed, woman as mother is at the center of macrobiotics.

All of these macrobiotic gender theories, many of which are profoundly conservative, seem to close down any gender experimentation within this diet. Women occupy two positions in this system: either woman's difference is elevated above the male, or it is critiqued and deemed inferior. This fundamental belief in difference manifests itself in two ways: sometimes women are unequal to men and confined to a separate inferior sphere; at other times, women are different from men and held up as superior. However, the appeal of macrobiotics can be understood best through the culture of "everyday life."[19] In macrobiotics, actual daily practices are the "site of struggle," as theorist John Fiske says, wherein living gender readjustments are made in the midst of foundational sexism. Theories are not entirely borne out in practice. It is lived experience that dictates how certain gender formations operate. Macrobiotics offers practitioners a system of yin/yang classification and practices that heal disease and offer a way out of sick gender paradigms, as it were. George Ohsawa says that one must become "a creative artist in the arrangement of Yin/Yang elements in your daily meals—the most fundamental and important art in your life" (*You Are All Sanpaku* 115). By eating certain foods cooked in certain ways, an individual can achieve a healthy new gender balance.

Recovering Gender Health: The Satisfactions of Daily Mechanics in Macrobiotics

In macrobiotics, calibrating one's gender means even more than preparing and cooking yin and yang foods in particular ways—it is about an entire yin and yang lifestyle. Yin and yang are finely tuned for good health from the first moment one comes to macrobiotics. From understanding disease, having a special diagnosis, and handling food cravings to chewing effectively to eliminating bad toxins and arranging one's home, practitioners regulate gender health through these ritualized daily practices.

Before a person discovers macrobiotics, the body is considered diseased, as is the gender. Because macrobiotic experts diagnose anyone who is not macrobiotic as diseased, they see the world as being full of sick individuals who wander around unstable because of extreme yin and yang energies (*Diet for Natural Beauty* 31). As Michio Kushi says, "Our red globules are yinnized from sugar, chemicals, and drugs—making them and us confused and uncertain of our direction" (*Macrobiotic Seminars of Michio Kushi* 65). Like in New Age culture generally, health becomes spiritual salvation, and disease is often regarded as an opportunity for spiritual enlightenment. Rosalind Coward has critiqued this notion that "total health is something to be actively pursued, a higher state than any of us had previously experienced" (44). She notes how this quest for perfect health has changed radically from the late nineteenth century:

> The corporeal body is no longer something which holds us back on our quest for perfectibility. Instead it has become the place where perfectibility can be found. Yet no less than with earlier views of the necessity to win salvation of the soul, now there is a sense of the necessity for the individual to work at, and win, the rewards locked in the human body. (43)

As Coward predicts, in macrobiotics, disease is viewed as a product of mis-education or ignorance that can be remedied to "win the rewards locked in the human body." Macrobiotic disease narratives have a "born-again" quality where life before macrobiotics was all sickness and life after macrobiotics all bliss.[20]

In order to alleviate gender "dis-ease," those new to macrobiotics must have what is called an "Oriental diagnosis." This diagnosis begins with an unconventional examination that closely observes the hands, feet, face, and pulse as well as gathers information about lifestyle, bowel movements, and ancestry. Assessing gender health can be done by simply looking at someone's face to read his or her "condition." Because women and men are seen as having essentially different natures and bodies, their diagnoses often follow their constitution. Women are often too yin, and men are too yang, and they need their opposite to "make balance" (*The Teachings of Michio Kushi* 55). When diagnosing, Eastern and Western standards of beauty and health can be at odds: fashion models with big, pouty lips are held up as an example of sick Western decadence; in Oriental diagnosis, big lips mean "poor intestines" and constipation (*The Teachings of Michio Kushi* 54). Macrobiotic experts argue that since health, like disease, is a material embodiment of a spiritual condition, as one becomes healthier (i.e., eating a macrobiotic diet to balance one's yin and yang), one's actual physiognomy changes. Big ears, small noses, clear skin, and pleasant-smelling perspiration all signal that one has a healthy constitution (*Macrobiotic Seminars of Michio Kushi* 46). Good gender health means that, in theory, one looks more like one's ancestors than "modern man." By going back in time, one slows down the rate of apocalypse. "It is better to eat foods that are farther back in biological history. They widen the scope of thinking, which means good memory" (Abehsera 205). This antimodern diagnosis initiates the consumption of appropriate and life-altering elements of yin and yang foods—a woman can turn around a sick "yin diagnosis" and attain better balance, that is, a stronger, more powerful self, even within constrained gender norms, by eating balanced food. A person's "vibrations, which are manifested in their words, expressions, and all of their actions," are also diagnosed. If a person's voice and actions are "quick, efficient, but quiet," then he or she is healthy (*The Teachings of Michio Kushi* 51). Gender is adjusted according to actions that are yin and yang: whistling for a woman is too yang, a sickness in the West where women are out of balance. Diagnosis simultaneously prescribes normative gender roles while implicitly encouraging each gender to scramble those roles by constantly manipulating yin and yang usage.

For example, pre-macrobiotics, a man might have one of the most yang diseases, known as a "man's cancer," such as cancer of the colon. According to macrobiotics, the colon, a cleansing organ deep in the body, is easily corrupted by the intake of extremely yang foods such as meat, especially organ or smoked meats, or dairy products, such as hard cheeses. A macrobiotic teacher would diagnose this man as fundamentally too yang because he would exhibit several of many yang traits: tense, with angry emotions, rigid belief systems, a lack of spiritual intuition, and perhaps even megalomania and impotence. For a man with colon cancer to rid himself of disease, he must rid himself of all the extreme yang foods, actions, and beliefs that brought on the disease in the first place. This is not just a matter of examining his "feminine" side; rather, he must orient himself to a spiritual order emphasizing a new gender identity founded on yin-ness.

"Yin-nizing" this man means that he must digest yin foods such as lettuce and apples and enact yin practices, such as singing a song or scrubbing his body in order to feminize himself. Because the macrobiotic ideal is peaceful balance, men defy their gender norm by consuming foods that pacify them. In order to stay well, he will have to spend the rest of his life ingesting "good yin" (squash and brown rice syrup) and rejecting bad yin (chocolates and soda). He can never presume that he is completely well, because in macrobiotics, disease exists on a continuum: everyone is more or less healthy, with the body always giving explicit warnings as to whether it is sick or not. Macrobiotic experts believe that you never just "get" cancer, but that numerous warning signs appear long before the body cries for help by exhibiting an extreme disease. Any disease that one exhibits indicates that gender imbalance is present as well. A yin disease such as breast cancer indicates yin gender dysfunction. And because disease is never static, gender dis-ease is never static: a person is never one fixed gender. Instead, gender health requires vigilance.

While in the macrobiotic spiritual world gender may be clearly defined, in the material world there are gender tensions and contradictions. For example, some macrobiotic men experience a tension between sexual drive or potency and a grain and vegetable diet. On the one hand, a nearly vegetarian diet creates "one peaceful world," as Kushi claims, but on the other hand, macrobiotic men must continue to be "manly." At the most prominent macrobiotic conference several years ago, I attended a men's health panel where jokes about potency dominated much of the hour—in defiance of the fear of impotency tied to vegetarianism, these men argue that they are cleaner, stronger, and more sexually active because of macrobiotics.[21] Therefore, the diet results in accentuated gender difference even while its daily practices undermine it. Men assert their potency even as they eat a marginalized diet that feminizes them in several different ways: by refusing the culturally sanctioned ingestion of masculinizing meat and cooking vegetables instead, by fetishizing an Orientalist culture in a dominant culture where what is Asian is implicitly feminized, by emphasizing peacefulness that matters more than aggressive male posturing, and by desiring spiritual attunement that is implicitly gender attunement.

However, until one is healthy, food cravings are interpreted as cravings for an unhealthy gender identity. Just as language precedes thought and forms gender identity, food precedes cravings and affects gender desire. Macrobiotics believes that most people have a "false consciousness" about food choices: Americans "believe" that they are choosing their food, when in fact their food is choosing them. "Cravings signify that our diet is imbalanced in the opposite yin or yang direction from the food which we are attracted . . . if we are attracted to fruit juice or ice cream, our diet is probably too salty, overcooked, and generally too yang" (*The Book of Macrobiotics* 191). The logic is that you crave the opposite food of what you just ate. For example, for most unhealthy Americans, if they eat a hamburger and french fries (extreme yang foods), then they will desire a cola drink (yin) or an ice-cream sundae (yin) to finish the meal. This theory of cravings has gender implications. If one has consumed a lifetime of hamburgers and has become outwardly yang (masculine, aggressive, hot, strong), then it is because one is inwardly yin (feminine, passive, cold, quiet). Behind every yang person is a yin person waiting to get out. Immediate sensual response to food cravings leads to instability. Pre-macrobiotics, gender fluctuates wildly in an unconscious way that leads to spiritual derangement. Post-macrobiotics, gender is conscious and moves smoothly on a peaceful continuum. Michio Kushi believes that "modern civilization itself can be viewed as an enormous mental health clinic, with hundreds of millions of people who are mentally disordered" (*The Book of Macrobiotics* 202). In contrast, peace is found when gender movement becomes predictable and controlled rather than chaotic.

In order to regulate gender, food cravings must be controlled. Cravings for food, while spontaneous, are never an expression of "pure" desire but understood as the product of one's last meal, of one's last gender orientation. Desire is constituted by food, and not the other way around. Until purged of bad yin and yang, one never has a legitimate desire. When toxins leave the body, "the discharged food particles often impress themselves in our consciousness and we experience them as cravings" (*The Book of Macrobiotics* 191). Our bodies indicate "disequilibrium." Cravings for McDonalds are cravings, not needs, and should be redirected toward whole-food options—options that are expensive and take longer to produce. In that way, macrobiotics critiques monopoly food producers, from conglomerates and large grocery stores to chain restaurants. An early critic of the industrialized food economy or the rise of factory farming and big agribusiness, macrobiotics believes that importing exotic fruits and vegetables from other economies throws local ecological and individual systems out of balance. Macrobiotics blames globalization for defiling citizens' bodies daily: people lose their minds by eating Westernized food, which renders them incapable of being good citizens. They cannot control their desires and do not understand their origins. Macrobiotics theorizes that those who are lost eating the standard American diet remain stuck in rigid gender roles. The national body and the gendered body are constituted by one another.

Chewing, the next step in food consumption, affects gender digestion and assimilation, as it were. Chewing is so important that Michio Kushi claims that chewing food at least fifty times per mouthful, and sometimes up to two hundred times per mouthful, distinguishes us from the "lower animals, such as the snake, [who] often bolt their food while more advanced animals chew" (*Macrobiotic Seminars of Michio Kushi* 65). Chewing serves at least two purposes: it increases spiritual capacity by turning eating into meditation, and it decreases the digestive workload. "Chewing makes digestion much easier, thinking clearer and advances evolution in the direction of happiness (An old Japanese word for 'chewing' is 'God's work')" (*Macrobiotic Seminars of Michio Kushi* 65). In contrast to the hasty and mindless food consumption of the West, the act of chewing rigorously does not allow one to talk, shovel food, or think of anything else—except one's meal. In fact, as one macrobiotic counselor suggests, chewing wards off Western decadence and cultural decay: "What am I eating? Indeed! I'm eating the days of the latter Twentieth Century. They're pretty hard to swallow; let's chew them well, and not swallow them whole" (qtd. in Albanese *Nature Religion* 196).

By chewing well, one can also alter one's gender. Chewing each mouthful hundreds of times is a metaphor for consuming and digesting the yin/yang cosmology. A fork (or chopstick) of well-chewed food is a daily affirmation of yang morphing into yin—through masticating, one can actively manipulate a gender substance. If one eats a yang steak but does not chew it, then it cannot be transformed thoroughly into yin and will rot in the colon. To have the smoothest digestion, one should "begin a meal with the most yang food and progress toward the most yin," which helps the flow of "juices" (*Macrobiotic Seminars of Michio Kushi* 66). In Kushi seminars, pictures of the digestive process display undigested food putrefying in the caverns of the body and creating disease. The gendered effects of food are also blocked if food is not chewed. When Kushi says, "We are our own masters, and no one else can chew for us," he implies that chewing fosters individual agency to regulate the food effects—and, by extension, the gender effects—on the body (*The Book of Macrobiotics* 83). Whereas gender identity is often projected onto a subject and interpellates others into gender ideology before birth, chewing is one of the many active steps in macrobiotics that give practitioners agency. If a woman wants to be healthy and powerful, then she can chew carefully to turn her food into more effective yin substances. Furthermore, as Kushi notes, "We should chew thoroughly in order to both physicalize and spiritualize what we are eating" (*The Book of Macrobiotics* 131). By usurping control of digestion, usually understood as passive, and converting yang to yin, gender balance is only a mouthful away.

Practitioners manipulate various macrobiotic practices—diagnosis of disease, cooking, chewing, and discharge—to determine their gender. A popular term for the elimination of toxic food and waste, "discharge," signals the completion of the initial macrobiotic cycle, which moves from disease, craving, food consumption, to elimination of bad food. Discharge also includes "culture," diagnosed as sick from woman's failure to stay in the home, rising divorce rates, and gender dysphoria from excessive Western dietary consumption. "To change our physical condition, we must first discharge any excessive or toxic substances, but in these situations, exaggerated psychological mechanisms resist such release" (*Macrobiotics and Oriental Medicine* 235). "These situations" indicates those for whom discharge is slow. Kushi claims that psychological factors may be resisting a "letting go" of the past. Here, food symbolizes the "abject," or that which cannot or will not be seen in one's psyche. The kinds and quality of "discharge" for those new to macrobiotics provide a kind of abject folklore: people claim to ooze toxic substances and pass fatty deposits. While material discharged is disgusting, it makes way for purification.

Spiritual enlightenment attained through food is a process of making the body clean. In Doris Witt's work on food and racial identity, she notes how African American "soul food" has signified all that is "dirty," "dark," and "primal" (81). In contrast, in macrobiotics, the racial fantasy is an exoticized spiritual fantasy: ordered, pure Eastern bodies have a holiness that Western bodies should emulate. Feminist theorist Deborah Lupton claims that the abject is also implicitly feminine: food is unclean, decaying, and a "source of great ambivalence" because it "forever threatens contamination and bodily impurity" (3). If discharge is conceived as a way to "reconstruct our past," to recreate our blood cells, then, spiritually, "reconstructing" the past means returning to a "better" gender self founded in Orientalism (*Macrobiotics and Oriental Medicine* 237).

If one eats well, then one can literally and figuratively flush out one's past and usher in a new life with entirely new blood cells. Materially, practitioners believe that new blood cells are created every seven days, seven weeks, and seven years (*The Book of Macrobiotics* 202). In order to create better "blood quality," practitioners religiously scrub their bodies, wear all-natural fibers, chew well, eat less, and eat discharge-inducing foods, such as the beloved carrot-daikon drink known as the "roto-rooter" of macrobiotics (*Macrobiotics and Oriental Medicine* 235). There is a thrill in being entirely transformed, or "saved," as Coward notes, by shedding the old body, with its unworkable, Western-gendered sensibilities, and inhabiting a new kind of health—particularly gender health.

After beginning to eat well, Kushi encourages people to make further lifestyle changes to foster spiritual growth, usually described as cultivating the "natural."[22] The natural is understood as both genders having "good" proportions of yin and yang. Kushi argues that "when we eat macrobiotically, we begin to recover our natural sensitivity and start to avoid synthetic clothing and artificial fabrics" (*The Book of Macrobiotics* 131). That is, a heightened sensitivity to "all-natural" or nontoxic dwellings, furnishings, technology, and "personal care" products increases as one eats the diet (132). In effect, this obsession with the "natural" means nothing short of revolution. Living in harmony with the seasons is paramount: "During the more yin winter season, we should emphasize more yang foods and cooking methods, while in the hot summer months, our diet should generally become more yin" (Esko and Esko 66). Nature is conceived as perfectly harmonious, even if we are not: "When we experience misery of any kind let us remember that nature and the universe are still constantly cycling, and our distress is caused only by our lack of harmony" (*The Book of Macrobiotics* 152). The natural is linked with the democratic, peace-loving, humanist society—if we all ate better, then there would be no oppression.

Practitioners have a "natural" sense of their gender that in the material realm is calibrated, adjusted, and controlled. Through food, one can be whatever gender one desires—that is "natural." While theorists have critiqued the idea that gender can be put on and taken off as a performance, ingesting gendered food is a similar kind of performance. However, in macrobiotics, gender is always already fluctuating in the daily—one does not have to "put on" a carrot's energy, because one will experience a number of "yin-nized" energies throughout the day. In macrobiotics, the "natural," which is a whole, primitive, and spiritually infused essentialism, exists alongside the material, where the "natural" is a daily practice of gender adjustment.

The Promise of Fluid Essentialism in Macrobiotics

All of these various macrobiotic practices—diagnosis of disease, cooking, chewing, and discharge—are manipulated by practitioners to determine their gender. While I agree that macrobiotic theories of yin and yang are based in a static essentialism, in macrobiotic *practice*, gender is a fluid essentialism, and therein lies its attraction. Macrobiotics is essentialist because yin and yang are naturalized as separate, distinct gender categories through the spiritual, but fluid because the practitioner controls these substances through daily ritual. Understanding this distinction is the key to recognizing the true limitations and possibilities of macrobiotics. Even if this sense of control over one's gender is illusory, it is important to understand one of the major appeals of this diet, and the satisfactions gained from it.

My contention is that these satisfactions do not fit within the traditional feminist understanding of diet. Whereas most diets encourage women to strive for an unattainable body image, macrobiotics not only rejects these perfect body standards but also gives women internal tools to navigate external gender demands. Through macrobiotics, one can create gender on a plate. By constantly adjusting the spiritual principles of yin and yang, which are manifested in the material world through everything from food itself to cooking practices, one gains control over one's gender. But when does "control" over gender mutate into being controlled by the diet itself? When does food cease to provide pleasure and only become that "which threatens human mastery" (Bynum 300)? Critic Kimberly Lau argues that macrobiotic eating "fragments the mind and body, further entrenches a mechanized model of the body, and advocates mental control to overcome bodily desires for various foods" (61). For many, it is a mystery why practitioners continue to follow a diet that is time consuming, intellectually demanding (one must always be thinking about yin and yang calibration), conservative in its gender politics, and difficult to maintain because of its purity and asceticism.

In this way, macrobiotics is a paradoxical phenomenon. It is profoundly deterministic because food intake determines identity entirely, but simultaneously voluntary because one can fashion a new identity by ingesting different foods. Macrobiotics offers transformation, just as other diets do, but in this case, the transformation is the promise of spiritual enlightenment and perfect health rather than external beauty. This possibility of transformation explains why, for many, macrobiotic principles are appealing in the face of valid feminist diet critiques. The spiritual sanctification of a mundane experience—eating food—means that boring, daily practices become holy. Manipulating gender is a spiritually exalted experience rather than a struggle in the material world for rights. Because macrobiotics is at once fundamentally conservative and yet open to daily adjustment, it gives women a tool to manipulate gender in the private sphere rather than the public one. Instead of taking up feminist public action and protest, women thrive on the spiritual satisfactions gained from gender equilibrium. Macrobiotics also gives spiritual meaning to traditional female practices, even while it explicitly attacks feminism. Furthermore, it offers female practitioners the satisfaction of feeling "countercultural." Practitioners feel that they live outside the bounds of Western culture by practicing Eastern spirituality. The countercultural status of macrobiotics provides a space and a community through which dominant values and ideologies can be inverted, parodied, and manipulated.

Because my argument is based largely on reading textual artifacts of the macrobiotic subculture, it only gestures toward the potential for gathering sociological or thorough ethnographic data regarding women's participation in and practice of macrobiotics. Even still, it is noteworthy that at every macrobiotic event I attended over the course of four years, white women made up roughly 70 percent of the participants.[23] Women participate in huge numbers in the Macrobiotic Women's Health Seminar and the Women's Macrobiotic Society, and they cook, lecture, teach, practice shiatsu, and diagnose clients. Though the most conservative macrobiotic theories about gender are foundational in the yin/yang philosophy, by and large they are ignored in macrobiotic communities, on

Web sites, and in books on general macrobiotic health. As one female macrobiotic teacher said to me, "I could not be teaching or have published books if it weren't for the power macrobiotics gave me." While many macrobiotic narratives indicate how women have reclaimed their lives through macrobiotic health, they also describe how women have taken on more public roles, even in the midst of conservative macrobiotic gender theory. Perhaps the ultimate power that macrobiotic women have is the power to heal themselves, as Gale Jack claims in "Ten Things Macrobiotic Women Do Well": "We may choose to see a doctor, an acupuncturist, a macrobiotic counselor . . . but we view them as co-creators of our wellness and do not give them ultimate power over our well being."

Even though, ultimately, control over one's gender may be elusive in macrobiotics, the pleasures of attempting to tinker with gender on a daily basis are manifold. Rather than reinscribing base essentialism, macrobiotic practices may provide new metaphors for understanding gender identity, even while that identity is founded on essentialist theories about gender. Macrobiotics gives women the chance to turn gender into a ritualized equation of daily life. Food rituals are holy ground: controlling them is not a disorder but a spiritually sanctioned enlightenment vehicle. By recognizing how gender is recalibrated through food rituals, we may understand better how the phenomenon of gender—part social, part biological, and often amorphous, painful, and unjust—becomes a practice of daily mechanics.

4

The Structure of Prehistorical Memory in the American Goddess Movement

> I bless the women of prehistory—
> the strong, the unnamed, the forgotten.
> —Barbara Ardinger, *A Woman's Book*
> *of Rituals & Celebrations*

With the rise of second-wave feminism in the 1970s, many women separated themselves from what they perceived as "patriarchal"— the state, the family, education, religion—in order to create distinct feminist spheres of influence. In the religious sphere, women developed gynocentric spiritual practices to counter alienating androcentric ones. As one female spiritual seeker said about male-dominated religious rituals, "Women get tired of hearing 'he-he-he' all the time" (qtd. in Harvey). Some women tried to reform the religions of their childhood, others sought out alternatives to mainstream religion, such as yoga or Scientology, and still others pursued Goddess worship, a spiritual practice in which women worship a female God, often called the Great Mother. Goddess worship presumes that roughly 10,000 years ago women ruled the earth peacefully, and that in a future time, women will rule again.[1] In the 1980s and 1990s, the proliferation of Goddess articles, books, Web sites, and groups indicated that "She," as the Goddess is called, was "making a comeback" (Lacher). In fact, the "Goddess movement" has grown to such a degree that conservative scholar Philip Davis called it "one of the most striking religious success stories of the late twentieth century" (4).

While Goddess worship is currently popular, theories about the existence of a matriarchy have been around for some time.[2] In the nineteenth century, several scholars, most famously J. J. Bachofen, posited that the beginning of history was matriarchal, and that "women's domination of state and family long remained undiminished" (107). Bachofen believed

113

that history went through several stages until matriarchy was "followed by patriarchy," which ushered in civilization (73). In the twentieth century, theorists such as James Frazier, Robert Graves, and Joseph Campbell also connected the matriarchal with a precivilized past, and depending on their bias, that past was either superior or inferior to the present (Eller, *Living in the Lap of the Goddess* 151). Presently, in order to legitimize their thriving "religion," Goddess worshippers have drawn on some of the same archaeological data and historical evidence to document the fact that women once ruled the earth.

According to Goddess worshippers, whole cultures celebrated the Goddess by performing seasonal rituals, creating cave paintings that represented Her power, and making statues in Her honor. In their vision of prehistory, women were revered by their cultures for their ability to give birth and "bleed without dying." Female power was omnipresent. The most well-known archaeologist of Goddess materials is Marija Gimbutas, who has interpreted hundreds of figurines from various digs as evidence for the existence of prehistorical Goddess worship and is known in some circles as the "mother of modern Goddess history." She argues that Goddess culture existed until "it was savagely destroyed by the patriarchal element and it never recovered" (238). Gimbutas's work is widely cited, and in books such as *The Great Cosmic Mother*, *The Chalice and the Blade*, and *When God Was a Woman*, Goddess worshippers claim Gimbutas's version of a matriarchal past as their "origin story," and they tell it repeatedly. As Goddess proponent Hallie Iglehart Austen says, "Research from every continent indicates that, from roughly 30,000 to 3,000 B.C.E., women and the Goddess were honored" (xvii). Historical goddess research of a past matriarchal society founds current Goddess worship beliefs today. Their history is so vital to their claims to legitimacy that it has been called "the central vehicle of feminist spirituality's evangelism to the cultural mainstream" (*Living in the Lap of the Goddess* 155). Indeed, the idea of a matriarchal prehistory now has enough popular resonance that even some outside of Goddess worship give it credence.

Though Goddess worshippers find their history indisputable, recent feminist academics are skeptical of their narratives and say that their evidence is deeply flawed. Many feminist academics argue that it is impossible to prove that a matriarchal past ever existed.[3] For instance, feminist archaeologists such as Margaret Conkey and Ruth Tringham assert that Goddess historians lack scientific proof and exhibit an "indifference to—and rejection of—historical specificity" (209). They argue that Gimbutas relies upon outdated and reductive methodologies that are invalid (Meskell 83). Goddess worshippers construct a "gynocentric" past, these critics claim, by reducing numerous possible interpretations of objects to a single "essentialist" one. For instance, the large-breasted, heavy-hipped figurines that Goddess worshippers claim as Goddess representations could be read in a number of ways—as sexual fantasy objects for men, for example. Protuberant breasts and pronounced hips do not a matriarchy make. Feminist anthropologist Micaela di Leonardo voices her frustration with Goddess worshippers who insist on their one reading when she criticizes a spiritual seeker whose essentialist impulses are "a potted combination of woman the gatherer, lunar cycles and goddess worship," and laments that "even feminists with no interest in specious evolutionary reasoning have fallen victim to the vision of an innately nurturant, maternal womankind" (27). Instead, feminist archaeologists say that Goddess worshippers should accept "ambiguity" when interpreting prehistory and its gender roles because no claims can be made with certainty (Conkey and Tringham 231). Ultimately, feminist academics have been disappointed by the Goddess movement, which they see as "a seemingly feminist social movement within popular culture [which] conflicts with many of the goals and hopes of . . . an explicitly feminist, engendered archaeology" (Conkey and Tringham 205).[4] Even feminist sociologist Cynthia Eller, who has written the most thorough account of the matriarchal prehistory thesis, suggests that while this myth may serve a "feminist function" by inspiring women in a way that political activism might not, in the end, the matriarchal myth harms contemporary feminism by living in an apolitical past instead of a political present (*The Myth of Matriarchal Prehistory* 18).

The fight over a matriarchal past provokes such strong arguments from feminist academics and Goddess worshippers that the dispute has reached a stalemate where "neither side speaks to the other" (Goodison and Morris 6). This stalemate exists because both sides are focused only on questions of evidence and historical argumentation rather than on the psychology of prehistorical memory. That is, they are concerned solely with debating the historical truth of matriarchal prehistory rather than with analyzing the social function that such "truths" play in contemporary Goddess culture. Goddess culture is an attempt to empower women as women outside of the constraints of modern-day feminism. Goddess worshippers may play fast and loose with history, but we need to understand why they take such liberties instead of simply critiquing them for doing so.

The Present Necessity of Prehistorical Memory

Goddess worshippers do not base their claims of matriarchy on historical "facts" alone. They claim to have repressed memories of the Goddess that can be recovered. Goddess worshippers argue that the trauma of being separated from the Goddess by patriarchy erased all memory of prehistorical matriarchy, but that these memories can be recuperated. Through reading Goddess myths, worshipping with other women, visiting Goddess sites, or holding figurines, worshippers believe that the lost memory will return. As Goddess psychologist Jean Houston says, "Tomorrow holds the promise of recovery of forgotten wisdom" (qtd. in Reis 34). Wisdom, like memory, is simply forgotten, not lost. For worshippers, excavating Goddess memories is a survival project: every memory of the Goddess ensures that She survives. It also guarantees that the trauma that caused the erasure of the memory in the first place will be healed.

This chapter argues that Goddess worshippers strategically use "memory" (whether true or not) to construct a prehistory that gives them access to bodily power. This approach to the past is directly counter to how liberal rights feminism has chosen to orient itself: while most feminists want to leave the past behind and create a new future, Goddess worshippers wish to abandon the future and go back to the past. For Goddess worshippers, power is unattainable in a progressive framework where history is an enlightened, emancipatory "march of progress." Because these prehistorical "memories" appear to be a deluded fantasy and a scientific impossibility, critics have not talked about the concept of memory in Goddess culture. Consequently, even while critics have focused on the difference between memory and history in the academy, this distinction has not been made in Goddess culture critiques. Instead, the psychological, political, and cultural signification of this memory meaning system has been rejected outright. Critics set history and Goddess memory against each other as antitheses; one is true, one is simply false. In contrast, I explore the structure of this "memory meaning system" and understand that what Goddess worshippers call memory is necessarily far more slippery, contingent, even "made up" than the historical evidence usually required in these debates.

In order to grasp why Goddess worshippers draw so frequently on "memory," which connotes "spirituality and authenticity" and is a "critical site for the generation and inflection of affective bonds," it is important to make distinctions between structures of memory (Klein 130). Christopher Castiglia says that people remember with two different orientations to the past: one, a progressive framework, wherein one believes that we should leave the past behind as "things are better now"; and two, a nostalgic framework, where the past is seen as a romantic utopia that is better than the present or the future. Castiglia argues that having a nostalgic version of the past is a kind of "strategic remembering," or, as Fou-

Past Goddess worshipping = death by human males, therefore heroic and highly emotionally charged

cault calls it, a "*countermemory*," which can serve as a "competing narrative of the past composed of memories that exceed official public history" (qtd. in Castiglia 168). Such *countermemories* "show disempowered people 'not who they were, but what they must remember having been'" (qtd. in Castiglia 168). For Goddess worshippers, "what they must remember having been" is powerful women who found pleasure in the body. By an instantaneous memory they can immediately claim the power that feminism could grant them only through an arduous historical progress of gradual assimilation into the public sphere. Rather than leave the past behind and work for a "better" feminism now, worshippers yearn for the community that once existed, and they do everything in their present power to go back and revel in it.

The right to memory exists within an embattled terrain over its legitimacy: What constitutes a valid memory? What is being remembered? And whose interests does the memory serve? In Goddess culture, it is important to understand the extent to which worshippers construct their memories in response to a perceived external threat. In other words, memories of prehistory are countermemories in part because they exist in the context of hostile reception by critics who believe these memories to be ludicrous, false, and aligned with a larger cultural trend of the hysterical.[5] Critic Robert Sheaffer dismissed a central beloved Goddess text, the documentary *Goddess Remembered*, by calling it, "A Case of False Memory Syndrome," thus comparing the recovery of matriarchal prehistory to the recovery of sexual abuse memories (qtd. in Davis 24). His critique implies that Goddess worshippers are simply "making up the past." Clearly, the experience of Goddess worshippers is very different from the experience of purported sexual abuse survivors; however, both describe their memories as a recovery from trauma felt in the body, and both should be taken on their own terms.

For Goddess worshippers, remembering is a gesture of reconciliation and unification with the past. Remembering takes one out of linear time, in which the Enlightenment subject is produced, and into prehistory, and a better "presubjecthood." When Goddess worshipper Christine Downing claims "to remember is to be remembered," she suggests that remembering the Goddess initiates a relationship with Her (4). The Goddess will both remember and love you back. Not only is there a homoerotic component to love for the Goddess, but also, demographically, lesbians participate in large numbers in Goddess worship. This is not surprising, given the focus in Goddess worship on women's love and appreciation for other women, even if in the form of female deities. "To be remembered" suggests that a Great Female Force in history is waiting longingly to recognize and love women in the present. Even if never recognized, the Great Mother will remain omnipresent. Psychologist Patricia Reis tells this story in her Goddess poem: "From the beginning, / We have been with you. / We are the ancient ones / And we remember" (36). In Reis's cosmology, not only have the "ancient ones" always been "there" from the beginning of time, but they also remember a woman's past for her, in case she has forgotten it. Friendly ancestral ghosts, not connected by blood but by an essential femaleness, remember the matriarchal past and pray for a matriarchal future. As Patrice Wynne reminds worshippers, we are "held as a prayer in the wombs of our ancestors" (xviii). By communicating with prehistory, Goddess worshippers access a benevolent, ancestral, and ancient female culture.

This body memory of prehistorical matriarchy is so powerful that Goddess worshippers try to live in prehistory rather than in the present. Though this quest is obviously impossible, worshippers still make it an active spiritual practice that they call "rememberfulness" (Ardinger 31). In contrast to the Buddhist practice of "mindfulness," where one attempts to live fully in the present moment rather than in the past or future, in "rememberfulness" worshippers attempt to live fully in the past. Worshippers are encouraged to "practice the presence of the Goddess" by stopping anytime during the day or night, at the office or at home, and "remember who you are"—"sheltered by the flowing blue cloak of our Mother, living on the skin of an organism named Earth, living as a child of the oldest goddess, who is Gaia" (Ardinger 31). In stories, interpretations of figurines, travel narratives to Goddess sites, and descriptions of Goddess rituals, worshippers dissolve the boundary between themselves and the past female "Other" by asserting a oneness with the past. Worshippers describe how the Goddess is "inside," "around," "calling through," and "always communicating" with women in the present.

In spite of being caught between the past and present, worshippers believe that their practices do not just reconnect them with the past but actually "reenact" it. As one worshipper said, rituals "are now as they have been for over 10,000 years" (Jamal 187). Because present rituals are thought to be exactly like prehistorical ones, worshippers believe that they experience prehistory *itself* through ritual. Goddess worshippers feel the past as a memory in their body, even as they live in the present. All the while, worshippers fantasize about this prehistorical space and time where they believe that these categories existed differently. If memory is "the story of double projection: the past is repeated and revered in the present, and the present is projected back onto the past," then the body is neither past nor present in Goddess culture, as it can travel between the two (Ramadanovic 61). To practice remembering is to meditate on a different body state with the goal of eventually becoming *that* prehistorical body.

The Racial Ideology of Prehistorical Memory

The body that Goddess worshippers fantasize about is a primitive body. Since "primitives" and/or people of color have been stereotyped as "all body" rather than mind by Western cultures, it is not surprising that worshippers express their desire for the body by turning to tropes of racial primitivism that reproduce suspect ideologies. As Marianna Torgovnick further explains, "the word *primitive*—with its aura of unchangeability, voicelessness, mystery, and difference from the West" (*Gone Primitive* 20, emphasis in original) gives New Age followers "a model of how to live a spiritual and harmonious life" (*Primitive Passions* 182). For Goddess worshippers, the primitive or "primal" is associated with sex, darkness, and earthiness, or sensibilities that white women do not believe they can access in the present.[6]

White Goddess worshippers take on the primitive body by following certain practices. In her Goddess art book, Hallie Iglehart Austen instructs worshippers on how to "return" to the body of prehistory. Next to a large photograph of a dark statue with prominent breasts, protruding bottom, and arms raised high, or the "Bird-Headed Snake Goddess, Africa, C. 4,000 B.C.E," Austen writes instructions on how to mirror the Goddess's posture and demeanor:

> Take the pose of this Goddess, for she can teach you about the union of earth and sky, spirit and body. Stand with your legs about a foot apart, knees slightly bent. Feel your feet firmly planted on the ground, the muscles of your genitals and anus relaxed. Thrust your buttocks out and your chest forward, making sure to keep breathing. Raise your arms to the sky. And now imagine that you have a bird's head. Open your mouth, and with your exhalation, let your breath become sound . . . let it be your song. How do you feel with your body undulating, grounded yet soaring? Continue to breathe fully, and sing the song of yourself as the Bird-Headed Snake Goddess. (8)

The ritual imperative is that worshippers should not just meditate on the Goddess but literally take on her form by assuming her pose. The fantasy that present ritual is literally prehistorical ritual enables women to capture not only the body memory of a prehistorical figurine but to inhabit the "actual" prehistoric body. By posing, or kinesthetically assuming the exact posture of the statue, women are shuttled into the past. Austen's instructions for the placement of the body indicate worshippers' beliefs about what the prehistorical female body does.

The prehistorical female body, like the figurine itself, is explicitly racialized. Since most Goddess worshippers are white, "taking the pose of the Bird-Headed Snake Goddess" means that white middle-class women, who may be alienated from their bodies in late capitalism, assume the position of a black figurine—a position that makes worshippers feel that power is in the past racialized female body, not the present one. Rita Gross acknowledges Western feminist attraction to the Hindu goddess, for example, since she appears "compelling, provocative, and inspiring" in part because she is usurped from her cultural context and speaks to the desired autonomy and release of anger that addresses white Western women's experience (105). By following a "spiritual quest" that they claim is imprinted in their memory, white worshippers consume the dark Goddess: they use and interpret figurines for their own needs, participate in tourism by traveling to Goddess sites, and analyze all caves, statues, and ruins as representatives of their particular Goddess paradigm. By fusing the primitive past with the present, women not only gain spiritual power but also create a spiritual lineage between white women and women of color. Many white Goddess worshippers even go so far as to claim a "genetic memory" of the past, or a racialized biological and ancestral tie to all prehistorical women. Notably, white women use memory to access a prepatriarchal time when they believe that women of color and white women coexisted peacefully, in contrast to the troubled history of white women and women of color in the United States. By constructing a fantasy of a harmonious racialized past they wish had existed, white worshippers imagine that they can reclaim this fantasy by honoring "dark" statues rather than working to end racism in the present. For them, worship is a kind of antiracist work. This racialized longing is tied up with their cathexis to the Great Mother: Goddess memories are founded on suspect essentialist beliefs about race and gender.

This vexed relationship between "rememberfulness" and primitivism can be documented in a number of moments where white women have claimed a prehistorical bond and lineage with women of color, often through the analogy of slavery. One of the most famous examples, touted as a wonderful construction of a matriarchal utopia, comes from Monique Wittig's *Les Guerilleres*. While Wittig's text is not explicitly a Goddess text, it is a fantasy of a lesbian matriarchal utopia, and one that is so beloved and often cited by Goddess worshippers that it is central to the construction of these fantasies:

There was a time when you were not a slave, remember that. You walked alone, full of laughter, you bathed bare-bellied. You say you have lost all recollection of it, remember . . . you say there are no words to describe it, you say it does not exist. But remember. Make an effort to remember. Or failing that, invent. (89)

By touching on four aspects of Goddess memory, this passage represents the tenor and content of Goddess prehistory descriptions. First, it makes an unproblematic connection between women and slavery, a connection that has been critiqued by feminist scholars such as Karen Sanchez-Eppler and Robyn Wiegman for falsely implying a union of white women and women of color in a mythical prelapsarian utopia.[7] Second, it suggests that women in matriarchy, who were not oppressed by the structures of patriarchy, existed in their "natural state" of Edenic happiness: they were safe from the threat of sexual assault and could "walk alone" or bathe naked. Third, it recognizes that women may have no memory or language of this time since "there are no words to describe it" because it "does not exist" (89). Memory constructs subjectivity by initiating language, but without a memory of the Goddess, one can have no language to describe her, and thus one is not fully "woman." And fourth, it assumes that women must "make an effort" to remember this matriarchy for the good of women everywhere (89). Finally, Wittig's suggestion to "invent" memory indicates the conflicting paradigms of "memory" and "history" at work in these debates. While history still hinges on "proof" rather than emotion, for Goddess worshippers "bodily feeling" is the spiritual justification or equivalent of proof in the pneumatic realm.

While always racialized, the fantasy of prehistorical and primitivist embodiment by definition extends beyond racial categories to include other aspects of physical reverie. The prehistorical female body is also a body that is strong and erotic. For Goddess worshippers, the "Bird-Headed Snake Goddess" is a mirror of empowerment—her arms are raised, her "mouth is open," and she "sings her own song." Looking at the photograph without the written text, however, the "Goddess" figurine has no mouth, we cannot know if she sings a song, and though her arms are raised, the potential meanings of the position are multiple, not singular. Most archaeologists would dismiss the figurine "empowerment" reading as a profound misreading. However, if we explore the use value of the figurine for Goddess worshippers, rather than its place in the historical record, then the symbolic structure of present-day Goddess ritual is illuminated.[8] The position of legs apart, "knees slightly bent," feet on

the ground, "genitals and anus relaxed," "buttocks out and chest forward," and arms raised suggests to contemporary worshippers a range of
physical movement, from squatting for menses or childbirth, to assuming
a prayer posture to the Goddess, to mirroring a martial arts stance for
self-defense. Importantly, the "genitals and anus" are "relaxed" as
opposed to "tense"—the assumption being that most women exist in a
tense body state, protecting their genitals from physical harm. The "prehistorical" physical posture of the figurine teaches twenty-first-century
women to stand still like a figurine at a historical moment when such a
task is near impossible; to breathe and sing like a bird, to have a "voice,"
as second-wave feminists so frequently described the gendered act of
claiming space and power; and to feel their "genitals" (or sexuality)
rather than ignore them.

Imagining an erotic and sexual prehistorical female body permits
present worshippers to personify these sexual qualities. As feminist
Sheila Ruth describes, "I love to imagine the Goddess sexing. I see Her

marvelous great body, all sinew and
steel, electrified with pleasure, curl-
ing and stretching, reaching for
touch. She howls and grunts, and
the world shakes" (151). Once
more, the Goddess is constructed as
a sexualized, primitive figure, similar to the bird-goddess figurine: she
is "sinew and steel," or hard and
strong as prehistorical women are
imagined to have been, and "grunt-
ing" or making a preverbal noise.
Ruth sees her own sexuality as link-
ing her with the Goddess: "When I
sex I am truly with the Goddess,
joined with all the wild things, they
who came before me and who will
follow. I see them, and I know
inside them, for they are me" (153).
The body, once again, bridges the

Figure 4.1. "Bird-Headed Snake Goddess, Africa,
c. 4,000 B.C.E." from Hallie Iglehart Austen, *The
Heart of the Goddess: Art, Myth and Meditations
of the World's Sacred Feminine.* Berkeley: Wingbow P, 1990.

historical gap between prehistorical past and present. When Ruth says "Sexing is a me-ness," her subjectivity, considered profoundly narcissistic by many critics of New Age spirituality, is transformed through an act which, for her, is communal (153). Her body is a vessel for the spiritual eroticism of all women in the prehistorical past, and specifically, in Goddess culture, her vagina is the entry point, figuratively and literally, for matriarchal worship.

The "yoni," as the vaginal opening is called by Goddess worshippers, becomes the bodily site for spiritual power. In his book on the "yoni" as symbol of the Goddess and women's power, Rufus Camphausen shows how statues, figurines, canyons, rocks, tombs, temples, rituals, and artwork celebrated vaginas in prehistoric women-centered cultures. He suggests that women's power "was strongly related to the Yoni and its unique ability to bleed in cycles with the moon (menstruation) and to give birth to new life (fertility)" (18). In Goddess culture, not only can one travel on a kind of "yoni vacation," but one can enact a ritual in an "empowerment retreat," where worshippers "individually and collectively enact menses and childbirth rituals through mime and dance. As a closing, they can mentally project a vision into the universe with the power that is in your womb" (Jamal 185). So-called "womb power," menses rituals, and yoni cave worship signal a return to difference feminism, where essential differences between the sexes are celebrated. Repeatedly, critics wonder how these practices give women power in any concrete or material sense. Such concerns may be well founded, but they do not account for worshippers' desire for a spiritual experience based on a vision of a prehistoric culture.

For many Goddess worshippers, remembering prehistory trumps working for women's rights in the present. Two paradigms are at work here: one in which feminists imagine abstract equalities gained in real historical time, and another in which worshippers remember a better prehistorical time, when the rewards of the body were the symbol of power. When worshipper Merlin Stone suggests that "we may find ourselves wondering to what degree the suppression of women's rites has actually been the suppression of women's rights," the implication is that women's rites are prior to women's rights (228). If women's rites had been practiced there would be no need for "rights": political action within state systems is necessary only because powerful female subjectivity was cut off in the past. While Kathleen Erndl and Alf Hiltebeitel note how the more recent interest in Hindu goddesses and the "existence of the Hindu Goddess has not appeared outwardly to have benefited women's position in Indian society," for most Goddess worshippers political action is a poor substitute for spiritual rejuvenation (11). The demands that

Goddess memory makes upon the present are spiritual ones—it insists on being legitimized through the fraught union of woman and body.

The Past Perfect: Interpellation into the Language of Memory

Memory gives Goddess worshippers a way to communicate with the Goddess through a language all their own. Worshippers describe how the Goddess communicates with them in two ways: either the Goddess communicates nonverbally with worshippers by "sending" messages through the body, or the Goddess communicates verbally through contemporary language. Most frequently, worshippers describe the former mode of communication—that they are in conversation with the past through a feeling of connection rather than actual language. As one worshipper describes, "The [Goddess] sites seemed so hungry for relationship, for communication with someone who could listen" (Castle xx). This passage indicates how worshippers share foundational beliefs about communicating with the past: first, that worshippers need to listen to the prehistorical Goddess; second, that they share a common language with Her, a language spanning centuries; and third, that the Goddess in the past wants to communicate with worshippers in the present. Whether or not one believes that this kind of communication with the past is possible is beside the point—Goddess worshippers rely on it spiritually. In short, they believe that the Goddess can actually talk to them, as worshipper Patricia Reis describes:

> The earliest Goddesses come to us without history, but not without story. *Their "language" is encoded in the bodies*: full breasts and bellies, egg-shaped hips and buttocks, exaggerated pubic triangles. . . . Understanding them poses a difficult task because we are so accustomed to using words to create meaning. If we are to "know" their messages, we must drop under the words to the preverbal place where images speak and the body expresses itself. (15, emphasis added)

Whenever they connect with the Goddess, worshippers go into a kind of preverbal reverie with Her. As Sheila Ruth explains: "Religious language, verbal and nonverbal, amounts then to a kind of 'signing'; its characters represent *primal* conceptualizations" (75, emphasis in original). The "*primal*" here would refer to the grunts of the body, the language of the body.

Through this mode of "primal communication," which is bodily communication, Goddess worshippers express their love for the Great Mother. Worshippers correspond by letting their present body "talk" to their prehistorical body. Critic Roberta Culbertson notes that for most survivors of trauma, "Ordinary narrative is simply inadequate" to describe their experience (170).[9] Since most Goddess worshippers believe that patriarchal trauma erased their memories, they long for a new language for their (old) experience—the language of matriarchal women found in past artifacts but felt in present rituals. While Goddess worshippers want recognition that matriarchal prehistory is the story before patriarchy, they also internalize and personalize their past experience, which is their body's knowledge of that time, a knowledge that exceeds the bounds of language.

Even though translating spiritual experience into everyday language is difficult, the preverbal past does "speak." As famous Goddess author Merlin Stone says, "I sensed, almost heard, the voices of women reciting the information that I had collected" (13). In therapeutic terms, being spoken to by past female ancestors may heal separation trauma from the Great Mother and from a destroyed matriarchy. In contrast, for women's and gender studies scholars, the figurines do not speak at all. However, worshippers believe that the language they receive in the present is the same language used in the past—though, once again, this is a historical impossibility. Just as present rituals take them back into prehistory, so too does present Goddess communication take them back where they always want to go—prehistory.

While worshippers try to leave the present time to experience a "better" prehistorical life, they frequently rewrite the past in the language of the present. As much as they try, Goddess worshippers cannot escape this tension between the past and present. In her utopic description, Michele Jamal reveals this tension:

> I can imagine a shamanic community in which women and men celebrate the body and spirit in daily life, and in dance and ritual. The intention of the community is to help each individual become empowered by initiation into shamanic consciousness. . . . I envision a community which encourages and nourishes values such as self-respect, esteem for others, and intercooperation. From what can be inferred from the archaeological records, these were values highly regarded in the agricultural communities of Old Europe and the Indus Valley. (177)

Jamal's fantasy wavers between the past and present. On the one hand, she wants to "celebrate the body" through the communal action of the past, an experience presumably absent in her current life; and on the other hand, she wants to "nourish" "self-esteem," a presentist fantasy shaped by individualism, rights, and therapeutic discourse. The "values" of "Old Europe," a term coined by Goddess scholar Marija Gimbutas to signify a prepatriarchal culture, turn out to be much the same as the values of the present. This slippage is precisely what feminist archaeologists find so frustrating: Goddess worshippers play fast and loose with history—they take liberties with their readings of past archaeological data. To even "infer" that in the Neolithic period, people would "celebrate the body . . . in dance and ritual," or that they had "self respect [and] esteem for others," is to rewrite prehistorical subjectivity in presentist terms as an autonomous liberal late-capitalist one (Jamal 177). Worshippers' fantasies about prehistory are often tripped up by their present linguistic and cultural limitations.

Since present language fails to describe a prehistorical fantasy, worshippers turn instead to the most desirable mode of communication—the language of the body. Worshippers make their own bodies the primary conduit for communicating with the Goddess: they *hear* the Goddess speaking, *see* her body and revel in it, *feel* the actual statue, *visit* the actual site in Greece, and *enact* a prehistoric ritual. Communicating with the past necessitates a physical response. Some worshippers even try to help other women heal emotional wounds in therapy by eliciting these physical responses. For example, when Patricia Reis says of her use of the Goddess in "woman-centered" therapy, "I imagine that these archaeological artifacts—the female images from prehistoric Paleolithic and Neolithic times . . . resonate and activate something deep within us. They help us to remember," she emphasizes how the figurines "activate something deep" *in the body* for her clients (13). As a therapist, Reis finds these artifacts that "trigger" or revive the memory of female ancestors so powerful that women become stronger by accessing them. The healing occurs in the body. For example, Reis describes what happened when she "came upon pictures of the Venus of Willendorf": "My body became electrified. I realized that this was the beginning of an answer. These objects seem to hold a haunting sacred mystery" (35). While viewing pictures of "Goddesses," women like Reis contend that these images spark a recognition of having lived a matriarchal past, though they have *forgotten it until seeing* the image of the Goddess. As Ardinger says, "We've been divided and conquered, and that's one reason I think we need to look at and hold a Willendorf Mother, to find the old power" (51).

The Memory of Prehistorical Union

Communicating with the past provides worshippers further evidence that the Goddess is real, and that She is always with them. In Goddess literature, practitioners are urged to ingest, merge with, or become one with the Goddess and Her body. As worshipper Carolyn Edwards says in her Goddess tales collection, "I had met the goddess; I was eating her; she was coming out of my pores" (xiv). Or, as in Ntozake Shange's famous quotation, beloved by Goddess worshippers, "I found god in myself / and loved her fiercely" (63). What it means for Shange, a black woman, and a white goddess worshipper to find "god in myself" is quite different. Not surprisingly, these racial differences are elided. Ironically, other racial distinctions may be unwittingly invoked: fantasies of the ever-present goddess in the past rely on a mammy-like, ever-loving dark goddess availability. It is not accidental that the omnipotent goddess in the past who loves worshippers in the present often has a big, dark face and body.

Goddess worshippers do not just want to be loved by Her, but they "often express a heartfelt desire to merge with the goddess, to be absorbed into her," notes Cynthia Eller in her Goddess culture study (*Living in the Lap of the Goddess* 144). This drive toward unification is a fundamental part of women's sacred journeys to Goddess sites glob-ally. Ethan Todras-Whitehill reported recently in the *New York Times* travel section that "new age-style sacred travel, or metaphysical touring, is a growing branch of tourism, particularly in countries like Egypt with strong ancient-civilization pedigrees. Tourists with an adventuresome spiritual focus—predominantly middle-aged, upper middle class and female—come together to improve themselves and the world." As wor-shipper Leila Castle describes, "Many of us were seeking healing, fol-lowing a dream or synchronicity, or were inspired by a vision as we entered the original altar, the body of the Goddess, in the form of a cave, mountain, spring, or tree. . . . We died and were reborn in her womb-caves, and knew we were no longer separate" (xxxi). The physical trip or tour to a Goddess site initiates another physical ritual based in memory—the "womb-cave" impresses upon the worshipper the essen-tial knowledge of oneness.

This homoerotic identification with Goddess objects, figurines, cave paintings and earth mounds is enacted cinematically in the documentary *Goddess Remembered*, one of the "most popular productions ever," according to the National Film Board of Canada (Davis 24). Throughout the documentary, the camera is a stand-in for the viewer: we never see the interviewer, though interviews happen; we rarely see anyone holding the camera, though the camera travels into difficult-to-reach places, such as obscure caves. The only time we see humans interacting on screen together in the documentary is when the footage of ancient monuments shifts to a table with the most prominent goddess historians and theorists together discussing their relationship to the Goddess. Besides their conversation with each other, the camera invites the viewer to participate as well by zooming in on individual women to invite the female viewer into an intimate oneness with Goddess supporters.

This documentary demonstrates perfectly what Goddess books, rituals, prayers, and worship seek to do—seamlessly suture the past and present to remedy the loss of the mother-connection and utopic female oneness. When the camera takes the viewer into a cave through a vulva-shaped opening ringed with red coloring to symbolize the menstruating woman, the viewer enters the cave with the camera as if she herself were entering the body of a woman. For worshippers, their "re-entry" is a physical union with past primitive women. Dubbed music of whispering voices—again, they portray the past as literally speaking to the present—overlays the cave tour as women witness multiple figurines of round, dark women. Though archaeologist Miranda Green insists that "it is the very 'other' nature of such iconography that renders it out of our interpretive reach," it is clear that "othering" is impossible when to cathect with the Goddess is essential (Goodison and Morris 195).

Worshippers claim that inanimate objects such as sites or statues "ask" women to be in relationship with them. "It was possible for us to receive teaching directly from them," notes Castle about a particular Goddess site (xviii). The belief that worshippers can be taught by objects that do not speak verbally is a function of prehistorical memory. Because worshippers feel that either they or their ancestors have lived in prehistory (often in a past life), communication with the past is a transfer of feeling through time. As one worshipper says, "I have come to know, to *feel*, oneness with all the millions of women who have lived, who live, and who will live. I contain those millions. Each of us does. Every moment. Such a power cannot be stopped" (Spretnak xxiv, emphasis in original). This power is the *countermemory* of female union, here achieved not through gaining rights in the present but through remembering the collective Goddess body existing in prehistory, prestatehood. When worshippers say, "I am / She is the powerful one," they long to draw on the Body/body in the past rather than on the seemingly fractured feminist community in the present (Ardinger 59). Prehistorical Goddess worship is prelapsarian feminism—the union of all women before the fall into modernity, which for Goddess worshippers is not rights gained but "rites" lost.

For worshippers, practices of "rememberfulness" are not metaphorical memories but literal ones. Indeed, the final ultimate connection to the prehistorical Goddess is the explicit biological linkage to the past. As Ardinger notes, "In 1987, geneticists presented evidence that we are all descended from an African 'mitochondrial Eve.' Her DNA lives in everyone alive today, so that means we really are all related" (35). Goddess theorist Christine Downing states that remembering the divine mother means "reawakening our phylogenetic memory" to "recover the key to the storehouse of racial memories" (6). Z. Budapest, one of the "founders of the Goddess movement" in the United States, is described as "gifted with an uncanny sense of genetic memory" (qtd. in Reiff 24). "This talk of genetic memory has unpleasant overtones," says critic David Reiff (24). For Reiff, the idea of "racial memory" recalls Nazism, where "genetic memory" served as the "antidote to the debilitating falsehoods of Jewish science and cosmopolitan, deracinated reason" (24). Mattias Gardell, in his work on paganism and white supremacy, notes how "racist pagans tend to biologize spirituality. Somehow, gods and goddess are encoded in the DNA of the descendents of the ancients" (17).

White women want a "genetic memory" that links them to a racialized, primitive past where multicultural Goddess circles ruled the world. The only way to be connected to "darkness" is to link to it historically and ingest it in the present—to lay claim to histories, figurines, and rituals that are not theirs. Goddess writer Hallie Iglehart Austen says, "All of us, no matter what our racial or spiritual heritage . . . have spiritual and blood ancestors who revered the Goddess. She is an important part of the heritage of every person on the planet" (qtd. in Eller 158). Austen believes that she is actually a biological descendant of the Goddess, whether it can be traced genealogically or not. Though archaeologists note that "the monolithic 'Goddess' whose biology is her destiny may to a large extent be an illusion, a creation of modern need," the "biologization of memory" signals the most powerful evidence of Goddess worshippers' "need" to make memory "theirs," when history cannot be (Goodison and Morris 21).

The Future of Past Goddess Memory

I have argued that Goddess worshippers articulate their prehistorical memories in terms of an embodied subjectivity in the past rather than seeking rights in the present. By establishing the importance of memory in Goddess culture and the practices to revive it, and by examining how memories operate—from fantasies of oneness with the Goddess, to constructing a primitive past, to feeling a worshipful speechlessness—these expressions are attempts to find a political utopia based in the body. When Carolyn Edwards says of the Goddess, "the stories are her voices, her faces, her thighs," she describes the process of transfiguration of narrative into body, so crucial to the circulation of memory and power in Goddess culture (xi). While "memory is not the property of individual minds, but a diverse and shifting collection of material artifacts and social practices," in Goddess culture it registers collectively through reflections, "artifacts," and rituals, and individually through the body rather than the "mind" (Klein 130).

The Goddess fantasy of prehistory is a fantasy of an embodied prefeminism—in contrast to a feminism that is equated to access to rights in a citizenry. Much modern feminism operates within a framework of improving the future while moving away from the past, and it seeks to grant women the same rights to modern liberal subjectivity as men. Other forms of feminism, from radical to Marxist to global, rarely look longingly backward to a female utopia but work actively for systematic gains in the future. In these paradigms, in order to be a feminist citizen, one must be interpellated into citizenship generally, where the body is often left behind and identity becomes a "liberal abstraction."[10] The "national body," as Lauren Berlant suggests, has "norms of privilege [that] require a universalizing logic of disembodiment" (238). Goddess worshippers remember prehistorical matriarchy as a resistance to liberal history, rational identity, and the state and, by extension, to those feminism(s) that wed gender rights to an abstract subjectivity divorced from the body.

In Goddess culture, "memories" of the past felt in the body grind against this lived existence as a disembodied citizen. They give women a separatist matriarchal orgiastic experience counter to their mundane experience of what Berlant calls "proper citizenship" (238). It is no wonder that it is so popular. Belief in the "memory" of a matriarchal prehistory changes worshippers' identity by restoring the body. Suddenly, a tired feminist community is resuscitated with a political utopian energy found in embodiment. Women feel the presence of the past in their bodies through matriarchal "ancestors" who speak through them. Women imagine themselves in naked, homoerotic reverie experiencing a freer sexuality and a safer physicality. Women worship Goddess sites, statues, and rituals and are so moved spiritually that they cannot speak, only feel. And white women celebrate a unified multicultural past in which they are connected physically to women of color. Rather than claim rights in a contemporary politic, Goddess worshippers use prehistorical memory to satisfy their longing for sensuality, Dionysiac reverie, erotic power, and racial union. Memories of prehistory are appealing precisely because they allow a different paradigm for gender identity, one in which the woman's body is positive, supportive, multiracial, sexual, and completely beyond the reach of the state.

However, the construction of Goddess memory is based on problematic beliefs about race, gender, and the primitive. Indeed, Goddess worshippers appear to be borrowing fantasies of primitive spirituality to enliven their own absent traditions. By analyzing why and how this memory is used, we may comprehend how longing for the spiritual transforms linear time in a gendered formation of the primitive past. By observing how white women imaginatively transport themselves back in time to a prehistoric utopia to cathect with the Great Mother and other women, I argue that women are not merely taking from the past but never wanting to leave it. By living memory now, as it were, Goddess worshippers not only alter their gender and racial identities but also their claims to spiritual power. The Goddesses and women in the past matriarchy are always speaking to them. Women in the present, in turn, collapse their subjectivity into the past to become one with it through "rememberfulness." Memory changes identity by constructing an identity that can waver between the postmodern subject and the prehistorical one. Or, as one Goddess historian describes the connection between the past, present, and future, "What if the memory of an age of peace and equality among all living creatures, a memory embodied in black Madonnas and other dark women divinities of submerged cultures, becomes a future celebrating equality with the beauty of differences, and justice?" (Birnbaum 15). The past memory is, as Eller suggests, linked to the state of feminism now—but it is memory, not history, that determines the future, a future expressed in the body, but not the "body politic."

It is not difficult to understand why white women use "strategic remembering" to construct a matriarchy throughout time rather than a disjunctive history where women appear and disappear. Women become all-powerful, central figures who mother well, shape their own history, and promote peaceful, egalitarian values. While some women want the Goddess because "it takes them beyond the political anger of feminism and work for women's rights 'to a deeper place,'" women's and gender studies scholars question such statements, which privilege elusive, mystical "woman identified" conjuring over the "political" (Robb). However, as feminist academics demystify archaeological facts and deconstruct spurious gender beliefs, Goddess worshippers continue to articulate their empowering relationship to the Goddess through nostalgic memory, however controversial that memory may be. Even though the matriarchal myth may be a "house of cards" that is "in imminent danger of collapse," as Eller argues, it is still held firmly together by the mortar of memory (*The Myth of Matriarchal Prehistory* 180).

Though feminist academics believe that Goddess worshippers' history is weak, the worshippers themselves feel that their memory is strong. For worshippers, this "strong memory" is more "real" to them

than history, even while it complicates the debate about the past by placing the burden of proof on the bodies of women in the present. As long
as the use-value and construction of Goddess memory are not considered in these debates, the divide between kinds of evidence of a matriarchal past will continue to grow. And for Goddess worshippers, as
history appears to be disputed outside of their community, memory—
however ideologically and racially suspect—remains for them the evidence that the female body can exist outside of time. In their minds, this
existence is a more powerful woman-identified state than the State could
ever provide.

5

New Age Soul

The Gendered Coding of New Age Spirituality on *The Oprah Winfrey Show*

Recently Oprah Winfrey held a Web seminar on New Age guru Eckhart Tolle and his book *A New Earth: Awakening to Your Life's Potential*. Tolle is a German-born, Cambridge-educated spiritual leader who writes about the "spiritual awakening" that he feels is the "next step in human evolution" ("About Eckhart Tolle" par. 4). Oprah touted his book as "her boldest choice yet" and raved about the book's ability to awaken readers to "the possibilities of their lives" ("Awaken Your Spirit" par. 4). She began the Web seminar by talking about Tolle's ideas and their central importance in her life, saying, "The one thing I know for sure is that you cannot even begin to live your best life without being connected to your spirit" ("Awaken Your Spirit" par. 5). When Oprah opened the field for audience participation, she received a question from a woman who asked how she should reconcile her religious faith with her spiritual seeking. What interests me about this question is less its content than its intended recipient: this was not a question fielded by Oprah for Tolle. Rather, the female audience member wanted to hear from the real guru on the set: Oprah.

This seeming confusion about who, exactly, is the spiritual authority here highlights how Oprah is not just a widely loved talk show host but a spiritual leader in her own right. When Oprah responded to the audience question on how to reconcile religion and spirituality, she filtered Tolle's spiritual message through her own black Baptist church experience. Apparently Oprah adored church until the day the minister said, "God is a jealous God," at which point God seemed distant and cruel.

Oprah cited that moment as pivotal in beginning to take "God out of a box" ("*A New Earth* Class" 11). Increasingly, Oprah not only created a god more in her own image but developed her own brand of spirituality. In the "church" of Oprah, she legitimizes and translates New Age philosophies by framing them in female experiences in general and "racializes" them through invoking her own church upbringing.

Oprah's beliefs have changed from that black Baptist church to her current embrace of New Age leaders. The traditional church order of a "jealous God" that Oprah split from has a radically different approach to authority than the New Age approaches she espouses. In the old church, there is a rigid hierarchy with power located only at the top; in Oprah's new belief system, the locus of power is diffuse and within each individual. Oprah summarized Elizabeth Lesser's argument in *The Seeker's Guide* that defines "old spirituality" this way:

> 1) The hierarchy has the authority. Church authorities tell you how to worship in church and how to behave outside of church. . . . 2) God, and the path to worship Him, have already been defined. All you need to do is follow the directions. . . . 3) There is only one path. It is the right way and all other ways are wrong. . . . 4) Parts of yourself—like the body, or ego, or emotions—are evil. . . . 5) The truth is like a rock. Your understanding of it should never waver. (Lesser par. 1)

Not surprisingly, Oprah embraces Lesser's definition of "new spirituality," in which, "You are your own best authority. . . . You listen within for your own definition of spirituality. . . . Many paths lead to spiritual freedom and peace. . . . Everything is sacred—your body, mind, psyche, heart, and soul. The truth is like the horizon—forever ahead of you, forever changing its shape and color" (Lesser par. 2). On *Oprah*, she validates the personal, which for women means not obeying a "jealous God," one rooted in a traditional, strict, religious upbringing, but listening for one's own truth. Women's spiritual experiences are primary on *Oprah*, not secondary. Essentially, Oprah filters white New Age ideas through her own black experience to make them legitimate, and through her experiences as a woman to make them speak most powerfully to other women.

Oprah Winfrey blends New Age culture with a racialized "sister sensibility" to create a unique ministry for her viewers on her talk show. Oprah's autobiography is a testimony of hardship, racism, and institutional poverty that establishes her credentials as "black enough" and therefore gives her the authority to preach New Age spirituality. Critics have observed that Oprah is "a compelling and successful spiritual teacher" who promotes her own "gospel" (Nelson, *Gospel According to Oprah* xv), and others have noticed that she popularizes New Age spirituality by focusing on "spiritual uplift, individual will, personal responsibility, and grand cosmic design" (McGrath 129). I am particularly interested in how Oprah manages to racialize and gender her translation of New Age spirituality. By analyzing the appearances of New Age experts on her talk show, I demonstrate how Oprah weds a New Age vision with the African American struggle and at the same time positions women at the center of it all.

Oprah's audience looks to her for spiritual truths and, in return, they get an experience not had at Sunday church hour. Oprah's church meets the needs of an audience dissatisfied with mainstream religions but still hungering for a spiritual outlet. Oprah's dramatic entrance on her show, her theme song, regal clothing, and focus on transformation make it nearly a complete Sunday hour. She also has the charisma, vocal intonation, and physical presence drawn from the black preaching tradition to make her that much more compelling. For example, her *Soul Series* radio show opens with a jazzy, gospel beat and Oprah's voice-over saying, "It's uplifting, enlightening, truly powerful—welcome to *Soul Series*" (Oprah's Soul Series). Her music, her entrance, her interests, and her charisma all frame her as a minister of self-help.

Rather than punish people into submission through pointing out their sins, Oprah's altar call is different. By using talk therapy and emphasizing women's agency in taking care of themselves, Oprah invents a kinder, gentler "confession booth." If you recognize, confess, and then become "intentional" about your problems, you can be in charge of your life, a mantra of New Age culture where mind and thought control is central. Through rhetoric, dialogue, her own story, and her audience relationship, Oprah translates white spirituality across a racial boundary.

Oprah's is no ordinary talk show—this is a ministry, and she uses some "old school" religion techniques to enhance her personal message. Oprah's rhetorical strategies and emotional rapport with audiences effectively establish her as an authority of the self-help gospel. Corrine Squire suggests that on *Oprah*, "The stress on communication recalls a religious commitment to testifying" (108). For example, Oprah punctuates the ideas of others on her show as the "testifier," the one who can attest to the importance of her invited guests. Her audiences often want to touch her clothing or get close to her, as the faithful have done with saints historically. But Oprah is not distant or ethereal, as the saints have been or as the "jealous God" has been. Oprah manages to both maintain her charismatic authority as a larger-than-life persona, and yet also come across as intimate and personal. By moving between speech registers of black vernacular, "girl talk," and spiritual advice, she makes her audience feel at once as if she knows them and they know her. Known for her brilliant interpersonal skills, Oprah comes across as genuine, accessible, and open. She marries the intimacy and individuality of the New Age movement with the adulation and power of a 700 Club-like ministry.

Oprah, Race, and the Female Godhead

If Oprah is a minister, then she is one who is decidedly female. Scholars have explored Oprah's ability to captivate viewers' attention through gendered communication. Laurie Haag notes that Oprah's communication patterns are consistently gendered feminine. For example, "She reacts, no holds barred, laughing, screaming, even crying at the appropriate times, and allows us to do the same" (119). Oprah is not an intellectually removed commentator, as the typically male host might be, but actively brings her emotions onto her show. Her "give-away" show, during which she gave a car to every audience member, is an especially good example of this: Oprah jumps up and down and yells with the audience as they move to mass hysteria. It is this emotional availability that allows female viewers to have the distinct feeling that Oprah is indeed "every woman," as she suggests, and that she appears to empathize with all levels of human experience. As New Age author Kathy Freston states on Oprah's radio show *Soul Series*, "Oprah, you are so empathic; that is why everyone loves you" (Oprah's Soul Series). Oprah's empathy has been taken to new heights as she relates across cultures to women in Saudi Arabia, where her show has recently begun airing. One conservative young Saudi woman, who is described as never leaving her home without a male chaperone, said, "I feel that Oprah truly understands me" (Zoepf A1). Oprah's ability to be eminently relatable makes her ordinary folk, or one of the girls, by narrowing the gap between herself as a high-profile celebrity and her audience.

Oprah also racializes spirituality through her choice of speech, music, guest roster, and general "sister" sensibility. She includes guests of color from Maya Angelou and Dr. Robin Smith to gospel stars such as BeBe and CeCe Winans, Yolanda Adams, Kirk Franklin, Oleta Adams, and Joshua Nelson, all of whom cite a higher power in their work. These figures further foreground the racialization of spirituality. But Oprah is not all talk, and like any good congregation leader, she also practices good works (shown on her "Change Your Life TV"). She is famous not just for her "random acts of kindness" but also for her Angel Network, founded in 1997. Oprah states that the "Angel Network works around the globe to give people the chance to live their best lives" ("Oprah's Angel Network" par. 1). This description marries the old-fashioned missionary work of reaching out to unenlightened others with the New Age goal of helping people not to salvation but to their "best lives" (aided by angels, no less). Perhaps even more importantly, beyond the naming and description of the network are the pragmatic works that help children at risk, and young girls and poor children of color especially. For example, she completed her school for girls in South Africa under her "Oprah Winfrey Leadership Academy Foundation," and she also helped draft and lobby for the 1991 National Child Protection Act. Her philanthropy is a kind of ministry that resembles traditional church outreach dealing with human and social needs. But Oprah tends to mobilize philanthropy around race and gender in ways that shore up her New Age feminist church. Her donations are "good works" that are usually women centered, which is precisely how she gets women glued to the screen every afternoon.

Oprah creates her own brand of New Age feminism that expresses feminist desires without overt feminist claims. Kathryn Lofton notes that Oprah has invented her own "'ritual of behaviors for helping others achieve personal goals. She urges fans to read, keep personal journals and purchase self-indulgent gifts'" (qtd. in Deggans par. 18). Through her Book Club she frequently chooses plots that function liturgically, moving from abuse to recovery for her church service. For example, Oprah's 1998 Book Club selection, Edwidge Danticat's *Breath, Eyes, Memory* (1994), follows a Haitian protagonist from sexual abuse to recovery through both therapy and reconciliation with her abuser. The book has a feel of redemption about it, as it moves the heroine from victim to agent, but it is a redemption that will resonate chiefly with women, as the story delves into relationships between women, body and weight issues, and sexual abuse. These female-centered issues are present in many of Oprah's book choices, along with her ever-constant concern over race. While some critics originally ridiculed the Book Club choices that reiterated Oprah's personal story, few complain now, especially since her audience has been riveted faithfully by her selections. As one guest said on the "Letters to Oprah's Book Club" show, "I could be the poster child for your Book Club at this point. I've read over 400 books since you started your Book Club" ("Letters to Oprah's Book Club" 13). Through her Book Club choices and the magazine, Oprah creates a home liturgy to empower women founded in "the spiritual practice of soulful reading" (Driedger 44). Oprah sells deliverance through these rituals. While her text is not the Bible, Oprah's Book Club choices and the urtext of her own life story make transformative reading enough.

Oprah makes women feel like they have an intimate relationship with her, almost like a "personal Jesus." She offers women a different home spiritual practice: she is a fan of personal space, altars, and special baths, all ways to encourage women toward better self-care. Jane Shattuc comments on how talk shows can reframe women's personal, private experiences as important, not frivolous. Shattuc suggests that talk shows "elicit common sense and everyday experience as a mark of truth which has been a central tenet of feminist claims of the personal being political and a mantra of its standpoint epistemology in particular" (Shattuc 169). In this forum women grapple with issues that are important to them and that are reflected in the show's program (or liturgy), while being largely absent from mainstream churches (Brooks Higginbotham 17). By eliciting women's daily and often mundane experiences and naming them as legitimate, Oprah provides a forum for the invisible, privatized lives that so many women lead.

White women do not gravitate to Oprah as another woman; their gravitation toward her is always informed by race. Oprah models a strong black female spirituality that appeals to followers of New Age culture. Historically, white women have found solace in the spiritual practices and religions of people of color. As many critics have suggested, Oprah provides the "love" for which many whites long. Barbara Grizzuti Harrison notes about Oprah:

> The oppressor wants to believe he's loved by the oppressed. The "majority" seeks proof that they are loved by the minority whom they have so long been accustomed to oppress, to fear exaggeratedly, or to treat with real or assumed disdain. They need that love, and they need that love in return in order to believe that they are good. (6)

Many white viewers (perhaps unwittingly) read her blackness as a sign of suffering and redemption. As the figure of the black female minister who has cultivated upper-class speech patterns and tastes in vestige, food, and material objects, such as her "favorite things," Oprah is both the woman whom white women want to emulate and the deep-feeling "Earth Mother" who knows their pain. White women in particular feel her forgiveness and kindness with a profound intensity built on racist assumptions. Tammy Johnson suggests that

> [Oprah] plays the wise black matriarch who redeems white people from their misdeeds and foibles by helping them embrace love and realize their true, good selves. Oprah seems to take on

the role of new-age mammy for suburban soccer moms. In the process, she safely reduces all things racial to the personal, side-stepping the hard questions of institutionalized racial oppression and white privilege. (par. 4)

By naming Oprah "new-age mammy," Johnson pointedly collapses Oprah's role with the historical and overdetermined mammy role of black caregiver, savior, and servant to white master, a role that shadows Oprah permanently.

New Age spiritualities take on another level of authenticity on Oprah's talk show, as they are resignified by her "blackness." She often uses the black vernacular and her own experiences to represent New Age figures on her show, refracting and overlaying their beliefs with a black feminist narrative of triumph through struggle. As Nelson notes, "Oprah's roots in the black church experience lend the television personality some of her authority" (*Gospel According to Oprah* xv). Through a blend of popular psychology and black spiritual tradition, the "church" of Oprah—with herself as its presiding minister—is constituted.

The Soul, Humanism, and Girl Power

Oprah's talk show filters New Age ideas in ways that personalize, racialize, and translate them for her female audience. While Oprah does not use the term "New Age" or locate herself in the movement specifically, she is nonetheless one of the most visible proponents of its thought, and many of her productions, especially the talk and radio show, endorse New Age philosophies. Though most of the New Age authors and teachers appearing on Oprah's show are white, Oprah's acceptance of what is considered a "white" subculture (New Age), imbues it with the authenticity of black experience. As Oprah's guests make grand, universal spiritual claims that appear to transcend identities, Oprah takes those same generic religious ideas and makes them particular to female experience and her own black struggle.

We can best understand this practice of "translation" by looking at how Oprah highlights and then transforms one New Age author's ideas, in this case, author Gary Zukav, one of Oprah's most frequent guests. In his most famous book *The Seat of the Soul*, Zukav describes how a coming new order will free us from past paradigms weighing down our souls. His apocalyptic tone is common in New Age writing, as is his belief that humans are not fundamentally flawed because of "original sin." He argues that by turning inward and becoming acquainted with our own emotions, intuition, and higher rational self, we can choose to not be controlled by the negative emotions of anger or fear. As humans, we can *choose* goodness at any moment, suggests Zukav (emphasis added). As Zukav notes, "An angry personality, for example, will create unpleasant, or even tragic situations, until its anger is faced and removed as a block to its compassion and love, to the energy of its soul" (Zukav 79). Because Zukav locates goodness internally rather than bestowed through "works or faith," as in many religions, he empowers readers and Oprah's viewers to transform their own psychology not by asking for external help but by righting one's inner emotional world.

Oprah reshapes New Age philosophies by modifying and refracting Zukav's ideas through her own voice and experience. In effect, Zukav's book becomes a new one on her show: Oprah uses his text to amplify her own beliefs. In a key Oprah episode entitled, "On How To Get Your Power Back," Zukav articulates a different kind of metaphysical power, one advocating "authentic power" rather than a lack of anger ("Gary Zukav on How To Get Your Power Back"). Oprah draws on Zukav to reimagine power. As the description on "Oprah.com" details, "When something happens that leaves you powerless, how do you recover? How do you create a power that can never be taken away?" ("Gary Zukav on How To Get Your Power Back"). Oprah begins this episode with the following, "This is a really important show, if you're ready for it," thus suggesting as she does with her spiritually oriented shows that she herself has found the advice powerful ("Gary Zukav on How To Get Your Power Back"). She now challenges the viewer to do the same, "if you're ready for it." Bruce Robbins suggests that Oprah "mediates between the expert's knowledge and a lay audience, in effect putting across that knowledge to a public whose resistance can be assumed" (Robbins 17).

In this particular episode, Oprah's gendered and raced glossing of universal spiritual ideas is quickly transparent. After Oprah's opening statement about the show, a young woman, Gina Cotroneo, says, "I was raped. It made me fearful, ashamed. I thought about committing suicide" ("Gary Zukav on How To Get Your Power Back"). Oprah then asks, "How do you recover?" Cotroneo answers: "Rape was a power struggle between two souls. I am more powerful than he is." Confronting her attacker in court, Cotroneo states:

> I told him that he had taken a piece of my soul and that I wanted it back. And I reached forward with my hand, and I kind of grabbed the air in front of him, in a symbolic gesture of taking my power. . . . I felt like the rape was a power struggle between

two souls. He may have been more forceful than I was, but I am more powerful than he is. ("Gary Zukav on How To Get Your Power Back")

It is important to note that not only is Cotroneo's story the center of this episode, but women's stories are the focus of most episodes. While there is the occasional male example or guest, everything about the show is female centered, from the language, examples, and advice to the look and feel of the program. It is not coincidental that Oprah highlights the example of taking back your power after being raped. She wants to address the epidemic of sexual violence through the plight of the individual.

Cotroneo succeeds in doing what Zukav teaches viewers, "Authentic power is building something inside of you that no one can take from you" ("Gary Zukav on How To Get Your Power Back"). When rape has been viewed historically as a violation, particularly one that "steals" a woman's virginity (her supposed worth), it is notable that Zukav suggests that although the body is ephemeral, the soul is not. The soul defines a woman's identity. However, rape is not simply a "power struggle between two souls," as Cotroneo notes, but the clear and violent dominance of one over the other in the material world ("Gary Zukav on How To Get Your Power Back"). Interestingly, Oprah draws on life examples to explore spiritual recovery from sexual trauma.

Oprah's repeated biographical narrative of suffering, redemption, and recovery—from sexual abuse, narrow ideas of God, issues with weight—racializes Zukav's ideas about power. By depicting her own experience, she also personalizes her relationship with the audience, affecting a semblance of emotional intimacy and implied trust between herself, these New Age spiritual teachers/gurus, and her audience. This church is not about a preacher pointing fingers at lay sinfulness, where spirituality can feel alienating or nonexistent. Rather, Oprah's appeal almost builds on black liberation theology, where suffering is a necessary vehicle for redemption—it is not an end in itself but an element of the redemption. And for her audience, comprised mostly of women of varying races, the feeling of suffering is all too familiar.

To inspire her often beleaguered audience, Oprah must translate ideas about power. Oprah continues to mold Zukav's notion of "authentic power" or "the alignment of your personality with your soul" by stating, "I love that definition. It's, actually, one of my favorite in the world" ("Gary Zukav on How To Get Your Power Back"). Oprah and Zukav play off one another, with Oprah personalizing and delighting over his philosophies. Oprah goes on to explain to viewers that they must use their "personality to serve the energy of your soul . . . with what your sole purpose here is on earth, then that is authentic empowerment" ("Gary Zukav on How To Get Your Power Back"). Oprah's "ministry" emphasizes that we are wholly in charge of our own empowerment to: (1) discern what we want in life, (2) work through all negative emotions to free ourselves from them, and (3) align our personality with positive energy. It is believed that focusing on negativity—especially loss, lack, and violence—only wastes energy that could be better spent loving and empowering ourselves ("Gary Zukav on How To Get Your Power Back").

Oprah uses Cotroneo's rape story—a woman's story—to demonstrate her version of women's power, yet she also introduces race to negotiate this tension between hope and anger. In regard to Cotroneo's personal agency, Zukav states: "[Cotroneo could have ended up] in an insane asylum consumed with grief, with anger or rage at men, with rage against the universe. That was an option. I heard a rap song once, and the young singer was . . ." ("Gary Zukav on How To Get Your Power Back"). Then Oprah interrupts in surprise: "You heard a rap song?":

> Zukav: Yeah.
> Oprah: Where were you?
> Zukav: I heard part of a rap song.
> Oprah: OK. OK.
> Zukav: And the part that I heard—the young man said, 'I got a
> right to be angry.' And I said, 'Yes you got a right to be angry.
> You've got a right to be loving too.' You have lots of rights.
> Which one are you going to take? ("Gary Zukav on How To
> Get Your Power Back")

This exchange simultaneously reminds viewers of the racial and cultural differences between Oprah and Zukav, *and* it closes this gap through a dialogic exchange that resembles the vernacular of black sisterhood. It has the effect of racializing Zukav's philosophy as a kind of "sister talk." Oprah asks Zukav to help audiences work through the difficulty of these moves when she notes, " 'Cause it's one thing to intellectually know it. It's another thing to work yourself through the process," thus further distinguishing Zukav's "intellectual" knowledge with her own lived "experience" ("Gary Zukav on How To Get Your Power Back"). While Oprah calls out Zukav's naïve whiteness when he refers to rap, she still agrees with him that anger—whether expressed through rap or the recovery from rape—is not effective ultimately. Even though she agrees with Zukav, the exchange about rap puts Zukav in his place: she is the authority on rap *and* on lived female experience.

Zukav needs Oprah to translate his otherwise abstract, naïve ideas situated in white, male privilege to be meaningful in any way. When Zukav suggests that someone can be free from this anger by listening to his or her "higher" self or intuition, Oprah responds that women often have difficulty listening to intuition because, in effect, they are conditioned to nurture others first. Oprah reconfirms her authority by particularizing Zukav's claim, declaring, "'Cause a lot of women say, for ex—I—I refer to women a lot 'cause I talk to a lot of them, and I am one, so I know that experience very well" ("Gary Zukav on How To Get Your Power Back"). Oprah's personalizing rhetoric, which establishes emotional intimacy with the guests and with the audience, filters New Age spirituality through the popular cultural figure of black female uplift that she typifies.

Even some viewers describe Oprah's singular ability to translate New Age ideas, and they use affective language to note her power. June Mears Driedger, a viewer and minister, describes the uplifting experience of watching an episode of *Oprah*: "I found solace in Oprah. She comes across as a best girlfriend, someone with whom one can both cry and laugh" (Driedger 41). Driedger discusses how she turned to Oprah and Zukav when she was depressed and "fighting to keep from drowning in feelings of uncertainty and powerlessness" (41). Driedger documents just how the relationship between Oprah and Zukav makes her *feel*, a feeling I would argue is based on Oprah's effective translation of Zukav:

> I smile as I watch them interact. Despite their distinctly different personalities—Oprah is outgoing and gregarious while Zukav is quiet and thoughtful—their mutual respect and affection for one another is obvious. Their collaboration as host and guest began a few years ago when she sought him out like a student seeking a spiritual master, after she read *Seat of the Soul*. . . . Their relationship has evolved to friendship, and Oprah often translates Zukav's more obscure statements into plain language for the viewing audience. They laugh easily with one another. (41)

Driedger finds more comfort in watching Oprah and Zukav than in many religious services (41). Part of this "comfort" comes from the racial subtext of Driedger's comments that relishes black-white spiritual interaction; Oprah and Zukav literally embody New Age integration. When Driedger, a minister herself, finds Oprah's "church of hope" more powerful than Sunday services, it is clear the extent to which Oprah performs a ministerial function. People trust her advice. My argument is built on

Driedger's very observation: Oprah's ability to make women feel like a member of a new church is based on her rendition of New Age ideas.

Obviously there are limits to the power that Oprah endorses, even as she particularizes it. Zukav and Oprah call Cotroneo's moving story of her rape recovery through overcoming anger a "perfect example," suggesting that if a woman can recover from rape, then she has the ability (power) to recover from anything, thereby conflating personal with political empowerment. There is never any mention of the political reform that allowed for Cotroneo to actually prosecute her rapist and thus have a powerful courtroom moment, perhaps unusual since so many rape charges not only never make it to trial but die when there. Because Oprah and Zukav do not highlight this fact, it is taken for granted that women will have a fair trial, that the police will act in their favor, and that they will not be punished or blamed as victims but be able to perform their empowerment publicly rather than hiding in secret shame. Critics Abt and Seesholtz argue that responses to rape are always inadequate in the talk-show medium, and they suggest that rather than offering "scientific evidence for the efficacy" regarding good trauma responses to rape, they are "simply mouthing mantras of pop-therapy" (Abt and Seesholtz 182). Franny Nudelman goes a step farther in observing that Oprah's show may highlight one woman's story at the expense of many: "The injured woman becomes the representative speaker, while women, deprived of a listening audience, find their ability to influence public life radically curtailed" (311).

Cotroneo draws on private spiritual growth rather than on public moments of activism and speech. Other than the courtroom moment, where she says she grabbed power back from her rapist by the gesture of pulling power toward her from the air, her power is personal. She says, "During the rape, I was looking at a picture on my wall in my bedroom of a guardian angel. And I just kind of silently called out to my guardian angels to help me. My guardian angel did help me. I was able to be cool enough to get some evidence that would eventually catch this person" ("Gary Zukav on How To Get Your Power Back"). Cotroneo mentions another popular New Age belief, that angels are present and can help us; she moves from the personal to the political—her belief in angels helps her locate her rapist. Eventually, Cotroneo learns how to be angry but says she did not dwell on it but used it to change to a job where she was valued. Zukav responds that "the difference was the rape. Now where could she have been after that rape—spiraling downward in despondency in victimhood. Angry" ("Gary Zukav on How To Get Your Power Back"). In a frightening twist that flattens any distinctions between trauma, Zukav seems to imply, as do many New Age believers, that in the end everything is a "lesson" and for the "good"—the rape was ultimately beneficial. Though these sentiments play into the worst stereotypes of New Age culture as hopelessly naïve, dangerous even, Oprah, again, tries to navigate around them through her specific use of her oppressed life story. While in New Age culture these examples might stand as universal expressions, Oprah tries to humanize them to make them particular, and thereby perhaps more political—even if through the personal, an interesting riff on the second-wave feminist slogan "The personal is political."

Intuition and the Body Politic

Oprah's pattern of racializing and gendering New Age spiritual philosophies operates across the spectrum of New Age guests—for example, when she translates the New Age ideas of Caroline Myss. Myss first came on the show as a "medical intuitive," or someone who can telepathically diagnose the diseases of others. She tells her life story (similar again to many Oprah Book Club plots) as a model of moving from being victimized and reveling in "woundology" to discovering her powers as an "intuitive." In both Myss's work *Sacred Contracts: Awakening Your Divine Potential* and the Oprah episode about the book called "On Discovering Why You Are Here," she suggests how to find your life purpose through archetypes. Oprah is the translator and the testifier who particularizes the universal archetype to her female audience.

While Myss argues that we all carry four basic archetypes—the child, the victim, the saboteur, and the prostitute—the ultimate goal, as Oprah interprets it, is to find a "purpose" (Myss, *Oprah Winfrey Show* 2). Once again, Oprah translates complex charts marking chakra points, horoscopes, and archetypes to their most basic premise. Oprah comments on these traditional archetypes in such a way as to repurpose the archetype even as she may not be able to fully recuperate Myss's limiting notions. It is not surprising when Oprah says, "For example, are you a diva. . . . If you're a diva, you would know it" (Myss, *Oprah Winfrey Show* 4). With bravado, Oprah claims her own positive archetype up front. By showing her "sassy" irreverent read as "black sister" side or her empathetic "I too have struggled with that side," Oprah literally creates a new archetype founded on blackness, one not articulated in Myss's white model that is supposedly universal (6). Myss argues that each archetype is complex; again, Oprah clarifies, "Each has a healthy form and a shadow form" (6).

Oprah goes on to say to the audience, "You're saying, OK, archetypes—I just want to know what my purpose is" (6). Oprah anthropomorphizes the archetypes; she even talks to them and asks them for help. If viewers had waded through Myss's book on the subject, they might have become dazed, but Oprah is there to mediate. Oprah establishes the classic frame of her show by turning to personal examples that translate to raced and gendered communities: first to explain the philosophy or problem and then to use a personal example, almost always geared toward women. Oprah uses this mode of sister talk—talk between women, particularly black women. She uses the vernacular to legitimize abstract concepts and then filters these philosophies through her own experience to literally color them.

The classic narrative of Oprah's show—female empowerment through spirituality—is usually demonstrated by several examples from particular women's lives, which Oprah uses to interpret abstract New Age ideas. On the Myss episode, this example is "Carrie," who is stuck and sabotaging her life. Myss tells Carrie that she "folds up" and is a child, "the cute little girl, the baby, the little innocent girl," a negative archetype, and that she is actually afraid of her own success, an interesting dilemma for many women who have struggled historically to succeed in the public sphere (Myss 8). Notably, Myss and Oprah equally exchange interpretations of Carrie's struggle: while Oprah has not created or written a new spiritual program, as Myss does in her book, she can *read*—that is, gloss, interpret, and comment on—women's personal experience in a way that legitimizes her interpretive power. Eventually Myss challenges Carrie to be okay with disappointing people and tells her to leave her toxic marriage, a frequent occurrence on the show, where women are counseled to learn the basics of self-esteem and to leave bad relationships.

However, once Oprah says to Carrie, "As long as you need other people's approval, then you are owned by them. . . . And slavery is dead, honey. It is way over," she hammers home the point in a way that Myss cannot (10). Though Oprah makes the classic troubled analogue between gender and race—that is, she equates a bad marriage and the experience of being "owned" emotionally with being "owned" physically—she also legitimizes white female struggle. Again, Oprah particularizes Myss's universal claims about archetypes and makes them about black female struggle. As with Zukav, Oprah refracts New Age beliefs through black feminine subjectivity to make them more accessible to her audience. Even though Myss deems her archetypes helpful, without an understanding of their specificity many women may claim universalist ideas about their identity that are unhelpful. Like a good teacher, Oprah explains the negative archetype concept through the concrete examples of the trapped woman's "little girl" voice and the saboteur that is a self-defeating woman. All of these examples help clarify and create a reference for understanding the spirituality of race and gender.

The Black Church of "New Age Feminism"

Critics have talked about Oprah's show as a women's space and as a spiritual space, but they have not put the two together to discuss exactly which feminized New Age messages are articulated. Oprah's spirituality is one of translation: she reinterprets and filters New Age philosophies through a gender and racial lens not necessarily to make them political but to make them particular. Oprah's seemingly slight modifications to universal New Age philosophies are not slight at all. They are constant and become the very reason her guests are understood. While certainly one could say that Oprah reinforces the most individualistic, conservative solutions to political problems, there are still more complex modes of communication and articulation involved in creating a particular spirituality. As one female minister said, "Oprah tells women they have value, that their words, their stories, are important. By contrast, the church's history of empowering women is brief, sporadic, and ambivalent, at best" (Driedger 46).

Ultimately, Oprah rewrites her New Age gurus to not only reflect daily struggle but also to recognize identity politics. Oprah occupies the uneasy terrain between drawing on and occupying a black female subject position while simultaneously attempting to appeal to a universal, transhistorical spirituality. Oprah moves back and forth between the particular and the universal—that is, between identifying how ideology and oppression have affected her life and the lives of others and denying the effects of oppression by emphasizing ideas such as "affirming one's innate goodness." She is not wholly apolitical or political but, rather, somewhere in between. Janice Peck argues, "Talk, in itself, is inadequate to the task of eliminating racism. But the frameworks through which we talk *about* racism do matter—they powerfully shape what we envision as problems and how we imagine solutions" (Peck 121, emphasis in original). Indeed, the "frameworks" for discussing spirituality on *Oprah* are more complicated than imagined. This "in-between space" that Oprah's New Age spirituality occupies is not merely self-indulgent but spiritually complex. Oprah is not merely individualistic and apolitical or antiracist and political—she is a black female preacher working from a pulpit and appealing to a massive female audience. Seen through this lens, Oprah's particular spirituality may provide a starting point to move past easy binary arguments about her and to begin to grasp the intricacy of the raced and gendered strategies at work in her complex translation of the New Age.

Conclusion

Is New Age Culture the New Feminism?

Several years ago, my mother began a "Women Who Run with the Wolves" group. She promptly bought a drum and jokingly howled at me while playing it, but I knew that this groundswell of female bonding, brought on by the huge success of Clarissa Pinkola Estes' book by the same name, was nothing to laugh at. After the early political high of feminism in the 1960s and 1970s, after the backlash against feminism during the Reagan era in the 1980s, and after the more permanent, though arguably more conservative, entrenchment of feminism in the 1990s, where was feminism to go but inward? As more women, particularly white and middle-to-upper-class women, assumed positions of power in the labor force, feminism did not seem to have the same urgency as before. Many women, therefore, did not seek external change through feminism but, rather, internal change through spiritual practice. Feminists lamented this increasing turn toward the personal and away from the overtly political: the "personal" was still supposed to be "*political*," wasn't it?

Initially, one might think that my mother's women-only group, which met weekly to share how fairy tales and cultural myths affected their female journeys, does not look so different from the consciousness-raising groups of the early feminist movement. Both groups support, educate, and empower women. Both groups look at how stories about women script a certain normative femininity. However, a profound difference exists. While my mother's group rekindled their anger by finding their "inner wolf," they never turned that anger outward to political action in the world. Early second-wave feminists were surrounded by

149

political activism as a forum to which to channel their energies, but my mother's group was surrounded by another movement altogether—the New Age movement. For many leftists, the historical narrative of feminism is one of a decline from its heyday of 1960s overt activism to the increasing personalization of today. True politics have been subsumed by a popular New Age rhetoric that at times may articulate political aims but has no movement behind it. However, this project suggests that by asking a different question, we may uncover a different narrative of the New Age: if, as critics have suggested, it has no "effect," then why do white women find it so empowering?

The New Age. The dawning of Aquarius. The Harmonic Convergence. Although the New Age movement has its roots in the early 1970s, by now its followers have taken it far past the fringe and into the boardroom and bedroom. From the *Tao of Leadership* and other New Age practices aiming to "humanize" business to relationship books such as *Mars and Venus in the Bedroom*, New Age speak is common parlance in elite seminars and popular talk shows. From Snapple beverage's "Made From the Best Stuff on Earth" advertisement to the beat of world music, the New Age has become its own buzzword: natural. "Everyone appears to be convinced of the virtues of eating 'naturally,' of living as 'natural' a life style as possible, of following 'natural' principles," suggests scholar Rosalind Coward in her critique of health fads (17). However, while New Agers tout the benefits of all things "natural," feminists have fought to "denaturalize" the very same term. From its insurgency, the New Age movement has run chronologically parallel to the feminist movement and its followers who have struggled to define womanhood as more than "nature," especially when man represents "culture." Interestingly, the intersection of these two movements has been ignored for several reasons: while feminists do not want to associate themselves with a movement perceived as irrational and apolitical, New Agers do not want to solve spiritual problems with material politics, and they often turn to a language of individualism instead. Furthermore, since academics dismiss the New Age as middlebrow and regressive—an apocalyptic sign of the return of the "premodern"—most academic work on the New Age that does exist usually has "the normative bias of an apologist, an opponent, or an apostate" (Bednarowski vii). The gender politics of the New Age movement and the spiritual politics of the feminist movement go unnoticed.

Perhaps one of the most ignored aspects of the intersection of the New Age movement and the feminist movement is the early interrelation between radical lesbian feminist beliefs and goddess/Wiccan spirituality.

While there is a frequent polarization between the spiritual and the political or New Age culture and feminism, there has been one area that overtly connected both New Age culture and second-wave feminism explicitly. For a brief window of time in the 1970s, some lesbians and radical feminists were involved in Goddess worship and Dianic Wicca in a seamless way that made the spiritual political, and vice versa. Perhaps the most famous proponent of Dianic Wicca is Z. Budapest, the head priestess of Susan B. Anthony Coven #1, author of numerous books, and "the founder of the Women's Spirituality Movement," as she notes on her Web site. In *Thesmophoria: Voice of the New Women's Religion*, Budapest's newsletter, she describes the importance of Dianic Wicca, which is the only Wiccan tradition that is fully female. Budapest says that it is a "wimmin only" practice, and that Diana is a "goddess of the wild" and not a "man lover. . . . It is the only men-free tradition we have in our name." As a priestess, Budapest performed over seventeen lesbian hand-fasts or Wiccan ceremonies a day at one point at the Michigan Womyn's Music Festival, indicating how from the early 1970s on, lesbians created commitment rituals outside of heteronormative government law. Lesbian separatism is central to the political sensibility of this spirituality. Other lesbians and radical feminists who participated in back-to-the-land movements incorporated spirituality into their rural, often separatist, or "womyn-only," lifestyle. Radical feminist and lesbian newspapers and periodicals, from *Womansource* to *Country Women*, indicate the extent to which Goddess worship and feminism were intertwined.

However, a telling moment occurred in 1976 that indicated the brewing split between the spiritual and the political in the feminist movement. Journalists Hope Landrine and Joan Regensburger, of *Off Our Backs*, a central second-wave newspaper, covered an important early feminist spirituality conference, only their article was called "Through the Looking Glass: A Conference of Myopics." They began their "news" story, "If the nature of the events at the April 23–25 women's conference in Boston ("Through the Looking Glass: A Gynergetic Experience") is an adequate representation of the state of the Women's Movement today, we are two feminists who seriously question committing our energies to that movement in the future." From their perspective, the conference was "little more than a frenzied confrontation between two groups of self-righteous, pompous myopics masquerading as serious philosophical, political, and spiritual discourse." They document "two camps" at the conference that they call "spiritualist" and "politicalist," and they quickly cast the spiritualists as hysterical and apolitical. Their description is worth citing at length because it is so bombastic:

> The spiritualist camp was composed of those women who more
> or less felt that women could do nothing to effect change in the
> system of patriarchy and, therefore, the future of the movement
> should be in the direction of withdrawal to worship the God-
> dess, practice magic, return to the Female Principle, reject any-
> thing associated with patriarchy, and cultivate psychic powers.
> This group of non-monogamous, non-smoking, vegetarian, anti-
> logic, spiritual right-on sisters . . . far outnumbered the political-
> ists, and thus exercised control over the content of the
> conference. (12)

As the article becomes even more damning toward the "spiritualists," it
dispels any utopic moment in which the spiritual could be political and
the political could be spiritual. The fantasy of integrating these elements
of the movement is over; discord and dichotomy ensue.

In more recent analyses of New Age spirituality, politics simply
vanish, to be usurped entirely by the personal, even though white New
Age women make a number of feminist and political claims. The myth is
that nothing political happens within New Age culture, and the New
Age is critiqued for its feminizing influences, without studying, compli-
cating, and attributing these influences to its powerful female voices.
Trysh Travis acknowledges that leftists and cultural critics struggle with
"how to conceptualize and make sense of utopian energies that resist
conscription into the familiar secular and materialist politics that are the
stock in trade of contemporary progressives" (262). If the personal and
political remain polarized, then the complicated practices of New Age
women, who may not self-define as feminist, drop out. My interest is in
creating a conversation between these two philosophies and movements,
feminism and New Age, both so wide-ranging and pluralistic, in order
for a broader picture to emerge. To conclude, I examine New Age guru
Louise Hay to see how spiritual power is manifested so often in New
Age culture for women and to understand how women in New Age culture are often "differently political" rather than apolitical. Feminists of
color have a different spiritual and religious lineage and tradition but
intersect with the New Age in some surprising ways that offer perhaps
the most integrated form of "spiritual activism." I also suggest that white
New Age women are still trying to make sense of power through several
main avenues all related to essentialism, including embodiment and primitivism, which are particularly troubling for any multiracial feminist
future. In closing, I return to the question: is New Age culture the new
feminism?

The Privatization of Power: Mind over Political Matter

"You must ask for more money," said the teacher of metaphysics who was concerned that I was living out of a "poverty consciousness." Metaphysics, a more extreme version of "self-help" philosophies and a contemporary form of the New Thought movement, believes that what you think has ultimate control over what you feel or do. Our group was rapt—we had all given over our weekend afternoons to figure out one simple problem: how to gain personal power. From eliminating negative thoughts to visualizing our vocation, Priscilla Okugawa, a trained metaphysics instructor, led us through a series of exercises demonstrating the extent to which the mind has control over the body, and over destiny.

Having control over one's life is a familiar slogan in the feminist movement: from "taking back the night" to "freedom of choice" concerning abortion, women have sought control over their lives for decades now. However, while many girls and women remained trapped in patterns of poor self-esteem and disempowerment, some metaphysical philosophies assert power and control in ways that would make feminists blush. While "power of positive thought" practices promote power over internal mental limits, many feminist practices promote power over external problems in the world: while the former movement is woefully weak in cultural analysis, the latter struggles with making the political powerful, sometimes at the cost of the personal. When even Gloria Steinem turns her attention to the *Revolution Within* to examine how her political actions make her ignore her own self-actualization, it is clear that the feminist movement still has much to learn about internalized oppression. Conversely, the powerful women in the metaphysical movement have no language for parts of their struggle, and thus simplify certain problems. It seems naïve at best that so many New Age women imagine that global problems can be addressed solely on an individual basis. It is clear that the mass political struggles of the 1960s have brought many gains to women but increasingly clear that spiritual movements have done the same: it remains to find a language to enable the two to speak with each other.

While New Age women imagine that the mind can control anything, second-wave feminists make sure women use their minds for advanced education. Feminists fought for better educational opportunities for women, and as universities and colleges went coed in the 1970s, and as students simultaneously protested for the right to have a voice in their education, many reforms became a reality. While experts in the 1950s had once said that "every year a girl spent developing her mind 'reduced the probability of a woman marrying,'" by the 1970s "a revolution in knowledge [had] occurred" as "feminist scholars began challenging the established lists—canons—of literature, art, music," and so on. Many women began going to school and entering professions (both blue and white collar) in record numbers (Rosen 40, 266). As women streamed into the workforce, and with the establishment of women's studies programs, various laws (Title XI), and groundbreaking research, including *Women's Ways of Knowing*, a feminist study on how women learn, and Carol Gilligan's classic work on women's ethics, *In a Different Voice*, it became possible for certain women, particularly middle-to-upper-class white women, to not only pursue higher education but also to imagine doing something with it. These reforms, now often taken for granted, made it possible for intellectual work on women's issues to be done in tandem with political organizing. Together, they helped produce an active feminist movement.

As the feminist movement was fighting to change the worlds of work and education, women in the New Age movement were testifying to the power of their minds to create a new world. While feminists most often understand the "mind" as something to be developed through equal opportunity education, New Age women understand the "mind" as a way to exceed one's gender limitations, though they do not articulate it in those terms. This New Age belief that one can manifest in reality whatever one desires in one's mind is actually a form of "agency," which is a central tenet of the women's movement. In metaphysics, New Thought, and "self-help," women are assumed to be equal to men in the mental realm. Guru Louise Hay is a perfect example of a woman who theorizes the mind's ability to manifest any desire or goal, and she has accumulated enormous power doing so.

Hay's written works mark only one part of her empire, which includes her own press, recorded books (a "must-have" for listening to her affirmations), workshops, organizations, and lecture tours. Journalist Mark Oppenheimer attests to this empire when he notes, "Louise Hay is one of the best-selling authors in history, and none of the women who have sold more—like J. K. Rowling, Danielle Steel and Barbara Cartland—owned a publishing empire" (Oppenheimer). Now in her eighties, Hay first began preaching at an alternative healing church in New York and soon after became a guru in the AIDS community. She believes not only in the power of the mind but also that the mind has control over emotions, which is a particularly important point for women, who have been stereotyped as being "too emotional." Essentially, Hay asserts that one can fulfill any desire by visualizing and affirming it, that one can turn disease into health, and that it may be subconsciously held negative beliefs that caused one's disease in the first place. With the publication of her first book *Heal Your Life*, Hay soon became an underground phenomenon: gay men flocked to her to find out how to release toxins from their bodies in order to be healed from AIDS, and also to recognize how they might have played a role in causing their disease in the first place. While criticism from others has caused Hay to temper her belief that we cause our own diseases, her work states repeatedly, "You are what you think." Hay believes that we choose our thoughts, and that whatever we believe is our destiny. She also claims that we choose our parents and must recognize the lessons that we need to learn from them. Hay has publicly come out as a rape and incest survivor. Rather than talk about anger or her legal rights for retribution against her attackers, she still feels that she "chose" her parents to learn a lesson, and that that lesson is to "love herself," including her sexuality. It is not difficult to understand why feminists and some gay activists have taken Hay to task for this profoundly naïve orientation to healing, which looks only at the personal, and not at how larger systems are at work.

But Hay is not so easy to pin down. As in many New Age texts, at moments it appears that Hay has no political concerns and that her message is solely personal, while at other moments, she articulates a politics that is largely about female power and how to access it. In a recent book, *Empowering Women*, Hay states that "from the level of emotional maturity, women are at the highest point in the evolution of this lifetime" (4). While initially it seemed that Hay was only interested in the "pure mind" to achieve its goals, she now articulates a strong "difference feminism" of women's superiority. Women's superiority, however, is hampered by external circumstances, and Hay argues that women must rewrite the laws so that they are "equally favorable to both men and women" (8). Notably, Hay does recognize that women cannot express their full spiritual potential if they are unequal on the material level.

If Hay is willing to grant that current laws are sexist, she argues that women should reclaim power not through feminist action but by not "being victims" (6). Hay says, "I know that when the feminist movement first came about, women were so angry at the injustices that were levied upon them that they blamed men for everything" (6). Though Hay acknowledges women's anger, for her the solution is not to act on it but to get over it. As she urges, "The best thing we can do for the men in our world is to stop being victims and get our own acts together" (4). Here she is strangely in accord with the many critics who suggest that women should stop being victims, such as Katie Roiphe, Camille Paglia, Christina Hoff Sommers, and Independent Women's Forum advocates. However, for Hay, women need to do this "for the men": this is a strange doublespeak, where, though women are "at the highest point" of emotional maturity, they are still chastised to get their "acts together" for *men*. It seems that for each step Hay takes toward some kind of feminism, she also takes one step back.

Scholar Elayne Rapping suggests that at least parts of the New Age movement stem from feminism. In her work on feminism and the "recovery movement" (twelve-step programs, confessional talk shows, and self-help books), she says the "roots of this movement are planted deep in the history of feminism itself" (11). Feminism also resides within New Age practices. As Michael Brown found, "Most women involved in channeling hold feminist positions on grassroots issues: equal pay, child care, sex discrimination, and abortion rights. As a group, they are precisely the sort of self-confident, forceful women one might expect to identify with a feminist agenda" (99). However, both Brown and Rapping conclude that few New Age women will claim the "F word." This is not surprising, since many college-age women in the United States do not self-identify as feminists, though they agree with many feminist platforms.[1] Given that so many women do not identify as feminists, what gender satisfactions do women get from spirituality that they do not get from feminism? I would suggest, perhaps to the surprise of many critics, that feminism is being actively figured out in New Age culture, though often with different terms and names.

Admittedly, many of Hay's claims about how to harness the power of the mind are shockingly retrograde. Hay claims that "one of the things we are capable of doing with our minds" is control pregnancy, and she says "I look forward to the time when we have learned to mentally accept or reject pregnancy" (61). Rather than demand that pharmaceutical companies and the government create birth control alternatives for men and women, Hay wants women to control it themselves. Hay crosses over still farther into the wacky and delusional by suggesting that "sending love to your breasts combined with positive affirmations has increased bust sizes for some women" (82). Again, Hay completely refuses to examine any systemic pressures that might have caused women to want larger breasts and focuses only on a simplistic optimism of mind power. The split is obvious between feminists who critique systems of oppression and Hay who critiques individuals. At the same time, Hay rightly asserts that at many moments, the individual may have more of a chance of healing herself or himself than depending on a failing and inadequate health care system, especially one that frequently ignores the needs of women. And in moderate form, many of her claims for power of the mind are being embraced by the mainstream medical profession, as more hospitals use visualization programs to help their patients heal.

While feminist and New Age women have one thing in common—they do not like patriarchal institutions—they do not protest them in the same way. What so many feminists fear is that Hay represents a "therapeutic feminism" that has taken the place of political feminism. Scholar Ruth Rosen defines "therapeutic feminism" as "programs of self-help that ignored the economic or sociological obstacles women faced, and instead emphasized the way in which each individual woman, if she only thought positively about herself, could achieve some form of self-realization and emancipation" (Rosen 316). Jillian Sandell further notes that with the rise of "therapeutic feminism," "there is a danger in confusing individual coping strategies with collective social change" (Sandell 22). In her history of second-wave feminism, Rosen claims that "therapeutic feminism" helped end *the* women's movement, for which she and many other feminists are nostalgic.

We know that "a singular feminist movement no longer exists" if it ever did, as Jennifer Wicke has argued (Wicke and Ferguson 33). If " 'academic feminism' is itself splintered into many domains, as is feminism in the supposedly real world outside the academy," then is it possible to understand New Age women's culture as one kind of feminism among many, however fraught that feminism might be (Wicke and Ferguson 33)? I suggest that claiming power is something feminists can understand, even if it comes in guises that may be unappealing, including certain theories that many feminists hoped were dead. Still, feminist theorists who look back nostalgically on second-wave feminism miss all of the viable and fascinating, though troubling, offshoots of feminism, such as New Age culture.[2]

Women of Color Spirituality Meets the New Age: Indigenous Forms of Spiritual Activism

What is the relationship of feminists of color to the New Age? As we have observed, when it comes to issues of appropriation, feminist academics of color are understandably outraged by white women's spiritual genocide and abuse. Some of these same critics have a deep investment in indigenous spirituality that often goes under the radar in the largely secular academy. Still others incorporate some New Age practices and philosophies into their spirituality, sometimes labeling it "New Age" and other times rejecting that label as white identified. By examining the largely overlooked spiritual writing of Akasha Gloria Hull, I observe how she overtly embraces though challenges the racial foundation of New Age culture. Hull is not alone as an African American feminist theorist in embracing elements of New Age culture, as we will see from Alice Walker and bell hooks. I then explore the more common perception that women of color spirituality has a different lineage tied to what Gloria Anzaldúa calls "spiritual activism." Understanding this lineage, which is also connected to "womanism," is crucial to grasping the fullness of authentic multiracial feminist spiritual expression.

"True Age" is the term Luisah Teish uses to describe a women of color spirituality that incorporates New Age beliefs within an indigenous paradigm exemplified in Hull's book *Soul Talk: The New Spirituality of African American Women* (book jacket). Hull, a scholar who authored a founding women's and gender studies text, *All the Women Are White, All the Blacks Are Men, but Some of Us Are Brave: Black Women's Studies,* with Patricia Bell-Scott and Barbara Smith (1982), argues that starting in the 1980s there was a new turn toward alternative spirituality among African American women (1). With conscious intention, Hull distinguishes this new spirituality from the New Age while still incorporating New Age practices. She suggests that there are "three interlocking dimensions" of this new spirituality:

> 1) the heightened political and social awareness of the civil rights and feminist movements, 2) a spiritual consciousness that melds black American traditions such as Christian prayer and ancestral reverence with New Age modalities such as crystal work and self-help metaphysics, and 3) enhanced creativity, especially as represented by the outburst of literature by Toni Morrison, Toni Cade Bambara, Alice Walker . . . literature that foregrounds supernatural material. (1)

Hull makes a case for including most of the female African American literary canon of the last forty years in her new spirituality paradigm. This move may surprise many; it is a clear divergence from New Age culture in which distinctions of "high" and "low" art mean that most of the popular New Age literature is hardly considered literary.

Hull's work is one of the only books addressing race and New Age culture specifically. Interestingly, *Soul Talk* is published by "Inner Traditions" which, together with Bear & Company, is one of the largest and oldest New Age publishers with a catalog ranging from books on alien abduction and Freemasonry to shamanism and indigenous traditions. Much of their catalog would be classified as New Age racist appropriation. Hull occupies an interesting space in that context, as her book is squarely marketed to/by/for New Agers while she critiques white New Age practices. Hull states, "On the surface, this New Age activity looked like a movement without much specific racial or gender content (since the 'norm' of whiteness goes unremarked) and black women, in particular, were not very visible in it. But this was far from the reality" (23). By simultaneously noting the whiteness of New Age culture and the invisibility of black women in it, she changes the very definition of New Age culture.

Hull aims to challenge categorizations within New Age culture at the same time that she points out the difference with which African American women experience New Age practices. Once Hull describes major New Age authors, from the work of Jane Roberts to Gary Zukav, she acknowledges that "none of us would think to call any of this material 'black.' In fact, all the authors are white, and the material itself is apparently raceless, that is, devoid of racial reference or implication" (27). While Hull acknowledges that spiritual practices can transcend time, space, and identity, she urges that "African American women's contributions remind us that consciousness about race and gender should exist among New Age thinking and agendas" (6).

"Politics, spiritual consciousness, and creativity," Hull argues, make a new spirituality paradigm for women of color (2). These three terms not only describe aspects of "womanism" but also describe works by women of color that women's studies practitioners may only define as scholarly, though they are also spiritual. For example, a founding women's studies text, *This Bridge Called My Back*, not only contains entries that address spirituality specifically, but the entire text is suffused with Hull's "big three": "politics, spiritual consciousness, and creativity." These spiritual qualities have largely gone unremarked for a variety of reasons: the secularity of the academy, the white, Western, feminist paradigms that often omit the spiritual from academic feminism, and a general discomfort with the spiritual when the political typically takes prominence in secular Western feminist theory.

In Hull's women of color genealogy, creativity is central to new spiritual consciousness, and *This Bridge*, along with its subsequent volumes, is an academic text valuing the creative as a legitimate theorizing mode. When Audre Lorde said "poetry is not a luxury" (36), this edict was taken to heart in women of color feminist and women's and gender studies texts of the 1970s to the 1990s. Form and content together express a spiritual sensibility atypical of most secular women's and gender studies academic scholarship. Alice Walker's definition of "womanism" includes the need for women of color to create; subsequent work related to "womanism" tends to be multigenred and to exist outside of the bounds of traditional academic scholarship.

"Womanism," a term vital to women's and gender studies, is another way of describing women of color spirituality as indispensable to political experience. Alice Walker coined the term "womanism" in 1981 and more thoroughly described it in 1983 as "1. From womanish. (Opp. of 'girlish,' i.e. frivolous, irresponsible, not serious.) A black feminist or feminist of color" who "loves other women" and "loves the spirit" (19). Lastly, "Womanist is to feminist as purple is to lavender" ("Womanist" 19). It is not accidental that theologians have taken up "womanism" prominently. Layli Phillips names "spiritualized" as one of womanism's five most important qualities (xxiv) and suggests that "womanism openly acknowledges a spiritual/transcendental realm with which human life, living kind, and the material world are intertwined" (xxvi). Womanism integrates women of color consciousness and spirituality so that there is no tension between the two but an essential and a productive interaction.

Some of the most prominent early African American feminist critics have taken a New Age or spiritual turn, perhaps to the surprise of feminist academics. Recently, Alice Walker and bell hooks have become active and public practitioners of Buddhism (some would argue a Westernized, New Age version at that). In interviews and articles, they speak about the internal self in some similar ways to white feminists who have been chastised for a turn to the "revolution within." Walker's most recent novel, *Now Is the Time to Open Your Heart,* was critiqued heavily for not only being too "New Agey" but for replicating the spiritual appropriation of indigenous people for the satisfaction of Western spiritual seekers. Michiko Kakutani gave a cringe-inducing review of Walker's novel: "In the end *Now Is the Time to Open Your Heart* is less a novel than a cloying collection of New Age homilies, multicultural pieties and trippy Carlos Castaneda-ish riffs, hung like politically correct Christmas ornaments on the armature of Kate's tortuous journey from self-pity to self-congratulation." Walker is unapologetic about her desire to integrate the spiritual and political on her own terms. In *We Are the Ones We Have Been Waiting For: Inner Light in a Time of Darkness: Meditations,* she notes how essential it is "to worship the Great Mystery, which is never static or dogmatic, but always evolving, ever unfolding" (133). Her collection of essays is based on talks given at meditation centers and to midwives, yoga groups, and alternative spiritual communities. She speaks openly about the importance of meditation in her life, and she also always integrates the spiritual with the political, but the spiritual in her later volumes tends to be foregrounded.

In *Where We Stand: Class Matters,* hooks critiques New Age culture for blaming "the poor for their plight" and for touting "economic prosperity" as "a sign of divine blessing" (44). While hooks continues to have concerns about the individualism and "prosperity consciousness" of New Age culture in *All About Love: New Visions*, there is a tension between her reliance on the numerous New Age authors she cites and her continued critiques of some New Age ideas. From Deepak Chopra and Thomas Moore to John Welwood and Marianne Williamson, most of hooks's evidence for her feminist work on love is New Age rather than overtly feminist. hooks notes, "Much as I enjoy popular New Age commentary on love, I am often struck by the dangerous narcissism fostered by spiritual rhetoric that pays so much attention to individual self-improvement and so little to the practice of love within the context of community" (76). Yet her dependence on New Age authors belies her discomfort with them. hooks has found a way to distance herself rhetorically from some of the white, bourgeois sensibilities of New Age culture while building many of her latest works on those same theories. She can complicate her relationship with New Age culture and yet still claim it on her terms, creating her own spirituality.

"What part does feminist spirituality have in taking back our own power?" asks Anzaldúa in *This Bridge Called My Back* (223), co-written with Cherríe Moraga. She later answers that question with the term "spiritual activism," which has become valuable to many feminists of color (223). Anzaldúa defines "spiritual activism" as "the work of *conocimiento*—consciousness work—which connects the inner life of the mind and spirit to the outer worlds of action. In the struggle for social change, I call this particular aspect of conocimiento spiritual activism" (*Interviews* 178). Anzaldúa's concept of "spiritual activism" is distinct from New Age culture in its indigenousness and outward activism, argues AnaLouise Keating:

> Unlike "New Age" versions of spirituality, which focus almost exclusively on the personal (so that the goals become acquiring increased wealth, a "good life," or other solipsistic materialistic terms), spiritual activism begins with the personal yet moves outward, acknowledging our radical interconnectedness. This is spirituality for social change. . . . What a contrast: while identity politics requires holding onto specific categories of identity, spiritual activism demands that we let them go. (*This Bridge We Call Home* 18)

Anzaldúa's "spiritual activism" is now a term taken up by other feminist scholars of color to mark a new theorizing of post-identity politics that draws on a different theoretical tradition altogether, in the vein of "womanist" to "feminist."

The link between indigenous religious tradition, feminism, and activism is an organic one for other feminist scholars of color. Andrea Smith, in *Native Americans and the Christian Right: The Gendered Politics of Unlikely Alliances*, describes how in Native communities "spiritual practices are not separate from everyday life" (83), and the Native women activists she interviewed "see spirituality as inextricably linked to their political activism" (268). In fact, the "concept of sovereignty is often understood as a spiritual as well as a political concept" (269). Smith explains that because sovereignty is the "dream of living outside the constraints of both U.S. colonialism and multinational capitalism," and it "entails a vision beyond what we can see now," it is by its nature spiritual (269). Smith's description of how the "dream" of sovereignty works in Native culture stands in marked contrast to many of the white female New Age practices we have observed that are based on a real longing for a transformed future but not on an ongoing experience of genocide that necessitates dreaming outside of the boundaries of the state.

M. Jacqui Alexander uses the sacred to redefine feminist and women's studies core terms because it is fundamental to the liberation of people of color. Experience becomes "sacred experience," the personal becomes "the personal as spiritual," work becomes "spiritual work," and so on (295). Labor, consciousness, and subjectivity are all made sacred. The body, as she says, "is not simply an encasement of the Soul, but also a medium of Spirit" (298):

> Experience is a category of great epistemic import to feminism. But we have understood it primarily as secularized, as if it were absent Spirit and thus antithetical, albeit indirectly, to the Sacred. In shifting the ground of experience from secular to the Sacred, we can better position, as Lata Mani has proposed, the personal as spiritual. (295)

Alexander bemoans feminism's secularism and imagines another way to inject the spiritual into the political. One cost of secularizing these core terms is to misunderstand the lives of immigrant women who do not inhabit divided lives built on a Western, secular model. "Healing work is the antidote to oppression" (311), suggests Alexander, and a transnational feminism without "sacred subjectivity" is anemic (300).

Saba Mahmood suggests that "to the degree that feminism is a politically prescriptive project, it requires the remaking of sensibilities and commitments of women whose lives contrast with feminism's emancipatory visions" (197). While Mahmood is advocating for women outside of the Western feminist paradigm, it is interesting to consider how Western

New Age women link their emancipation to the spiritual when Western feminist paradigms have been distinctly secular. For Mahmood, like Alexander, all of feminism's most dear terms fail to speak to women's experience outside of the West, in part because they are secular. Ideas of time, the state, identity, alliance building, histories—many feminist political terms—must be theorized anew in light of their secular "neutrality."

Clearly these theorists of color, who are invested in critical race analysis and spirituality, though on a spectrum from less to more invested in the New Age, suggest that white feminist spiritual paradigms are not only inadequate, but that "spiritual activism" signifies a different tradition altogether. Some of the feminist theorists of color embrace New Age culture but qualify that embrace within the same sentence or even text, something white New Age writers rarely do. Fundamentally, for most feminist theorists of color, there is no division between the spiritual and the political, as we have so often witnessed within the second-wave feminist movement and critiques of New Age culture. The future of a more integrated spiritual-political feminism rests in part on recognizing the places where such dichotomies do not exist and acknowledging that the spiritual and political cannot be divorced in women of color consciousness theory.

The Essentialist Satisfactions of the White New Age: Gender Identity, Embodiment, and Primitivism

The very appeal of New Age culture for white women is unsurprisingly the source of the main criticisms against it: its use of essentialism, embodiment, and primitivism. While "difference feminism" is no longer fashionable in the academy, it remains alive and well in popular culture, especially in New Age culture. In nearly every part of this project, we have seen the reemergence of an essentialism that claims women as superior: women believe they have a special calling because they are more attuned to spirituality. Women believe that they live closer to the earth and cycles of nature, and thus they can protect the environment. Women believe that they have special spiritual powers that mark them as oracles for a new millennium. Women believe that they have privileged insight into rejecting a mind/body dualism and can help others think holistically. Women believe that because they are more willing to integrate their male and female sides, they can teach men to do the same. Women believe that they understand the interrelatedness of all life better because they have superior qualities such as nurturance, understanding, and patience. And many white women believe that a more powerful spiritual gender identity is found in the superior spirituality and indigenous traditions of women of color.

Indeed, just as it seemed that essentialism had gasped its last breath in academia, John Gray's *Men are from Mars, Women are from Venus* (and its more reputable twin, Deborah Tannen's *You Just Don't Understand*), stayed on the best-seller list for almost a decade. By turning on any talk show, one can see gender differences played out over and over: emotionally, men are quiet, withdrawn, and in their "caves," while women need to talk, share, and connect. While academics and feminists may be appalled by the essentialist scripting of such conservative gender formations, Diana Fuss has pointed out that "to insist that essentialism is always and everywhere reactionary is, for the constructionist, to buy into essentialism in the very act of making the charge; *it is to act as if essentialism has an essence*" (21, emphasis in original). Though I will not rehash here this academic "war" between "constructionists" and "essentialists," I do suggest that what appears unabashedly "essentialist" at the outset in daily practices has other possibilities.

New Age women continue to use essentialist arguments to testify to their authority in the religious sphere. As in the nineteenth century, when women turned "virtues" such as "piety" and even "passivity" into vehicles for spiritualism, so too do New Age women draw on stereotypes of women as "more spiritual" to make quasi-feminist critiques "without the anger," as one practitioner said. New Age women say over and over that they have inherited a world that "men have ruined," and that only women have the special power to fix it. Ironically, as many second-wave feminists have lamented the old days of political action, when anger was focused on a single problem—men—it is in New Age culture that these single critiques of men still appear. Whether in the fluid essentialism that macrobiotics offers, or in the more static essentialism of Goddess culture, women draw on these notions of women's superiority to empower themselves.

Rather than work within the state as second-wave feminists sometimes did, however, New Age women more often turn if not to the "gifts of women" then to the essentialist fantasy that the answers are found in women's bodies. New Age culture allows for an experience—indeed, a celebration—of embodiment. Goddess culture, for example, seeks to reunite with the Goddess through rituals based on the body and a "worshipful speechlessness." Women are guided by their own "intuition," a crucial term in New Age culture that refers to an inner voice felt in the body rather than an external authority. Intuition arises in the body, and by listening carefully to what we feel within us, women can access it. As famous self-help teacher Shakti Gawain says, "The knowingness that resides within each of us can be accessed through what we usually call our intuition. By learning to contact, listen to, and act on our intuition, we can directly connect to the higher power of the universe" (10). In Goddess worship, this "intuition" is found in physical "rememberfullness" with the Goddess. Macrobiotics also elevates the body, though it does so not through intuition but by carefully codified dietary systems of yin and yang.

In New Age culture, women are encouraged to be in their bodies and pay loving attention to their bodies; in contrast, feminism has understandably wanted to disassociate women from sole identification with their bodies. As in so many New Age practices, the way to integrate the male and female is through the *body*. Rosalind Coward suggests that in New Age culture "it is as if the body has become the site of all innocence, which for a while was attributed by religions to the soul of the child" (30). For most New Age women, the body is the site of all wisdom—and it is through the body that one can perform spiritual acts such as accessing the paranormal or traveling in the Sisterhood of Shields.

Yet often the body is celebrated not just as body but as *primitive* body, and not just as essentially wise but also as essentially dark. All of the New Age communities that I have observed fetishize the ancient ancestors of remote origin: from Lynn Andrews and Mary Summer Rain, who long for a romantic Indian past, to macrobiotic women who long for an Asian pastoral, to Goddess worshippers who long to "return" to the black body and a perfect matriarchy. White women fantasize a utopian harmony wherein they already have the "primitive" within.

As second-wave feminism grappled with race issues, it is not surprising that these popular manifestations of racial appropriation seem outmoded, frustrating, and racist. However, while New Age women are using perverse forms of racial fetishization, their critics have overlooked the complex dynamics of power, embodiment, and altered gender identities. In the case of Andrews and Summer Rain, I suggest that their longings are longings for female bonding—for a New Age "feminism" if you will, rather than particularly for Indianness. Gender and race are bound up together in these New Age cultures, and though their fetishization is deeply troubling, their aims should be more clearly parsed.

While many New Age practitioners use race to access gender, they also try to create a racial harmony that has largely been rejected by contemporary feminists. One of the key historical narratives of second-wave feminism is that there was a body of burgeoning feminist criticism oblivious to race politics until feminists of color came along to critique it, and helpfully so. When critic Susan Gubar suggested in her controversial piece "What Ails Feminist Criticism?" that feminists of color had made the use of the word "woman" impossible and were partly to blame for the sorry state in feminist criticism, there was an outcry. Robyn Wiegman, among others, suggested that Gubar had misunderstood epistemologically that feminism was white first and "colored" second. To grant feminism an originary status in history before race is to imagine that feminism is not always about race, and that women of color have not also always had a feminist past. In the contentious politics of failed alliances and histories between white women and women of color in the United States, New Age women stake an interesting place. They argue romantically and unapologetically for a better multiracial past often accessed through the spiritual, whether it be Goddess rituals or the paranormal. They argue, in fact, for an inclusive multiracial past rather than subscribe to liberal feminist narratives of female progress through time. They long for that past because the feminist present of fraught—and necessarily so—racial politics is once again "about anger" rather than about harmony.

Of course, nearly every New Age practice is founded on suspect, complicated racial dynamics; of course, these New Age multiracial utopias are predicated on an elision of racial difference. Recognizing these racial logics should be our starting point for discussion, not our ending point, as they have been. New Age culture gives women the space to act out idealized multiracial women's community in ways that women's and gender studies scholars see as flawed and impossible. Jean Wyatt states, "In many academic circles the notion of interracial community is dismissed as naïve, idealistic, and inevitably exclusionary" (896). Are New Age women acting out a failed dream of multicultural feminism? If so, how are they doing it? We need to examine why so many New Age women take their dreams and fantasies of race harmony out of the nation and into the past and future where they remain ideal rather than fractured in the real present.

The Future of "New Age Feminism"

In conclusion, I return to the second half of my originary question for this project: "Why are white women interested in New Age culture and not feminism?" If we take as foundational what this project has shown—that New Age culture is a women's culture where the modes of production and consumption, demographic, history, and philosophical foundations are gendered—then it is a close step to seeing the New Age as perhaps the most popular face of feminism. However, the constant question remains: Are they or are they not feminists?

Feminism's many divisions have been depicted by the media and by many feminists as breaking down into two significant factions: on the one side are those who are often referred to pejoratively as "babe feminists," "do-me feminists," "lipstick feminists," or, to some, just plain "antifeminists" such as Katie Roiphe, Rene Denfield, and even Naomi Wolf who are on the side of self-power over politics; on the other side are the "victim" feminists or "good girl" feminists who "grumpily" hold onto the "pure politics of the street" and eschew any connection to consumption, sex, or popular culture (Baumgardner and Richards 258).[3] Obviously these dichotomies are simplistic and unhelpful. Less obviously, they also manage to leave out of the picture altogether New Age women and their battle for empowerment as women.

What I have observed in numerous narratives, ethnographies, and cultural practices is that many of the claims that New Age women articulate are the same claims that feminism makes, without the rhetoric of feminism: New Age women want community, and they want empowerment as women. What is troubling to me is that without an overt political platform, many of these women will be unable to make demands as a community. Even more troubling is the unacknowledged imperialism and racism of most New Age practices that undermine claims for gender justice. What is most fascinating to me is that New Age culture is "so visible that it is invisible," as one journalist said, and that women are implicitly articulating the claims of feminism within a community wholly other from traditional feminist communities. While I am not suggesting that New Age culture's feminism has the same force as more overt forms of feminism, I am suggesting that unless we recognize how women respond to New Age allures, we will not be able to fully understand how gender and racial identities have been fashioned in the twenty-first-century United States.

I return now to a phrase that has haunted me throughout this book: as one woman said about New Age practices, "It's power without the anger." In New Age literature and culture, white women repeatedly see feminism as the angry "other," even as they espouse feminist views themselves. Katherine, a channeler interviewed by Michael Brown, describes her longing for a kind of "gentle power": " 'All the feminist stuff that we talked about in divinity school, that doesn't work for me anymore' (referring to feminism's focus on the coercive power of patriarchal institutions and attitudes). 'In channeling, there isn't any agenda. There's no power in a negative sense' " (100). While New Age women might not want "anger," they often have a striking desire for unadulterated spiritual power.

It is in the best interest of women's and gender studies scholars and other critics to understand the complicated ideological and aesthetic appeal of New Age culture, a culture that infiltrates almost every aspect of American life. Indeed, "religion might be on the decline, but spirituality—perceived to be less dogmatic, more tolerant and flexible, and better suited to the pursuit of personal inner quests—is waxing" (Davie, Woodhead, and Heelas 2). New Age is just one part of a spiritual revolution that multiplies, mutates, and shows no signs of slowing down (2). Though some argue, as Catherine Albanese notes, that there are shifting signs that the story of the New Age (capital N and A) has not at the millennium been as "compelling as it had two decades earlier," still the "distinct repertoire of beliefs and practices that acquired the New Age label tumbled over boundaries . . . to become more or less public property" (*A Republic of Mind and Spirit* 511). Albanese states finally that "in the early twenty-first century, arguably, a renewed and far more encompassing metaphysical spirituality was abroad in the land" (511).

If critics continue to ignore New Age/spiritual/metaphysical appeals, then they may be further alienated from a huge number of Americans who in some way subscribe to New Age tenets. Women's and gender studies scholars in particular must look closely at the ever-increasing move toward the "personal" at this juncture in American culture. To ignore the New Age as one of America's most prominent answers to spirituality is to ignore an all-too-large portion of America at our recent fin de siècle. As scholar Beryl Satter suggests: "Today's New Age and self-help authors represent not a national wallowing in self-indulgence, but an eerily accurate barometer of the nation's most pressing personal and political concerns" (254). New Age and alternative spiritualities have "highlighted democracy's contradictions," as Leigh Schmidt has suggested, rather than simply signaled one clear dire national outcome or another (290).

In 1848 the Fox sisters heard rappings from the dead, and in the same year Elizabeth Cady Stanton and Susan B. Anthony organized the Seneca Falls convention to lobby for women's right to vote. In the nineteenth century these movements were wedded, but in this century there is barely a conversation between them. Not only has feminism profoundly influenced New Age culture, but New Age culture has profoundly influenced the public conversation about women's power, even if it has not influenced feminism directly. I am not suggesting that the New Age is liberatory—in the most profound sense, its racial politics prevent it from ever being so—but I am suggesting that its all-pervasive rhetorical platforms need to be understood as real ways that some women navigate power. As Lynn Andrews says, "Power is female" (Staubs 28). However troubling it might be, that power still needs to be reckoned with. Yet for any possible authentic multiracial feminist community, we must attend not just to the spiritual realm but to the material one as well: as Jean Wyatt points out, "antiracism based on the all-too-real lack of social justice could provide a more solid grounding for crossrace feminist solidarity than the imaginary yearning for identification" (899). The spiritual is, almost by definition, a space for "imaginary yearning," but it must be coupled with a greater self-consciousness about white women's suspect desire for a "racially innocent" feminism. As we have seen, spirituality and politics have yet to be truly integrated in most feminist conversations, but that integration represents the future of a multiracial and global feminism. That kind of "New Age" feminism has an eye to its racialized, material past even as it struggles for its dreamed-of future.

Notes

Introduction

1. While scholars date various "Awakenings" differently, Ruth Engs suggests that the current "millennial Awakening" runs from 1970 to 2000 (3).
2. See Elayne Rapping; Wendy Simonds.
3. See R. Laurence Moore; David D. Hall; Harry S. Stout and D. G. Hart; Thomas A. Tweed.
4. In a diatribe against New Age culture, Arthur Versluis draws the connection between earlier movements and the New Age: "The pseudoreligious potpourri" found across the United States in the late nineteenth century is "clearly a predecessor of the 'New Age' movement during the late twentieth century. Just as the New Thought movement represented diluted Emersonian transcendentalism for the masses, the New Age movement pandered to a materialist interpretation of what originally were authentic traditional teachings" (314).
5. Examples of a few famous mediums include Mrs. Lenora Piper, who was discovered by William James in 1885 and was a highly investigated trance-medium. Patience Worth, known as the housewife Pearl Lenore Pollard Curran, began to receive communications from a "personality claiming to be a 17th century English girl who had come to America and been killed by Indians" (Berger 99). Through the Ouija board, Mrs. Curran, who had no formal education, began to write "literary composition of the highest quality," such as *The Sorry Tale*, *Telka*, and *Hope Trueblood*. See Arthur S. Berger.
6. Scholar Andreas Huyssen uses this term to name a similar demonization of "the feminine" in relation to the Modern (53).

Chapter 1. "Touched by an Angel"

1. The wide-ranging effect of Douglas's study cannot be underesti-
mated. It is the religious narrative of the nineteenth century; even
within this chapter, almost all religious historians cite Douglas's
study without complication. Among them are Kenneth Woodward,
Robert Bellah, Gary Wills, Bryan LeBeau, and Leon J. Podles.

2. By now Douglas's "feminization" thesis has been challenged by several generations of critics—from Jane Tomkins and Linda Kerber to
Leonard Tennenhouse, Dana Nelson, and Robyn Wiegman—for
misunderstanding the relationship between gender, history, and the
sentimental. Initially, critics such as Tompkins and Kerber sought to
reclaim the popular texts and values attributed to women, which
Douglas critiqued as redemptive. These critics see the "separate
spheres" theory of gender, wherein women inhabit the domestic private sphere and men the public political one, as relevant insofar as
women's sphere is positive, equal, and sometimes even superior to
the male sphere. However, more recent critics such as Tennenhouse
and Nelson have tried to move "beyond the masculine-feminine
opposition that structures any theory of feminization, good or bad"
(Tennehouse 4). These critics see "sentiment as a widely circulating
cultural discourse in both male and female writings" (Gould iii).

3. Scholar Wendy Simonds notes about women and self-help: "I saw
journalists' professional displeasure with the [self-help] genre as
symptomatic of the general disdain usually accorded by the intellectual elite to 'women's culture'—all forms of media directed to an
audience of women, or media utilized (whether explicitly directed or
not) primarily by women" (2).

4. For a larger discussion on the feminization of Christianity, see Leon
J. Podles.

5. For further identification of current spiritual seeking as a "Great
Awakening," see Jennifer Harrison 22–28; David Kinghoffer 32–34;
Ruth Engs. Engs marks the historical movements as "Great Awakenings of the Jacksonian (1830–1860), the progressive (1890–1920), and
the current millennial (1970–2000) reform eras" (3).

6. Belief in the paranormal has only increased over the last thirty years.
In 1988, "A full 67 percent of Americans report having experienced
ESP, according to the National Opinion Research Council of the
University of Chicago, and 42 percent say they've had unexplained
contact with the dead. Those numbers have increased from 58 percent and 27 percent, respectively, in 1973" (Wilson 37). According to
a *Time* magazine poll, "69 percent of people polled believe in angels,

and 46 percent believe they have their own guardian angel." See Nancy Gibbs 56–64; William L. MacDonald 35–43.

7. New Age culture has also been critiqued, documented, or promoted by five diverse communities: popular journalism, fundamentalist Christians, "skeptical" literature, sociological theories, and "literature written from New Age perspectives" (Hanegraaff 3). Of these five communities, the first three—popular journalism, fundamentalist Christians, and "skeptical" literature—are largely negative about the New Age; sociological theories attempt to be evenhanded and offer more description of the New Age than analysis or critique; other academic studies range between considering the New Age as worthy of study and dismissing it as corrupting rational discourse; and, finally, "literature written from New Age perspectives" is almost overwhelmingly positive about New Age philosophies, with the exception of a few practitioners who critique elements of the New Age while still self-identifying with the culture.

8. Statistical and anecdotal evidence also suggests that women make up the largest consumer base of New Age culture. "Middle-aged women make up the majority of their large New Age bookstore's customers" (Kinsella 42). It is clear, as one critic said, that "one can get a feeling for the subculture . . . by spending an hour browsing in a New Age bookshop" (Bloch 4), and at a channeling workshop featuring J. Z. Knight, "Most are middle-aged women." See Katherine Lowry 47.

9. There are certainly exceptions to the access to power women have felt in New Age culture. At the Esalen Institute in the 1970s, a major conference was conceived that featured no women as panelists. Although feminists protested, such institutions were quite androcentric until confronted by the women's movement in the 1970s. See Walter Anderson.

10. Even while the New Age and Christian fundamentalism seem polarized, several polls indicate otherwise. A Princeton Religion Research Center study showed that "a surprisingly high number of Christians identify beliefs generally described as New Age. At the same time, however, many have doubts that New Age spirituality is compatible with Christianity. Among Catholics, 59 percent said they consider New Age beliefs to be compatible with Christianity, compared with 23 percent of Protestants." See Randall Balmer.

11. Scholar Erling Jorstad argues that "the decade coheres into a meaningful pattern when its religious expression is seen in a threefold design: 1) mainline [religion] moves into frontline, 2) evangelicalism moves toward popular religion, and 3) privatization moves into New

Age religion" (x). Critic Harold Bloom has suggested that the New Age "may have achieved its greatest prominence throughout the 1980s" (183).

12. See Michael Korda.

13. See William Powers 16–28; Judy Quinn 12–13; Mike Hofman; Marilyn Johnson 32–36.

14. "Gender was a minor theme in Bellah and his colleagues' (1985) study," note Blaine J. Fowers, Brooks Applegate, Michael Tredinnick, and Jason Slusher 159–75. See also M. Elizabeth Albert 84–96.

15. This "individualistic" spiritual seeking, which is confirmed by a number of studies, clearly has a class dimension. Interestingly, while later studies mark a historical lineage of white middle-class women discovering God within, they do not investigate gender, though they mention social class. Wolfe finds that in late twentieth-century middle-class white America, even fairly religious Americans "ignore religious sectarianism," and even while debates rage between secular and orthodox camps, "moderation and tolerance . . . are the bedrock moral principles of the American middle class" (63, 72).

16. Many critics lament this change in contemporary U.S. culture. "America is becoming more and more a therapeutic society," says Mark Edmundson. Some argue that therapy is nothing more than "a hegemonic discourse that shapes and contains responses to structural injustice" (Cloud 158).

17. The same critiques leveled at New Age women are leveled at feminism by conservative critics. Elizabeth Powers claims that because feminism has encouraged women to take "days and years devoted to self-maintenance" in order to "fulfill themselves" that, ultimately, feminism has made many women egocentric.

18. But, as sociologists Daniel Mears and Christopher Ellison suggest, "One might suspect that New Age materials in fact are more popular among less affluent and/or less educated persons, or among un(der)employed persons. These groups may view New Age materials as leading to insight and self-empowerment (e.g., a central goal of many New Age books, journals, tapes, and so forth) that in turn might facilitate, if indirectly, upward mobility" (290).

19. Though Brooks argues that Bobos have learned lessons about individualism and the rejection of "spiritual authority" from "Sheila," they are moving back toward community rather than away from it (236). However, Brooks suggests that this sense of community is not a surrender to God or a willingness to choose one religion strongly over another. In the end, the spirituality of Bobos might be conceived as "Sheilaism" within a community of "Sheilas."

20. While this purchasing power is not entirely typical of New Age consumption, which is filled with the kitsch many people associate with middle-to-lower class taste—it is noteworthy that the spiritual life of upper middle-class white Americans is described in such gendered materialist terms.

21. Because Kaminer's concern is the decline of rationalism, it has an unusual leveling effect on the differences between religion and New Age culture. New Age beliefs are not so different from established religions; it is just that one set of beliefs is "socially acceptable" while another set is not (35). The differences between the two are "organizational" rather than truly theological (35).

22. As in Janice Radway's pivotal study *Reading the Romance*, where women use romance novels strategically, sometimes to take a break from housework or carve out private time alone, New Age women use books to explore spirituality without leaving home. See also Wendy Simonds.

23. Anecdotally it appears that women have New Age diseases such as chronic fatigue syndrome, environmental illness (EI), and fibromyalgia more often than men. In a recent study of Swedish office workers, women reported "sick building syndrome" (SBS) in 12 percent of cases as compared to 4 percent among males. See Berndt Stenberg and Stig Wall 491–503.

24. See "Suzanne Somers and Breast Cancer Treatment" and "Suzanne Somers' Use of Iscador Treatment."

Chapter 2. "The Indian Way is What's *Inside*"

1. While I did not personally take part in the "Native rituals" weekend, I have observed white appropriation and/or use of Native practices in a variety of settings, from workshops to New Age bookstores.

2. For information, see Helene E. Hagan; Mark Havnes; Ines Hernandez-Avila 329–53.

3. Andrews and Summer Rain are not oblivious to racist critiques. At the beginning of her book *Woman at the Edge of Two Worlds*, Andrews has this disclaimer: "The ceremonies portrayed in this book originate from the ancient history of the Sisterhood of the Shields and not from tribal customs and traditions of the Native American" (frontispiece). She eventually becomes aware of the accusations against her, though it does not change her practices. In Summer Rain's life, these accusations have taken on sinister tones. She notes that because of "continuing death-threat letters and the

more recently manifested premonition dreams of kidnapping incidents that contain vivid location details that were verified by doing some extensive investigative footwork, I currently have a live-in security person who is with me twenty-four hours a day" (*Bittersweet* 242). Though Summer Rain does not state specifically that these "death-threat letters" are coming from those accusing her of appropriation, it is clear that the most negative critiques she receives are from those accusers. For example, on both Andrews's and Summer Rain's Web sites, letters appear regularly that critique their Indian appropriation. Summer Rain's *Bittersweet*.

4. Fetishizing primitivism, especially the Indian primitive, certainly has a long history. I am interested in the *gendered* desire for the Indian primitive. For more on the Indian primitive and the Indian as fetish object, see Roy Harvey Pearce; Richard Berkhofer Jr.; Brian W. Dippie; Daniel Francis; Helen Carr.

5. For feminist articles that criticize analogizing white women's oppression with racial oppression, see Robyn Wiegman; Karen Sanchez-Eppler 28–59.

6. Andrews colonizes the Yucatan with so much zeal and purple prose that it may seem ironic. Critics of her work respond with a vehemence and contempt that may be inspired by her aesthetics as much as her imperialism. For work on tourism imperialism, see James Clifford.

7. See Vine Deloria Jr. and Jace Weaver for different Indian perspectives on Indian religion and the myth of the "spiritual Indian."

8. Due to several New Age hits like Summer Rain's and Neale Donald Walsch's best-seller series *Conversations with God*, Hampton Roads Publishing Company has a successful independent New Age publisher. Their books reflect a more alternative New Age sensibility that emphasizes the paranormal—life-after-death experiences, channeling, prophecy, out-of-body experiences, and communicating with aliens. Thus the press charts a gradual movement toward the paranormal in Summer Rain's work, and in New Age culture generally.

9. At first glance, it is unclear whether the story of No-Eyes is fact or fiction. On the one hand, Summer Rain includes the story of Sacajawea, specific tribal names, and actual dates that anchor the story in real time. On the other hand, the highly wrought prose and the embellishing narrative commentary encourage the reader to consume the story as fiction. Summer Rain frequently miswrites history. For example, She-Who-Sees's vision of the disappearance of her tribe through miscegenation in the nineteenth century is less probable

than the obliteration of her tribe through disease, war, and removal. See Ward Churchill.

10. While in her narratives Summer Rain appears to have feminist agency—she confronts sexist remarks, acts independently in spiritual seeking, and meets the men in her works and marriage as peers—a contradiction exists between understanding redress in political rather than spiritual terms. How can one at once believe in the spiritual equality of all souls yet have to repair material inequality in the present? This dilemma is navigated by theorizing gender through the paranormal and past lives. For example, her refusal to accept same-sex relationships is conceptualized in terms of a gender imbalance in past lives: "Homosexuality is evidence of a spirit's excessive lifetimes as the opposite sex resulting in a current inability to reverse roles. Homosexuality *extends* the spirit's 'return cycle.' It represents a wasted lifetime in respect to the spirit's ultimate purpose and advancement. . . . The male/female *balance* must be equalizing" (*Daybreak* 343). A single lifetime is "wasted" in a same-sex relationship because the balance of male/female is off: a male soul has been a male soul too often and is trapped, therefore, loving another man. This unusual homophobic logic provides a gender parallel to her racial logic: one moment she sets up pure and rigid boundaries, and the next she confuses them. Though stating that the male/female balance is essential and cannot be thrown off, on many other occasions she insists that souls matter, not identities.

11. This idea of memory provides a strange twist on scholar Walter Benn Michaels's critique of constructionism, which he says concretizes race on the basis of history, not biology, but ends up being essentialist anyway. After dismissing biological essentialism, Benn Michaels states that we now use the category of history rather than blood to claim what we perceive to be our own: "Why should learning something about the past that we have never known be described as remembering it?" (178). See Walter Benn Michaels.

Chapter 3. Gender on a Plate

1. In 1965, a young woman named Beth Ann Simon died from macrobiotic diet number seven. Serious macrobiotic practitioners sometimes go on a range of "progressively restrictive" diets, from one to seven, to achieve greater purity and spiritual enlightenment (Raso 27). On the number seven, the most extreme of the diets, one eats

only brown rice and small amounts of liquid. Regardless of whether or not macrobiotics killed Beth Ann Simon, her death became the case against it, especially for critics such as Dr. Stare. Some say that Simon remained on diet number seven for "nine months" instead of the prescribed seven days (Levenstein 183). Others say that perhaps she died from a drug overdose. See "The Kosher of the Counterculture"; "Zen Diet Assailed by A.M.A. Council as Peril to Health"; Jack Raso; Harvey Levenstein; Donna Maurer.

2. See Hilda Bruch; Joan Jacobs Brumberg; Kim Chernin; Susie Orbach.

3. See Dr. Steven Bratman for more information on orthorexia.

4. See Ronald E. Kotzsch; Warren J. Belasco; Harvey Levenstein; Kimberly J. Lau.

5. Yin and yang represent the kind of static essentialism that has been dismissed by feminist theorists such as Judith Butler, Diana Fuss, and Donna Haraway in the past twenty years. These theorists have critiqued essentialism and come out on the side of social construction. Having declared that essence is dead, believing in a gender essence is now considered out of vogue at best, and idiotic at worst. Also see Linda Nicholson.

6. The following are the seven "basic principles" of the macrobiotic diet, as quoted in Michio Kushi:

> 1. More complex carbohydrates, fewer simple carbohydrates
>
> 2. More vegetable-quality protein, less animal food protein
>
> 3. Less overall fat consumption, more unsaturated fat and less saturated fat
>
> 4. A balance of various naturally occurring vitamins, minerals, and other nutritional factors
>
> 5. Use of more organically grown, natural quality food; more traditional food processing techniques and fewer artificial and chemically processed foods
>
> 6. Consumption of as much food remaining in whole form as possible and less of refined and partial foods
>
> 7. Greater consumption of food that is rich in natural fiber, and less of food that has been devitalized by over-processing. (9)

7. Originally, Kushi settled in New England and founded the Kushi Institute in Becket, Massachusetts, because of its history of movements such as "Abolitionist, Transcendentalist, women's suffrage,

Mormonism, etc.," and because, according to Oriental philosophy, "the northeast direction or region governs thought and conscious-ness" (*One Peaceful World* 39). The Kushi Institute is known as the premier place to study macrobiotics. The fees are high (thousands of dollars for one week), and access to the center itself is difficult. Most of the people drawn there have crisis-level health issues ranging from cancer, AIDS, heart disease, and diabetes to more difficult-to-cure sicknesses such as environmental illness. Typically, they come for one week and learn the basics of the diet and philosophy. In the summer of 1997, I lived as a full-time member of the Kushi Institute. From working for the administration, to assisting in cooking classes, to helping prepare meals for the roughly sixty-person community, to sitting in on teaching and counseling sessions, I observed macrobi-otic life.

8. This nostalgic pastoral utopia is founded on myths of nation build-ing: "This is the story of modern America. Our ancestors built this country with strong bodies and clear judgment nourished by grains. They were cooking oatmeal, baking their own bread. . . . They were strong and they knew their purpose of life intuitively" ("Humanity's Traditional Food").

9. Social historian Todd Gitlin remarks that "This lack of confidence, anxiety, even incoherence about what the national [U.S.] identity is and ought to be, or even whether there ought to be one at all, today crops up everywhere in American culture" (41). Gitlin glosses over how this "anxiety" for many in the white middle-class, particularly in New Age culture, becomes a racially inflected longing for what is "not-American," that is, primitive, exotic, Eastern, and ancient. Harvey Cox notes how "the West projects reverse images of its own deficiencies": "This mythical Orient once consisted almost entirely of sages and fakirs, magical talismans and esoteric lore, serpents weaving to nasal flutes, infinite holiness, wisdom and inner peace" (149).

10. The growth and treatment of food is particularly fetishized in Japan-ese culture—people tell romantic stories of visiting Japanese food factories where miso or umeboshi plums are made. Often, macrobi-otic practitioners try to reproduce "ancient" methods of fermenting, pickling, and so on to again bring more balance to the food cycle. Author Michel Abehsera answers the question: "Why is it called Zen macrobiotic cooking?" "It is the traditional food of ancient Japan, now preserved fully only in the Zen Buddhist monasteries. The rest of Japan, unfortunately, moves more and more away from this tradi-tional cuisine as it becomes more and more like the West. Zen monks are the longest-lived and healthiest people in Japan, while, at the

other end of the scale, Westernized physicians and restaurant owners die early." (9).

11. White fish meat, on the other hand, is considered a less extreme "yang" and an acceptable "meat" alternative. Practitioners eat fish in part because of the Orientalist fantasy that Eastern cultures, which are fish-eating cultures, are superior to Western cultures.

12. "Neutralizing poisons from meat" is just one of many food remedies prescribed in macrobiotics. "When we eat too much meat, or eat meat cooked in a wrong way (such as undercooked), acute forms of 'intoxication' can be created. . . . Foods supplying the opposite energy can therefore offset the effects of meat: scallions, mushrooms, brown rice vinegar, sake or wine, and barley" (47). See Michio Kushi's *Macrobiotic Home Remedies.*

13. Christine Pirello, Jessica Porter, Elaine Nussbaum, and Wendy Esko, among others, are all women who have cooked their way into careers of macrobiotic book publishing, consulting, and small business.

14. From symptoms ranging from fatigue, poor self-esteem, and "loss of self-discipline" to more extreme symptoms leading to degenerative illnesses, feminists argue that a sense of powerlessness in the world leads to illness. For resources that connect women's oppression to health problems, see Lesley Doyal and other more popular authors such as Christiane Northrup.

15. Ironically, while sugar may "enslave" women, it is an ancient system of enslavement of people of color. Kushi further critiques the quest for sugar for moving the world from a preindustrial to industrial culture; the loss of the pastoral is tied to an addictive substance that weakens, especially weakening the imperialist cultures that consumed it. Kushi argues that when Toussaint l'Overture and the Black Freedom Fighters rebelled against French troops, they were able to conquer the French because of their "simpler, more well-balanced diet" (*One Peaceful World* 155). The French, on the other hand, became sick with yellow fever because of their "weak constitutions" (a popular macrobiotic phrase).

16. In order to popularize the concept of yin/yang in the West, Ohsawa reversed the Chinese understanding of yin and yang and applied it to diet in a way that had not been done before (Colbin 65).

17. The most misogynist or conservative gender teachings are not espoused publicly by popular macrobiotic practitioners such as Warren Kramer, Christina Perillo, Carrie Wolf, and Wendy Esko. In their writing, Perillo and Esko do not overtly mention gender. Rather, they promote the already gendered philosophy of yin and yang, thereby implicitly supporting a philosophy of gender differ-

ence. Interestingly, on the Kushi Institute's Web site, there are a few articles that try to find a balance, as it were, between antifeminist macrobiotic theory and theory influenced by feminism.

18. In a twist on both conservative and liberal politics, woman should both stay at home and yet be paid for it: "Society should pay their [caregiver's] retirement and pay them a salary for staying home to care for the next generation" (*Women's Health Guide* 47). The emphasis is on empowering women in the domestic sphere, a desirable place for them.

19. For theories on "everyday life," see Michel de Certeau; Pierre Bourdieu; John Fiske.

20. For macrobiotic conversion narratives, see Elaine Nussbaum; Dr. Anthony J. Satilaro; William Dufty.

21. The Kushi Institute Summer Conference is the largest gathering of macrobiotic teachers and followers and takes place yearly at a designated college campus in the Northeast. I attended this conference both in 1995, where I heard the panel on men's health, and in 1997.

22. This idea of the "natural" is related to what Catherine Albanese calls an American obsession with "nature religion." She cites the Hutchinson Family Singers, an American nineteenth-century antislavery singing group, who participated in health-reform movements, natural healing, vegetarianism, phrenology, and a host of other modalities, as prime examples of those who worship "nature religion." For the Hutchinsons, the "natural" is used to describe everything from demanding temperance to upholding American democracy: "Drunkenness eroded families, and slavery obstructed the natural relation of men and women to the land in wholesome agricultural work" (*Nature Religion* 8, 9).

23. As well as working as a cook at the Kushi Institute in the summer of 1997, I attended numerous macrobiotic events over the course of four years. I participated in two International Conferences, had three individual health consultations, and attended many workshops, ranging from weekend conferences such as "How to Start Your Own Macrobiotic Cooking School" and "Hypoglycemia—How to Beat It" to individual workshops on cooking for women's health and strategies for environmental change.

Chapter 4. The Structure of Prehistorical Memory in the American Goddess Movement

1. Cynthia Eller notes helpfully that the "rough consensus" that a matriarchy existed for Goddess worshippers was formed under "the

pressure of three key developments: (1) the steadfast rejection of matriarchal myth by most feminist anthropologists; (2) a burgeoning feminist spirituality movement intent on placing goddess worship in prehistory; and (3) the pioneering archaeological work of Marija Gimbutas" (34).

2. See Johann Jacob Bachofen; Frederick Engels; for current critique and synopses of that work, see Rita Felski; Cynthia Eller.

3. Critics such as scholar David Reiff argue that Goddess worshippers are narcissistic, have "fantasies of redemption," and have "an intuition that is contemptuous of reason and of neurochemistry," which he sees as "one of the most worrying things about the Goddess movement" (31, 24). Conservative scholar Philip Davis believes that the decline of Western civilization is predicated on the flourishing of Goddess culture and that it is used to "recruit and encourage people to work for the New Age of gender feminism" (352).

4. I am not interested in, nor capable of, contradicting specific archaeological claims that others do elsewhere in an excellent manner (e.g., Ruth E. Tringham). Furthermore, as many archaeologists recognized the contingent nature of their prehistorical knowledge claims, reconstructing prehistory became best understood as a "simulacrum" or an "identical copy for which no original has ever existed" (qtd. in Conkey, "Original Narratives" 116). Since the past is not an "original" but a fabrication, most archaeologists make claims hesitantly about what can be known about prehistoric life. Archaeologist Margaret Conkey suggests that in prehistory, "subsistence and economics are 'fairly easy' to know, whereas social organization and religious and spiritual life are close to impossible to know" ("Original Narratives" 110).

5. Several books suggest that the rise of New Age culture, of which Goddess worship is frequently considered a part, is essentially the "fault" of women who are too emotional, spiritual, and hysterical. See Philip G. Davis; Mel D. Faber; Elaine Showalter.

6. Several books and articles celebrate the "dark goddess" specifically. For more, see Marion Woodman and Elinor Dickson; China Galland; Demetra George; Lucia Chiavola Birnbaum.

7. See Robyn Wiegman; Karen Sanchez-Eppler 28–59.

8. Conkey and Tringham point out that the figurines that Goddess worshippers interpret as female deities were once analyzed by misogynist archaeologists as male sex objects. Either reading perpetuates interpretive inaccuracies (*Feminisms in the Academy* 213). Archaeologist Karel van der Toorn notes that in relation to early Israelite figurines of women, "there is no unambiguous indication

that these various types of figurines are in fact goddesses. Their nudity does not make them divine, neither do their protruding breasts or other symbols of physical beauty and fertility" (Goodison 92).

9. Culbertson speaks about the narratives of survivors of extreme violence and war, especially the Holocaust. I am in no way suggesting that Goddess worshippers and Holocaust survivors have commensurate experiences, only that most of the critical work on memory and trauma is relevant in describing memory in Goddess culture.

10. Michael Warner, Lauren Berlant, and others have critiqued both the notion of the citizen as a liberal abstraction (that is, a certain kind of public citizen—necessarily white, male, Protestant, and land owning—stands for the nation and reifies citizenship as such), and the notion that public acts, such as saluting the flag, constitute citizenship rather than private acts.

Conclusion

1. "Just a quarter of women say they consider themselves a feminist; 70 percent do not" states a CBS poll in 2005. See Sean Alfano.

2. For one of the best examples of nostalgia for second-wave feminism, see Gayle Greene and Coppelia Kahn.

3. But spirituality as it trickles out becomes "cool" when it takes on "girl power" connotations. In *Manifesta*, Jennifer Baumgardner and Amy Richards write about constructing their own ritual through an all-female dinner party where "for two years, we had a makeshift coven . . . [and] cast freestyle spells. . . . Most of us had left our own religion or allowed it to lapse, and we were searching for spiritual rituals that had meaning for us" (16). Baumgardner and Richards eventually find meaning in their community of women, and not the "Wicca stuff," which they "ditched." Here politics and community have become their religion, though some women want the community more than the politics (16).

Works Cited

Abehsera, Michel. *Zen Macrobiotic Cooking: Oriental and Traditional Recipes*. New York: Avon, 1968. Print.

Abt, Vicki, and Mel Seesholtz. "The Shameless World of Phil, Sally, and Oprah: Television Talk Shows and the Deconstructing of Society." *Journal of Popular Culture* 28.1 (1994): 171–92. Print.

Adams, Carol J. *The Sexual Politics of Meat: A Feminist-Vegetarian Critical Theory*. New York: Continuum, 1990. Print.

Aihara, Herman. *Kaleidoscope: Macrobiotic Articles, Essays, and Lectures 1979–1985*. Oroville, CA: George Ohsawa Macrobiotic Foundation, 1986. Print.

Albanese, Catherine. *Nature Religions in America: From the Algonkian Indians to the New Age*. Chicago: U of Chicago P, 1990. Print.

———. *A Republic of Mind and Spirit: A Cultural History of American Metaphysical Religion*. New Haven: Yale UP, 2007. Print.

Albert, M. Elizabeth. "In the Interest of Public Good? New Questions on Feminism." In *Community in America: The Challenge of "Habits of the Heart,"* ed. Charles H. Reynolds and Ralph U. Norman. Berkeley: U of California P, 1988. 84–96. Print.

Aldred, Lisa. "'Money Is Just Spiritual Energy': Incorporating the New Age." *Journal of Popular Culture* 35.4 (2002): 72. Academic Search Complete. EBSCO. Web. 1 May 2011.

———. "Plastic Shamans and Astroturf Sun Dances: New Age Commercialization of Native American Spirituality." *American Indian Quarterly* 24.3 (2000): 329–52. Print.

Alexander, M. Jacqui. *Pedagogies of Crossing: Meditations on Feminism, Sexual Politics, Memory, and the Sacred*. Perverse Modernities. Durham: Duke UP, 2005. Print.

Alfano, Sean. "Poll: Women's Movement Worthwhile." *CBS News.com*. CBS, Oct. 23, 2005. Web.

Althusser, Louis. "Ideology and Ideological State Apparatuses." *Lenin and Philosophy and Other Essays.* New York: Monthly Review P, 1971. Print.

Anburajan, Aswini. "Breaking Down Oprah's Numbers." *MSNBC.com.* NBC, 7 Dec. 2007. Web. 1 May 2011.

Anderson, Sherry Ruth, and Patricia Hopkins. *The Feminine Face of God: The Unfolding of the Sacred in Women.* New York: Bantam, 1992. Print.

Anderson, Walter Truett. *The Upstart Spring: Esalen and the American Awakening.* Reading, MA: Addison-Wesley, 1983. Print.

Andrews, Lynn V. *Crystal Woman: The Sisters of the Dreamtime.* New York: Warner, 1987. Print.

———. *Dark Sister: A Sorcerer's Love Story.* New York: HarperCollins, 1995. Print.

———. *Flight of the Seventh Moon: The Teaching of the Shields.* New York: Harper & Row, 1984. Print.

———. *Jaguar Woman: And the Wisdom of the Butterfly Tree.* New York: Harper & Row, 1985. Print.

———. *Love and Power: Awakening to Mastery.* New York: Harper-Collins, 1997. Print.

———. *Medicine Woman.* New York: Harper & Row, 1981. Print.

———. *Star Woman: We Are Made from Stars and to the Stars We Must Return.* New York: Warner, 1986. Print.

———. *Teachings around the Sacred Wheel: Finding the Soul of Dreamtime.* San Francisco: HarperCollins, 1990. Print.

———. *Windhorse Woman: A Marriage of Spirit.* New York: Warner, 1989. Print.

———. *Woman at the Edge of Two Worlds: The Spiritual Journey of Menopause.* New York: Warner, 1993. Print.

Anzaldúa, Gloria. *Interviews/Entrevistas.* Ed. AnaLouise Keating. New York: Routledge, 2000. Print.

Anzaldúa, Gloria, and AnaLouise Keating. *This Bridge We Call Home: Radical Visions for Transformation.* New York: Routledge, 2002. Print.

Ardinger, Barbara. *A Woman's Book of Rituals & Celebrations.* San Rafael, CA: New World Library, 1992. Print.

Aupers, Stef, and Dick Houtman. "Beyond the Spiritual Supermarket: The Social and Public Significance of New Age Spirituality." *Journal of Contemporary Religion* 21.2 (2006): 201–22. Academic Search Complete. EBSCO. Web. 1 May 2011.

Austen, Hallie Iglehart. *The Heart of the Goddess: Art, Myth and Meditations of the World's Sacred Feminine.* Berkeley: Wingbow P, 1990. Print.

Bachofen, J. J. *Myth, Religion, and Mother Right*. Trans. Ralph Manheim. Princeton: Princeton UP, 1967. Print.

Balch, Robert. "The Evolution of a New Age Cult: From Total Overcomers Anonymous to Death at Heaven's Gate." *Sects, Cults & Spiritual Communities: A Sociological Analysis*, ed. William W. Zellner and Marc Petrowsky. Westport, CT: Praeger, 1998. 1–27. Print.

Balmer, Randall. "New Age Beliefs Are Really Quite Old." *Los Angeles Times*, 11 Jan. 1992: F15. Print.

Basil, Robert, ed. *Not Necessarily the New Age: Critical Essays*. Buffalo, NY: Prometheus, 1988. Print.

Baumgardner, Jennifer, and Amy Richards. *Manifesta: Young Women, Feminism, and the Future*. New York: Farrar, Straus and Giroux, 2000. Print.

Bednarowski, Mary Farrell. *New Religions and the Theological Imagination in America*. Bloomington: Indiana UP, 1989. Print.

Belasco, Warren J. *Appetite for Change: How the Counterculture Took on the Food Industry, 1966–1988*. New York: Pantheon, 1989. Print.

Bell, David, and Gill Valentine. *Consuming Geographies: We Are Where We Eat*. New York: Routledge, 1997. Print.

Bellah, Robert N., ed. *Habits of the Heart: Individualism and Commitment in American Life*. Updated ed. Berkeley: U of California P, 1996. Print.

———. University of Virginia. 15 Nov. 2000. Lecture.

Berger, Arthur S. *Lives and Letters in American Parapsychology: A Biographical History, 1850–1987*. Jefferson, NC: McFarland, 1988. Print.

Berger, Michele Tracy, and Kathleen Guidroz. *The Intersectional Approach: Transforming the Academy through Race, Class, and Gender*. Chapel Hill: U of North Carolina P, 2009. Print.

Berkhofer, Richard Jr. *The White Man's Indian: Images of the American Indian from Columbus to the Present*. New York: Knopf, 1978. Print.

Berlant, Lauren. *The Queen of America Goes to Washington City: Essays on Sex and Citizenship*. Durham: Duke UP, 1997. Print.

Bird, S. Elizabeth. "Savage Desires: The Gendered Construction of the American Indian in Popular Media." *Selling the Indian: Commercializing and Appropriating American Indian Cultures*, ed. Carter Jones Meyer and Diana Royer. Tucson: U of Arizona P, 2001. 62–98. Print.

Birnbaum, Lucia Chiavola. *Black Madonnas: Feminism, Religion, and Politics in Italy*. Boston: Northeastern UP, 1993. Print.

Bloch, Jon P. *New Spirituality, Self, and Belonging: How New Agers and Neo-Pagans Talk about Themselves.* Westport, CT: Praeger, 1998. Print.

Bloom, Harold. *The American Religion: The Emergence of a Post-Christian Nation.* New York: Simon & Schuster, 1992. Print.

Bourdieu, Pierre. *Distinction: A Social Critique of the Judgment of Taste.* Trans. R. Nice. Cambridge, MA: Harvard UP, 1984. Print.

Bowers, Cynthia. "Breaking the Stained Glass Ceiling." *CBSNews.com.* CBS, 11 Nov. 2007. Web. 1 May 2011.

Bratman, Steven. *Health Food Junkies.* New York: Broadway, 2001. Print.

Braude, Ann. *Radical Spirits: Spiritualism and Women's Rights in Nineteenth-Century America.* 2nd ed. Bloomington: Indiana UP, 2001. Print.

Brooks, David. *Bobos in Paradise: The New Upper Class and How They Got There.* New York: Simon & Schuster, 2000. Print.

Brown, Michael F. *The Channeling Zone: American Spirituality in an Anxious Age.* Cambridge, MA: Harvard UP, 1997. Print.

Brown, Slater. *The Heyday of Spiritualism.* New York: Hawthorn, 1970. Print.

Bruch, Hilda. *Eating Disorders: Obesity, Anorexia Nervosa, and The Person Within.* New York: Basic, 1973. Print.

Bruchac, Joseph. "'Return of the Bird Tribes' (or Daffy Duck in Buckskins)." n.p., 4 April 1999. Web. 1 May 2011.

Brumberg, Joan Jacobs. *Fasting Girls: The Emergence of Anorexia Nervosa as a Modern Disease.* Cambridge, MA: Harvard UP, 1988. Print.

Budapest, Z. "What Is the Dianic Tradition?" *Thesmophoria: Voice of the New Women's Religion* 3.7, Spring Equinox, 1982. Print.

———. "A Witch's Manifesto: Goddess Religion in Feminism." *Whole Earth Review* 74 (1992): 34–42. Print.

Butler, Jon, Grant Wacker, and Randall Herbert Balmer. *Religion in American Life: A Short History.* New York: Oxford UP, 2008. Print.

Butler, Judith. *Gender Trouble: Feminism and the Subversion of Identity.* New York: Routledge, 1990. Print.

Bynum, Caroline Walker. *Holy Feast and Holy Fast: The Religious Significance of Food to Medieval Women.* Berkeley: U of California P, 1987. Print.

Campbell, Eileen, and J. H. Brennan. *Body, Mind and Spirit: A Dictionary of New Age Ideas, People, Places and Terms.* Boston: Tuttle, 1994. Print.

Camphausen, Rufus C. *The Yoni: Sacred Symbol of Female Creative Power.* Rochester, VT: Inner Traditions, 1996. Print.

Carr, Helen. *Inventing the American Primitive: Politics, Gender and the Representations of Native American Literary Traditions, 1789–1936.* New York: NYU P, 1996. Print.

Carrette, Jeremy, and Richard King. *Selling Spirituality: The Silent Takeover of Religion.* London: Routledge, 2005. Print.

Carroll, Brett E. *Spiritualism in Antebellum America.* Bloomington: Indiana UP, 1997. Print.

Castiglia, Christopher. "Sex Panics, Sex Publics, Sex Memories." *boundary 2* 227.2 (2000): 149–75. Print.

Castle, Leila. "Serpent Tales: A Personal Journey into the Sacred Feminine at Sacred Sites around the World." *Earthwalking Sky Dancers: Women's Pilgrimages to Sacred Places*, ed. Leila Castle. Berkeley: Frog, Limited, 1996. xiii–xxviii. Print.

Chernin, Kim. *The Hungry Self.* New York: Times, 1985. Print.

Churchill, Ward. *Fantasies of the Master Race: Literature, Cinema and the Colonization of American Indians.* Ed. M. Annette Jaimes. Monroe, ME: Common Courage P, 1992. Print.

Clemetson, Lynette. "Oprah on Oprah." *Newsweek,* 8 Jan. 2001: 39–48. Print.

Clifford, James. "Traveling Cultures." *Cultural Studies*, ed. Lawrence Grossberg, Cary Nelson, and Paula Treichler. New York: Routledge, 1992. 96–116. Print.

Cline, Sally. *Just Desserts: Women and Food.* London: Andre Deutsch, 1990. Print.

Cloud, Dana L. *Control and Consolation in American Culture and Politics: Rhetorics of Therapy.* Thousand Oaks, CA: Sage, 1998. Print.

Colbin, Annemarie. *Food and Healing.* New York: Ballantine, 1986. Print.

Conkey, Margaret W., and Ruth E. Tringham. "Archaeology and the Goddess: Exploring the Contours of Feminist Archaeology." *Feminisms in the Academy: Rethinking the Disciplines*, ed. Donna C. Stanton and Abigail J. Stewart. Ann Arbor: U of Michigan P, 1995. 199–247. Print.

Conkey, Margaret W., and Sarah H. Williams. "Original Narratives: The Political Economy of Gender in Archaeology." *Gender at the Crossroads of Knowledge: Feminist Anthropology in the Postmodern Era*, ed. Micaela di Leonardo. Berkeley: U of California P, 1991. 102–39. Print.

Cope, Stephen. "Standing Psychotherapy on Its Head." *Yoga Journal*, May/June 2001: 102–05. Print.

Counihan, Carole M. *The Anthropology of Food and Body: Gender, Meaning, and Power.* New York: Routledge, 1999. Print.

Counihan, Carole M., and Steven L. Kaplan, eds. *Food and Gender: Identity and Power.* Amsterdam: Harwood Academic P, 1998. Print.

Coward, Rosalind. *The Whole Truth: The Myth of Alternative Health.* London: Faber and Faber, 1989. Print.

Cox, Harvey. *Turning East: The Promise and Peril of the New Orientalism.* New York: Simon & Schuster, 1977. Print.

Culbertson, Roberta. "Embodied Memory, Transcendence, and Telling: Recounting Trauma, Re-establishing the Self." *New Literary History* 26.1 (1995): 169–95. Print.

Davie, Grace, Linda Woodhead, and Paul Heelas. *Predicting Religion: Christian, Secular, and Alternative Futures.* Aldershot, UK, and Burlington, VT: Ashgate, 2003. Print.

Davis, Philip G. *Goddess Unmasked: The Rise of Neopagan Feminist Spirituality.* Dallas: Spence, 1998. Print.

de Certeau, Michel. *The Practice of Everyday Life.* Berkeley: U of California P, 1984. Print.

Deggans, Eric. "Oprah Fans Get into the Spirit." *St. Petersburg Times Online. St. Petersburg Times,* 21 June 2003. Web. 1 May 2011.

de Grazia, Victoria, and Ellen Furlough, eds. *The Sex of Things: Gender and Consumption in Historical Perspective.* Berkeley: U of California P, 1996. Print.

Deloria, Philip J. *Playing Indian.* New Haven: Yale UP, 1998. Print.

Deloria, Vine Jr. *For This Land: Writings on Religion in America.* New York: Routledge, 1999. Print.

Di Leonardo, Micaela. *Exotics At Home: Anthropologies, Others, American Modernity.* Chicago: U of Chicago P, 1998. Print.

———, ed. "Gender, Culture, and Political Economy: Feminist Anthropology in Historical Perspective." *Gender at the Crossroads of Knowledge: Feminist Anthropology in the Postmodern Era.* Berkeley: U of California P, 1991. 1–48. Print.

Dippie, Brian W. *The Vanishing American: White Attitudes and U.S. Indian Policy.* Middletown, CT: Wesleyan UP, 1982. Print.

Di Veroli, Robert. "New Age Adherents Labeled as Products of Counterculture." *The San Diego Union-Tribune,* 4 Aug. 1990: B4. Print.

Donaldson, Laura E. "On Medicine Women and White Shame-ans: New Age Native Americanism and Commodity Fetishism as Pop Culture Feminism." *Signs* 24.13 (1999): 677–96. Print.

Douglas, Ann. *The Feminization of American Culture*. New York: Knopf, 1977. Print.

Downing, Christine. *The Goddess: Mythological Images of the Feminine*. New York: Crossroad, 1981. Print.

Doyal, Lesley. *What Makes Women Sick: Gender and the Political Economy of Health*. Basingstoke, England: Macmillan, 1995. Print.

Driedger, June Mears. "Spirituality According to Oprah." *Vision: A Journal for Church and Theology* 1.1 (2000): 41–47. Web. 1 May 2011.

Dufty, William. *Sugar Blues*. New York: Warner, 1975. Print.

Eagle Feather, Ken. Personal interview. 22 June 1999.

Easthope, Gary, and Lisa Rayner. "Postmodern Consumption and Alternative Medications." *Journal of Sociology* 37.2 (2001): 157–78. Print.

Edmundson, Mark. *Nightmare on Main Street: Angels, Sadomasochism, and the Culture of the Gothic*. Cambridge, MA: Harvard UP, 1997. Print.

Edwards, Carolyn McVickar. *The Storyteller's Goddess: Tales of the Goddess and Her Wisdom from around the World*. New York: Marlowe & Company, 2000. Print.

Ehrenreich, Barbara, and Deirdre English. *For Her Own Good: 150 Years of the Experts' Advice to Women*. New York: Anchor, 1978. Print.

Eller, Cynthia. *Living in the Lap of the Goddess: The Feminist Spirituality Movement in America*. Boston: Beacon P, 1995. Print.

———. *The Myth of Matriarchal Prehistory: Why an Invented Past Won't Give Women a Future*. Boston: Beacon P, 2000. Print.

Engels, Frederich. *The Origin of the Family, Private Property, and the State*. New York: Penguin, 2010. Print.

Engs, Ruth. *Clean Living Movements: American Cycles of Health Reform*. Westport, CT: Praeger, 2000. Print.

Erndl Kathleen M., and Alf Hiltebeitel, eds. *Is the Goddess a Feminist?: The Politics of South Asian Goddesses*. New York: NYU P, 2000.

Esko, Edward, and Wendy Esko. *Macrobiotic Cooking for Everyone*. Tokyo: Japan Publishing, 1980. Print.

Estes, Clarissa Pinkola. *Women Who Run With The Wolves: Myths and Stories of the Wild Woman Archetype*. New York: Ballantine, 1992. Print.

Evans, Karen. "Journey of the Spirit." *Health*, April 2001: 119ff. Print.

Faber, Mel D. *New Age Thinking: A Psychoanalytic Critique*. Ottawa, Canada: U of Ottawa P, 1996.

Felski, Rita. *The Gender of Modernity*. Boston: Harvard UP, 1995. Print.

————. "On Nostalgia: The Prehistoric Woman." *The Gender of Modernity*. Boston: Harvard UP, 1995. Print.

Ferguson, Marilyn. *The Aquarian Conspiracy: Personal and Social Transformation in the 1980s*. Los Angeles: J.P. Tarcher, 1980. Print.

Fields, Rick. *How the Swans Came to the Lake: A Narrative History of Buddhism in America*. Boulder: Shambhala, 1981. Print.

Fiske, John. "Cultural Studies and the Culture of Everyday life." In *Cultural Studies*, ed. Lawrence Grossberg, Cary Nelson, and Paula A. Treichler. New York: Routledge, 1992. 154–73. Print.

Flammang, Janet A. *The Taste for Civilization: Food, Politics, and Civil Society*. Urbana: U of Illinois P, 2009. Print.

Fowers, Blaine J., Brooks Applegate, Michael Tredinnick, and Jason Slusher. "His and Her Individualisms? Sex Bias and Individualism in Psychologists' Responses to Case Vignettes." *The Journal of Psychology* 130.2 (1996): 159–75. Print.

Francis, Daniel. *The Imaginary Indian: The Image of the Indian in Canadian Culture*. Vancouver: Arsenal P, 1992. Print.

Fredrickson, George M. *The Black Image in the White Mind: The Debate on Afro-American Character and Destiny, 1817–1914*. Hanover: Wesleyan UP, 1987. Print.

Fuller, Robert C. *Spiritual, But Not Religious: Understanding Unchurched America*. New York: Oxford UP, 2001. Print.

Fuss, Diana. *Essentially Speaking: Feminism, Nature & Difference*. New York: Routledge, 1989. Print.

Gagne, Steve. *Energetics of Food: Encounters with Your Most Intimate Relationship*. Santa Fe: Spiral Sciences, 1990. Print.

Galland, China. *Longing for Darkness: Tara and the Black Madonna*. New York: Penguin, 1990. Print.

Gallup Poll. "Americans' Belief in Psychic and Paranormal Phenomena Is Up Over Last Decade." *Gallup*. Gallup, 8 June 2001. Web. 1 May 2011.

————. "Does Congregation Membership Imply Spiritual Commitment?" *Gallup*. Gallup, 9 Aug. 2005. Web. 1 May 2011.

————. "Three in Four Americans Believe in Paranormal." *Gallup*. Gallup, 16 June 2005. Web. 1 May 2011.

Gardell, Mattias. *Gods of the Blood: The Pagan Revival and White Separatism*. Chapel Hill: Duke UP, 2003. Print.

Garrett, Lynn, and Bridget Kinsella. "New Age Is All the Rage: Despite an Irksome Label, This Broad Segment of Publishing Is Partnering with Most Mainstream Categories." *Publishers Weekly*, 10 March 1997: 33–41. Print.

Gawain, Shakti. *Living in the Light: A Guide to Personal and Planetary Transformation.* San Rafael, CA: New World Library, 1986. Print.

George, Demetra. *Mysteries of the Dark Moon: The Healing Power of the Dark Goddess.* San Francisco: HarperCollins, 1992. Print.

Gibbs, Nancy. "Angels Among Us." *Time,* 27 Dec. 1993: 56–64. Print.

Gilligan, Carol. *In a Different Voice: Psychological Theory and Women's Development.* Cambridge: Harvard UP, 1982. Print.

Gimbutas, Marija. *The Goddesses and Gods of Old Europe.* Los Angeles: U of California P, 1982. Print.

Gitlin, Todd. *The Sixties: Years of Hope, Days of Rage.* New York: Bantam, 1987. Print.

Gomez-Pena, Guillermo. "The New Global Culture Somewhere between Corporate Multiculturalism and the Mainstream Bizarre (a border perspective)." *TDR: The Drama Review* 45.1 (2001): 7–30. Print.

Gonser, Sarah. "O the Incredible, Sellable." *Folio: The Magazine for Magazine Management.* Feb 2001. Web. 1 May 2011.

Goodison, Lucy, and Christine Morris, eds. *Ancient Goddesses: The Myths and the Evidence.* London: British Museum P, 1998. Print.

Gould, Philip. "Revisiting the 'Feminization' of American Culture." *Differences* 11.3 (1999): i–xii. Print.

Greene, Gayle, and Coppelia Kahn, eds. *Changing Subjects: The Making of Feminist Literary Criticism.* New York: Routledge, 1993. Print.

Grimes, Dorothy G. " 'Womanist Prose' and the Quest for Community in American Culture." *Journal of American Culture* 15.2 (1992): 19–25. Print.

Grogan, Sarah. *Body Image: Understanding Body Dissatisfaction in Men, Women, and Children.* New York: Routledge, 1999. Print.

Gross, Rita. "Is the Goddess a Feminist?" *Is the Goddess a Feminist?: The Politics of South Asian Goddesses,* ed. Kathleen M. Erndl and Alf Hiltebeitel. New York: NYU P, 2000. 104–12. Print.

Gubar, Susan. "What Ails Feminist Criticism?" *Critical Inquiry* 24.4 (1998): n. pag. Print.

Haag, Laurie L. "Oprah Winfrey: The Construction of Intimacy in the Talk Show Setting." *Journal of Popular Culture* 26 (1993): 115–21. Print.

Hagan, Helene E. "The Plastic Medicine People Circle." *Sonoma County Free Press.* Sonoma County Free P, Sept. 1992. Web. 1 May 2011.

Hall, David D., ed. *Lived Religion in America: Toward a History of Practice.* Princeton: Princeton UP, 1997. Print.

Hanegraaff, Wouter J. *New Age Religion and Western Culture: Esotericism in the Mirror or Secular Thought*. New York: Brill, 1996. Print.

Haraway, Donna. *Simians, Cyborgs, and Women: The Reinvention of Nature*. New York: Routledge, 1991. Print.

Harrison, Barbara Grizzuti. "The Importance of Being Oprah." *New York Times Magazine*, 11 June 1989: 6. Print.

Harrison, Jennifer. "Advertising Joins the Journey of the Soul." *American Demographics* 19.6 (1997): 22–28. Print.

Hart, D. G., and Harry S. Stout, eds. *New Directions in American Religious History*. New York: Oxford UP: 1997. Print.

Harvey, Bob. "In Goddess We Trust." *The Ottawa Citizen*, 10 July 1999: I1. Print.

Hay, Louise. *Empowering Women*. Santa Monica, CA: Hay House, 1999. Print.

Havnes, Mark. "Indian Leaders Decry 'Plastic Medicine Men.'" *The Salt Lake Tribune*, 12 Dec. 1997. Print.

Heelas, Paul. *The New Age Movement: The Celebration of the Self and the Sacralization of Modernity*. Cambridge: Blackwell, 1996. Print.

———. *Spiritualities of Life: New Age Romanticism and Consumptive Capitalism*. Malden, MA: Blackwell, 2008. Print.

Heelas, Paul, and Linda Woodhead, with Benjamin Seel, Bronislaw Szerszynski, and Karin Tusting. *The Spiritual Revolution: Why Religion Is Giving Way to Spirituality*. Oxford: Blackwell, 2005. Print.

Hernandez-Avila, Ines. "Mediations of the Spirit: Native American Religious Traditions and the Ethics of Representation." *American Indian Quarterly* 20.3/20.4 (1996): 329–53. Print.

Higginbotham, Evelyn Brooks. *Righteous Discontent: The Women's Movement in the Black Baptist Church 1880–1920*. 1993. Cambridge, MA: Harvard UP, 1993. Print.

Hirsch, J. M. "Diet Right?: Cooking Show Host Touts Macrobiotic Benefits." *Associated Press*, 1997. Print.

Hofman, Mike. "Oprah Gets Psyched." *Inc.* 1 Sept. 2001. Print.

hooks, bell. *All About Love: New Visions*. New York: HarperCollins, 2001. Print.

———. *Where We Stand: Class Matters*. New York: Routledge, 2000. Print.

Hughes, Dennis. "An Interview with Lynn Andrews: Best-Selling Author, Renowned Retreat Leader, and Teacher in the Field of Personal Development." *Share Guide: The Holistic Health Magazine and Resource Directory*. Share Guide, n.d. Web. 1 May 2011.

Huhndorf, Shari M. *Going Native: Indians in the American Cultural Imagination*. Ithaca: Cornell UP, 2001. Print.

Hull, Gloria T. *Soul Talk: The New Spirituality of African American Women*. Rochester, VT: Inner Traditions, 2001. Print.

Hull, Gloria T., Patricia Bell-Scott, and Barbara Smith. *All the Women Are White, All the Blacks Are Men, but Some of Us Are Brave: Black Women's Studies*. Old Westbury, NY: Feminist P, 1982. Print.

Huyssen, Andreas. "Mass Culture as Woman: Modernism's Other." *After the Great Divide: Modernism, Mass Culture, Postmodernism*. Bloomington: Indiana UP, 1986. Print.

Jack, Alex. "Macrobiotics and America's Destiny." *Macrobiotics Today* 34.5 (1994): n. pag. Print.

Jack, Gale. "Ten Things Macrobiotic Women Do Well." *CyberMacro Articles*. CyberMacro, n.d. Web. 1 May 2011.

Jack, Gale, and Wendy Esko, eds. *Women's Health Guide*. Becket: One Peaceful World P, 1997. Print.

Jacobs, Margaret D. *Engendered Encounters: Feminism and Pueblo Cultures, 1879–1934*. Lincoln: U of Nebraska P, 1999. Print.

Jacoby, Susan. *The Age of American Unreason*. New York: Pantheon, 2008. Print.

Jamal, Michele. *Shape Shifters: Shaman Women in Contemporary Society*. New York: Arkana, 1987. Print.

James, William. *The Varieties of Religious Experience (1902)*. New York: Penguin, 1982. Print.

Johnson, Marilyn. "The Book Club: Women Linked by Reading Groups." *Life*, Aug. 1998: 32–36. Print.

Johnson, Tammy. "It's Personal: Race and Oprah." *ColorLines*, Winter 2001–02. Web. 1 May 2011.

Jones, Margaret. "Publishing for 'Spiritual Seekers.'" *Publishers Weekly*, 6 Dec. 1993: 45–49. Print.

Jorstad, Erling. *Holding Fast/Pressing On: Religion in America in the 1980s*. New York: Praeger, 1990. Print.

Jurca, Catherine. *White Diaspora: The Suburb and the Twentieth-Century American Novel*. Princeton: Princeton UP, 2001. Print.

Kakutani, Michiko. "Books of the Times; If the River Is Dry, Can You Be All Wet?" *New York Times*, 20 April 2004: 7. Academic Search Complete. EBSCO. Web. 1 May 2011.

Kaminer, Wendy. *Sleeping with Extra-Terrestrials: The Rise of Irrationalism and Perils of Piety*. New York: Pantheon, 1999.

Kannapell, Andrea. "In Person: Unlocking the Energy Within." *The New York Times*, 14 June 1998: 4. Print.

Kasee, Cynthia. "Identity, Recovery, and Religious Imperialism: Native American Women and the New Age." *Women & Therapy* 16.23 (1995): 83–93. Print.

Keating, Analouise. "'I'm a citizen of the universe': Gloria Anzaldúa's Spiritual Activism as Catalyst for Social Change." *Feminist Studies* 34.1/2 (Spring/Summer 2008): 53–69. Academic Search Complete. EBSCO. 1 May 2011.

Kelly, Keith J. "Adweek Crowns Oprah Mag Queen." *NYPost.com*. New York Post, 5 Mar. 2007. Web. 1 May 2011.

Kerr, Howard. *Mediums and Spirit Rappers and Roaring Radicals: Spiritualism in American Literature, 1850–1900.* Champaign Urbana: U of Illinois P, 1972. Print.

King, Laurel. *Women of Power: Ten Visionaries Share Their Extraordinary Stories of Healing & Secrets of Success.* Berkeley: Celestial Arts, 1989. Print.

Kinghoffer, David. "Ghost Story: New Age Spirituality in the United States." *National Review* 50.6 (1998): 32–34. Print.

Kinsella, Bridget. "Gayle & Howard Mandel." *Publishers Weekly*, 14 June 1999: 42. Print.

Klein, Kerwin Lee. "On the Emergence of Memory in Historical Discourse." *Representations*, Winter 2000: 127–50. Print.

Korda, Michael. *Making the List: A Cultural History of the American Bestseller, 1900–1999.* New York: Barnes & Noble, 2001. Print.

Kotzsch, Ronald E. *Macrobiotics: Yesterday and Today.* New York: Japan Publications, 1985. Print.

Kripal, Jeffrey J. Esalen: *America and the Religion of No Religion.* Chicago: U of Chicago P, 2007. Print.

Kushi, Aveline. *Aveline Kushi's Complete Guide to Macrobiotic Cooking for Health, Harmony, and Peace.* New York: Warner, 1985. Print.

Kushi, Aveline, and Wendy Esko. *Diet for Natural Beauty: A Natural Anti-aging Formula for Skin and Hair Care.* Tokyo: Japan Publishing, 1991. Print.

Kushi, Michio. *The Book of Macrobiotics: The Universal Way of Health, Happiness, and Peace.* New York: Japan Publishing, 1986. Print.

———. *Guide to Standard Macrobiotic Diet.* Becket, MA: One Peaceful World P, 1995. Print.

———. *Humanity at the Crossroads: Dietary and Lifestyle Guidelines for the Age of Cloning, Genetically Engineered Food, Mad Cow Disease, Microwave Cooking, Electromagnetic Fields, and Global Warming.* Becket, MA: One Peaceful World P, 1997. Print.

———. "Humanity's Traditional Food." *MacroChef*, Winter 1998: 20. Print.

———. *Macrobiotic Home Remedies.* Ed. Marc Van Cauwenberghe, M.D. New York: Japan Publishing, 1985. Print.

———. *Macrobiotic Seminars of Michio Kushi.* Becket: One Peaceful World, 1998. Print.

———. *The Teachings of Michio Kushi: The Way of Life in the Age of Humanity.* Ed. Edward Esko. Becket, MA: One Peaceful World P, 1993. Print.

———. "What Is Love?" *MacroChef*, Fall/Holiday 1998: 20+. Print.

Kushi, Michio, and Alex Jack. *One Peaceful World.* New York: St. Martin's P, 1987. Print.

Kushi, Michio, and Edward Esko. *Spiritual Journey: Michio Kushi's Guide to Endless Self-Realization and Freedom.* Becket, MA: One Peaceful World P, 1994. Print.

Kushi, Michio, and Phillip Jannetta. *Macrobiotics and Oriental Medicine: An Introduction to Holistic Health.* Tokyo: Japan Publishing, 1991. Print.

Kyle, Richard. *The Religious Fringe: A History of Alternative Religions in America.* Downers Grove, IL: InterVarsity P, 1993. Print.

Lacher, Irene. "She Worship: Return of the Great Goddess." *Los Angeles Times*, 19 Sept. 1990: E1. Print.

Lander, Christian. *Stuff White People Like.* Wordpress. 18 Jan. 2008. Web. 1 May 2011.

Landrine, Hope, and Joan Regensburger. "Through the Looking Glass: A Conference of Myopics." *Off Our Backs.* Washington, DC: Off Our Backs. June 1976: 12–14. Print.

Larson, Rebecca. *Daughters of Light: Quaker Women Preaching and Prophesying in the Colonies and Abroad, 1700–1775.* New York: Knopf, 1999. Print.

Lasch, Christopher. *The Culture of Narcissism: American Life in an Age of Diminishing Expectations.* New York: Norton. 1978. Print.

———. "Soul of a New Age." *Omni* 10.1 (1987): 78ff. Print.

Lasch-Quinn, Elisabeth. *Race Experts: How Racial Etiquette, Sensitivity Training, and New Age Therapy Hijacked the Civil Rights Revolution.* New York: Norton. 2001. Print.

Lau, Kimberly J. *New Age Capitalism: Making Money East of Eden.* Philadelphia: U of Pennsylvania P, 2000. Print.

LeBeau, Bryan F. *Religion in America to 1865.* New York: NYU P, 2000. Print.

Lee, Josephine, and Tom Ferguson. "Coin of the New Age." *Forbes*, 9 Sept. 1996: 86–88. Print.

Lesser, Elizabeth. "Excerpt from *The Seeker's Guide.*" *The Oprah Winfrey Show.* Prod. Harpo Productions, Inc., 9 June 2008. Web. 1 May 2011.

"Letters to Oprah's Book Club." Lexis-Nexis. Web. Transcript. 1 May 2011.

Levenstein, Harvey. *Paradox of Plenty: A Social History of Eating in Modern America*. New York: Oxford UP, 1993. Print.

Lippy, Charles H. *Being Religious, American Style: A History of Popular Religiosity in the United States*. Westport, CT: Praeger, 1994. Print.

Lipsitz, George. "The Possessive Investment in Whiteness: Racialized Social Democracy and the 'White' Problem in American Studies." *American Quarterly* 47.3 (1995). Print.

Long, Marion. "In Search of a Definition: New Age Theory." *Omni* 10.1 (1987): 80. Print.

Lorde, Audre. *Sister Outsider: Essays and Speeches*. The Crossing Press Feminist Series. Trumansburg, NY: Crossing P, 1984. Print.

Lott, Eric. *Love and Theft: Blackface Minstrelsy and the American Working Class*. New York: Oxford UP, 1995. Print.

Lowry, Katherine. "Channelers." *Omni* 10.1 (1987): 47. Print.

Luft, Rachel E. "Intersectionality and the Risk of Flattening Difference: Gender and Race Logics, and the Strategic Use of Antiracist Singularity." *The Intersectional Approach: Transforming the Academy through Race, Class, and Gender*, ed. Michele T. Berger and Kathleen Guidroz. Chapel Hill: U of North Carolina P, 2009. Print.

Lupton, Deborah. *Food, the Body, and the Self*. London: Sage, 1996. Print.

MacDonald, William L. "The Popularity of Paranormal Experiences in the United States." *Journal of American Culture* 17.3 (1994): 35–43. Print.

Mahmood, Saba. *Politics of Piety: The Islamic Revival and the Feminist Subject*. Princeton: Princeton UP, 2005. Print.

Mankiller-Mendoza, Lclair. *Lynn Andrews Website Forum*. 15 April 1999. Web. 1 May 2011.

Marty, Martin E. "Not-So-New-Age." *Christian Century* (8 Sept. 1999): 879+. Print.

"Mary Summer Rain." *The Pyramid Bookstore*. Hampton Roads, 2003. Web. 1 May 2011.

Maurer, Donna. "Too Skinny or Vibrant and Healthy? Weight Management in the Vegetarian Movement." *Weighty Issues: Fatness and Thinness as Social Problems*, ed. Jeffery Sobal and Donna Maurer. New York: Aldine De Gruyter, 1999. 209–29. Print.

Mcgee, Micki. *Self-Help, Inc.: Makeover Culture in American Life*. Oxford: Oxford UP, 2005. Print.

McGrath, Maria. "Spiritual Talk: The Oprah Winfrey Show and the Popularization of the New Age." *The Oprah Phenomenon*, ed. Jennifer Harris and Elwood Watson. Lexington: U of Kentucky P, 2007. 125–46. Print.

Mears, Daniel P., and Christopher G. Ellison. "Who Buys New Age Materials?: Exploring Sociodemographic, Religious, Network, and Contextual Correlates of New Age Consumption." *Sociology of Religion* 61.3 (2000): 289–313. Print.

Melton, J. Gordon, and James Lewis, eds. *Perspectives on the New Age*. Albany: SUNY P, 1992. Print.

Melton, J. Gordon, Jerome Clark, and Aidan A. Kelly. *New Age Encyclopedia: A Guide to the Beliefs, Concepts, Terms, People, and Organizations That Make Up the New Global Movement toward Spiritual Development, Health and Healing, Higher Consciousness, and Related Subjects*. 1st ed. Detroit, MI: Gale Research, 1990. Print.

Meskell, Lynn. "Goddesses, Gimbutas and New Age Archaeology." *Antiquity* 69.262 (1995): 74–86. Print.

Michaels, Walter Benn. *Our America: Nativism, Modernism, and Pluralism*. Durham: Duke UP, 1995. Print.

Mintz, Sidney W. *Tasting Food, Tasting Freedom: Excursions into Eating, Culture, and the Past*. Boston: Beacon P, 1996. Print.

Moore, R. Laurence. *In Search of White Crows: Spiritualism, Parapsychology, and American Culture*. New York: Oxford UP, 1977. Print.

———. "Reinventing American Religion—Yet Again." *American Literary History* 12.1, 12.2 (2000): 318–26. Print.

Moraga, Cherrie, and Gloria Anzaldúa. *This Bridge Called My Back: Writings by Radical Women of Color*. New York: Kitchen Table, Women of Color P, 1983. Print.

Myss, Caroline. *Sacred Contracts: Awakening Your Divine Potential*. New York: Harmony, 2001. Print.

———. *Why People Don't Heal and How They Can*. New York: Three Rivers P, 1998. Print.

Nelson, Dana. "No Cold or Empty Heart": Polygenesis, Scientific Professionalization, and the Unfinished Business of Male Sentimentalism," *Differences* 11.3 (1999): 29–56. Print.

Nelson, Marcia Z. *The Gospel According to Oprah*. Louisville, KY: Westminster John Knox P, 2005. Print.

———. "Oprah on a Mission: Dispensing a Gospel of Health and Happiness." *The Christian Century*. (Sept. 25–Oct. 8 2002): 20–25. Web. 1 May 2011.

Nesbitt, Paula. *Feminization of the Clergy in America: Occupational and Organizational Perspectives.* New York: Oxford UP, 1997. Print.

Nicholson, Linda J., ed. *Feminism/Postmodernism.* New York: Routledge, 1990. Print.

Noll, Mark A. *America's God: From Jonathan Edwards to Abraham Lincoln.* New York: Oxford UP, 2005. Print.

Northrup, Christiane. *Women's Bodies, Women's Wisdom: Creating Physical and Emotional Health and Healing.* New York: Bantam, 1998. Print.

Nudelman, Franny. "Beyond the Talking Cure: Listening to Female Testimony on *The Oprah Winfrey Show.*" *Inventing the Psychological: Toward a Cultural History of Emotional Life in America,* ed. Joel Pfister and Nancy Schnog. New Haven: Yale UP, 1997. 297–315. Print.

Nussbaum, Elaine. *Recovery from Cancer.* New York: Avery, 1980. Print.

Official Website of Lynn V. Andrews. Lynn Andrews Productions, n.d. Web. 1 May 2011.

Ohsawa, George. *Essential Ohsawa: From Food to Health, Happiness to Freedom.* Ed. Carl Ferre. New York: Avery, 1994. Print.

———. *You Are All Sanpaku.* Trans. William Dufty. New York: Citadel P, 1965. Print.

Oppenheimer, Mark. "The Queen of the New Age." *The New York Times Magazine,* 4 May 2008. Web. 1 May 2011.

Oprah's Angel Network. 2008. Web. 1 May 2011.

Oprah's Book Club. "About Eckhart Tolle." Web. 1 May 2011.

———. 2008. "A New Earth Class." Web. Transcript. 1 May 2011.

———. "Awaken Your Spirit." Web. 1 May 2011.

Oprah's Soul Series. 2008. XM Radio. Web. 1 May 2011.

Orbach, Susie. *Fat Is a Feminist Issue: The Anti-Diet Guide; Fat Is a Feminist Issue II: Conquering Compulsive Eating.* London: Arrow, 2006. Print.

Pearce, Roy Harvey. *Savagism and Civilization: A Study of the Indian and the American Mind.* Baltimore: Johns Hopkins UP, 1967. Print.

Peck, Janice. "Talk about Race: Framing a Popular Discourse of Race on Oprah Winfrey." *Cultural Critique* 27 (Spring 1994): 89–126. Print.

Perkes, Kim Sue Lia. "Crystals, Wellness, and the Cosmic Forces: Followers of New Age Religion." *U.S. News & World Report,* 4 April 1994: 54. Print.

Pew Research Center. "Many Americans Mix Multiple Faiths: Eastern, New Age Beliefs Widespread." The Pew Forum on Religion & Public Life. Pewforum.org. 9 Dec. 2009. Web. 1 May 2011.

Phillips, Debra. "Coming of Age." *Entrepreneur*, July 1996: 98–101. Print.

Phillips, Layli. *The Womanist Reader*. New York: Routledge, 2006. Print.

Pike, Sarah M. *New Age and Neopagan Religions in America*. New York: Columbia UP, 2004. Print.

———. *Earthly Bodies, Magical Selves: Contemporary Pagans and the Search for Community*. Berkeley: U of California P, 2001. Print.

Podles, Leon J. *The Church Impotent*. Dallas: Spence, 1999. Print.

Possamai, Adam. *In Search of New Age Spiritualities*. Burlington, VT: Ashgate, 2005. Print.

Powers, Ann. "New Tune for the Material Girl: I'm Neither." *The New York Times*, 1 Mar. 1998: 34. Print.

Powers, Elizabeth "A Farewell to Feminism." *Commentary*, Jan. 1997: 23–31. Print.

Powers, William. "Oprah Waldo Emerson." *National Journal* 32.21 (2000): 16–28. Print.

Quinn, Judy. "A New Twist—and Test—for the 'Oprah Effect.'" *Publishers Weekly*, 15 Sept. 1997: 12–13. Print.

Radway, Janice A. *Reading the Romance: Women, Patriarchy, and Popular Literature*. Chapel Hill: U of North Carolina P, 1984. Print.

Ramadanovic, Peter. "When 'to die in freedom' Is Written in English." *Diacritics* 28.4 (1998): 54–67. Print.

Rapping, Elayne. *The Culture of Recovery: Making Sense of the Self-Help Movement in Women's Lives*. Boston: Beacon P, 1996. Print.

Raso, Jack. *Mystical Diets: Paranormal, Spiritual, and Occult Nutrition Practices*. New York: Prometheus, 1993. Print.

Reich, Charles A. *The Greening of America: How the Youth Revolution Is Trying to Make America Livable*. New York: Random House, 1970. Print.

Reiff, David. "Designer Gods." *Transition* 0.59 (1993): 20–31. Print.

Reis, Patricia. *Through the Goddess: A Woman's Way of Healing*. New York: Continuum, 1991. Print.

Rimke, Heidi Marie. "Governing Citizens through Self-Help Literature." *Cultural Studies* 14.1 (2000): 61–78. Print.

Robb, Christina. "In Goddesses They Trust." *Boston Globe*, 9 July 1990: 32. Print.

Robbins, Bruce. "Celeb-Reliance: Intellectuals, Celebrity, and Upward Mobility." *Postmodern Culture* 9.2 (1999): 17. Print.

Roberts, Brent W., and Ravenna Helson. "Changes in Culture, Changes in Personality: The Influence of Individualism in a Longitudinal Study of Women (Personality Processes and Individual Difference)." *Journal of Personality and Social Psychology* 72.3 (1997): 641–52. Print.

Rosaldo, Renato. *Culture and Truth: The Remaking of Social Analysis.* 1989. Boston: Beacon P, 1993. Print.

Rose, Stuart. "New Age Women: Spearheading the Movement?" *Women's Studies* 30 (2001): 329–50. Print.

Rosen, Ruth. *The World Split Open: How the Modern Women's Movement Changed America.* New York: Viking, 2000. Print.

Ross, Andrew. "New Age Technoculture." *Cultural Studies,* ed. Lawrence Grossberg, Cary Nelson, and Paula Treichler. New York: Routledge, 1992. 531–55. Print.

Ruth, Sheila. *Take Back the Light: A Feminist Reclamation of Spirituality and Religion.* Lanham, MD: Rowman & Littlefield, 1994. Print.

Safe. Dir. Todd Haynes. Perf. Julianne Moore, Xander Berkeley, and Peter Friedman. Sony Pictures Classics, 1995. Film.

Safransky, Sy. "Whose Spirituality Is Whose?" *The Sun,* May 1995: n. pag. Print.

Sanchez-Eppler, Karen. "Bodily Bonds: The Intersecting Rhetorics of Feminism and Abolition." *Representations* 24 (1988): 28–59. Print.

Sandell, Jillian. "Adjusting to Oppression: The Rise of Therapeutic Feminism in the United States." *"Bad Girls"/"Good Girls": Women, Sex, and Power in the Nineties,* ed. Nan Bauer Maglin and Donna Perry. New Brunswick: Rutgers UP, 1994. 21–35. Print.

Satilaro, Anthony J. *Recalled by Life.* Boston: Houghton Mifflin, 1982. Print.

Satter, Beryl. *Each Mind a Kingdom: American Women, Sexual Purity, and the New Thought Movement, 1870–1920.* Berkeley: U of California P, 1999. Print.

Scanlon, Jennifer. *Inarticulate Longings: The Ladies' Home Journal, Gender, and the Promises of Consumer Culture.* New York: Routledge, 1995. Print.

Schmidt, Leigh E. *Restless Souls: The Making of American Spirituality.* San Francisco: HarperSanFrancisco, 2005. Print.

Shange, Ntozake. *For Colored Girls Who Have Considered Suicide, When the Rainbow Is Enuf: A Choreopoem.* New York: Macmillan, 1977. Print.

Shanley, Kathryn W. "The Indians America Loves to Love and Read: American Indian Identity and Cultural Appropriation." *The American Indian Quarterly* 21.4 (1997): 675–702. Print.

Shattuc, Jane M. "The Oprahfication of America: Talk Shows and the Public Sphere." *Television, History, and American Culture: Feminist Critical Essays*, ed. Mary Beth Havalovich. Durham: Duke UP, 1999. 168–80. Print.

Shoemaker, Nancy. "Imaginary Indians in Modern Times." *Reviews in American History* 29.2 (2001): 222–27. Print.

Showalter, Elaine. *Hystories: Hysterical Epidemics and Modern Media.* New York: Columbia UP, 1997. Print.

Simonds, Wendy. *Women and Self-Help Culture: Reading Between the Lines.* New Brunswick: Rutgers UP, 1992. Print.

Smith, Andrea. *Native Americans and the Christian Right: The Gendered Politics of Unlikely Alliances.* Durham: Duke UP, 2008. Print.

Snell, Marilyn. "The World of Religion According to Huston Smith." *Mother Jones*, Nov./Dec. 1997: 40–44. Print.

Spretnak, Charlene, ed. *The Politics of Women's Spirituality: Essays on the Rise of Spiritual Power within the Feminist Movement.* New York: Anchor P, 1982. Print.

Squire, Corinne. "Empowering Women? The Oprah Winfrey Show." *Feminist Television Criticism: A Reader*, ed. Charlotte Brunsdon, Julie D'Acci, and Lynn Spigel. Oxford: Clarendon P, 1997. 98–110. Print.

Srivastava, Sarita. "'You're calling me a racist?' The Moral and Emotional Regulation of Antiracism and Feminism." *Signs: Journal of Women in Culture & Society* 31.1 (2005): 29–62. Academic Search Complete. EBSCO. Web. 1 May 2011.

Stare, Fredrick J. "The Diet That's Killing Our Kids." *Ladies Home Journal*, Oct. 1971: 70–76. Print.

Staubs, Rose Marie. "Andrews's Sisters." *Omni* 10.1 (1987): 28. Print.

Stenberg, Berndt, and Stig Wall. "Why Do Women Report Sick Building Symptoms More Often Than Men?" *Social Science & Medicine* 40.4 (1995): 491–503. Print.

Stephens, Chuck. "Gentlemen Prefer Haynes." *Film Comment*, July/Aug. 1995: 76–81. Print.

Stone, Merlin. *Ancient Mirrors of Womanhood: A Treasury of Goddess and Heroine Lore from Around the World.* Boston: Beacon P, 1984. Print.

Stout, Harry S., and D. G. Hart, eds. *New Directions in American Religious History.* New York: Oxford UP, 1997. Print.

Sullivan, Shannon. *Revealing Whiteness: The Unconscious Habits of Racial Privilege.* Bloomington: Indiana UP, 2006. Print.

Summer Rain, Mary. *Ancient Echoes: The Anasazi Book of Chants.* Norfolk, VA: Hampton Roads. 1993. Print.

———. *Bittersweet.* Charlottesville, VA: Hampton Roads, 1993. Print.

———. *Daybreak: The Dawning Ember.* Charlottesville, VA: Hampton Roads, 1991. Print.

———. *Dreamwalker: The Path of Sacred Power.* West Chester, PA: Whitford P, 1988. Print.

———. *Earthway.* New York: Simon & Schuster, 1990. Print.

———. *Fireside.* Charlottesville, VA: Hampton Roads, 1998. Print.

———. *Phantoms Afoot: Journeys into the Night.* Charlottesville, VA: Hampton Roads, 1989. Print.

———. *Soul Sounds: Mourning the Tears of Truth.* Norfolk, VA: Hampton Roads, 1992. Print.

———. *Spirit Song: The Introduction of No-Eyes.* Charlottesville, VA: Hampton Roads, 1985. Print.

Sutcliffe, Steven. *Children of the New Age: A History of Spiritual Practices.* New York: Routledge, 2003. Print.

"Suzanne Somers and Breast Cancer Treatment." *EZBoard,* 12 March 2002. Web. 1 May 2011.

"Suzanne Somers' Use of Iscador Treatment." *The Cancer Cure Foundation.* Cancer Cure Foundation. May 2001. Web. 1 May 2011.

Tacey, David. *The Spirituality Revolution: The Emergence of Contemporary Spirituality.* New York: Routledge, 2004. Print.

Taylor, LaTonya. "The Church of O." *Christianity Today,* 1 April 2002. Web. 1 May 2011.

Tennenhouse, Leonard. "Libertine America." *Differences* 11.3 (1999): 1–28. Print.

The Goddess Remembered. Dir. Donna Read. National Film Board of Canada, 1989. Film.

"The Kosher of the Counterculture." *Time,* 16 Nov. 1970: 59–63. Print.

The New Age. Dir. Michael Tolkin. Perf. Judy Davis, Peter Weller, Patrick Bachau, and Corbin Bernsen. Warner Bros. Pictures, 1994. Film.

The Oprah Winfrey Show. *Caroline Myss on Sacred Contracts.* Prod. Harpo Productions, 15 Aug. 2002. Web. Transcript. 1 May 2011.

———. *Gary Zukav on How to Get Your Power Back.* Prod. Harpo Productions, 13 Sept. 2000. Web. 1 May 2011.

Todras-Whitehill, Ethan. "Touring the Spirit World." *New York Times,* 29 April 2007: 1. Academic Search Complete. EBSCO. Web. 1 May 2011.

Tolkin, Michael. *The Player; The Rapture; The New Age: Three Screenplays*. New York: Grove P, 1995. Print.

Torgovnick, Marianna. *Gone Primitive: Savage Intellects, Modern Lives*. Chicago: U of Chicago P, 1990. Print.

———. *Primitive Passions: Men, Women, and the Quest for Ecstasy*. New York: Knopf, 1997. Print.

Travis, Trysh. *The Language of the Heart: A Cultural History of the Recovery Movement from Alcoholics Anonymous to Oprah Winfrey*. Chapel Hill: UNC P, 2009. Print.

Tringham, Ruth E. "Households with Faces: The Challenge of Gender in Prehistoric Architectural Remains." *Engendering Archaeology: Women and Prehistory*, ed. Joan M. Gero and Margaret W. Conkey. Cambridge, MA: Basil Blackwell P, 1991. Print.

Tumber, Catherine. *American Feminism and the Birth of New Age Spirituality: Searching for the Higher Self, 1875–1915*. New York: Rowman & Littlefield, 2002. Print.

Tweed, Thomas A., ed. *Retelling U.S. Religious History*. Berkeley: U of California P, 1997. Print.

Vara, Richard. "Defining the Future: Bookstores on Alternative Spiritualities Continue to Grow." *Houston Chronicle*, 18 Oct. 1997: E13. Print.

Versluis, Arthur. *American Transcendentalism and Asian Religions*. New York: Oxford UP, 1993. Print.

Walker, Alice. *Now Is the Time to Open Your Heart: A Novel*. New York: Random House, 2004. Print.

———. *We Are the Ones We Have Been Waiting For: Inner Light in a Time of Darkness: Meditations*. New York: New P, 2006. Print.

———. "Womanist." *The Womanist Reader*. Ed. Layli Phillips. New York: Routledge, 2006. Print.

Wallis, Claudia. "Why New Age Medicine Is Catching On." *Time*, 4 Nov. 1991: 68–76. Print.

Walsch, Neale D. *Conversations with God: An Uncommon Dialogue*. New York: G.P. Putnam's Sons, 1996. Print.

Warner, Michael. "Franklin and the Letters of the Republic." *Representations* 0.16 (1986): 110–30. Print.

Weaver, Jace, ed. *Native American Religious Identity: Unforgotten Gods*. Maryknoll, NY: Orbis, 1998. Print.

Wicke, Jennifer, and Margaret Ferguson, eds. *Feminism and Postmodernism*. Durham: Duke UP, 1994. Print.

Wiegman, Robyn. *American Anatomies: Theorizing Race and Gender*. Durham: Duke UP, 1995. Print.

Wills, Gary. *Under God: Religion and American Politics*. New York: Simon & Schuster, 1990. Print.

Wilson, Lillian. "The Aging of Aquarius." *American Demographics* 10.9 (Sept. 1988): 37. Print.

Winston, Kimberly. "Women Warriors Lead the Charge: In Spirituality, Women's and Men's Titles Are Flexing Their Sales Muscle." *Publishers Weekly*, 13 April 1998: 26–29. Print.

Witt, Doris. *Black Hunger: Food and the Politics of U.S. Identity*. New York: Oxford UP, 1999. Print.

Wittig, Monique. *Les Guerilleres*. New York: Avon, 1976. Print.

Wolfe, Alan. *One Nation, After All: What Middle-Class Americans Really Think About: God, Country, Family, Racism, Welfare, Immigration, Homosexuality, Work, The Right, The Left, and Each Other*. New York: Viking, 1998. Print.

Woodman, Marion, and Elinor Dickson. *Dancing in the Flames: The Dark Goddess in the Transformation of Consciousness*. Boston: Shambhala P, 1996. Print.

Woodward, Kenneth L. "Gender & Religion: Who's Really Running the Show?" *Commonweal*, 22 Nov. 1996: 9–14. Print.

———. "The Rites of Americans." *Newsweek*, 29 Nov. 1993: 80. Print.

Wuthnow, Robert. *After Heaven: Spirituality in America Since the 1950s*. Berkeley: U of California P, 1998. Print.

Wyatt, Jean. "Toward Cross-Race Dialogue: Identification, Misrecognition, and Difference in Feminist Multicultural Community." *Signs: Journal of Women in Culture & Society* 29.3 (2004): 879–903. Academic Search Complete. EBSCO. Web. 1 May 2011.

Wynne, Patrice, ed. *The Womanspirit Sourcebook: A Catalog of Books, Periodicals, Music, Calendars & Tarot Cards, Organizations, Video & Audio Tapes, Bookstores, Interviews, Meditations, Art*. San Francisco: Harper & Row, 1988. Print.

Yankelovich, Daniel. *New Rules: Searching for Self-Fulfillment in a World Turned Upside Down*. New York: Random House, 1981. Print.

Young, James O., and Conrad G. Brunk. *The Ethics of Cultural Appropriation*. Chichester, UK: Wiley-Blackwell, 2009. Print.

York, Michael. *The Emerging Network: A Sociology of the New Age and Neo-Pagan Movements*. London: Rowman & Littlefield, 1995. Print.

Zaidman, Nurit. "The New Age Shop—Church or Marketplace?" *Journal of Contemporary Religion* 22.3 (2007): 361–74. Print.

"Zen Diet Assailed by A.M.A. Council as Peril to Health." *New York Times*, 19 Oct. 1971: 29. Print.

Ziff, Bruce, and Pratima V. Rao. "Introduction to Cultural Appropria-
    tion: A Framework for Analysis." *Borrowed Power: Essays on
    Cultural Appropriation*, ed. Bruce Ziff and Pratima V. Rao. New
    Brunswick: Rutgers UP, 1997. 1–27. Print.
Zoepf, Katharine. "Dammam Journal: Saudi Women Find an Unlikely
    Role Model: Oprah." *The New York Times*, 19 Sept. 2008. A1.
    Print.
Zukav, Gary. *The Seat of the Soul*. New York: Simon & Schuster, 1989.
    Print.

Index

Hughes, Dennis, 65; "An Interview
with Lynn Andrews: Best-Selling
Author, Renowned Retreat Leader,
and Teacher in the Field of Personal
Development," 65
Huhndorf, Shari, 60, 85–86; *Going
Native: Indians in the American
Cultural Imagination*, 60, 85–86
Hull, Akasha Gloria, 157–59; *All the
Women Are White, All the Blacks
Are Men, but Some of Us Are
Brave: Black Women's Studies*, 158;
*Soul Talk: The Spirituality of
African American Women*, 158–59
humanism, 109, 139–45
humanistic psychology, 30, 50
Hutchinson, Anne, 35
Huyssen, Andreas, 45, 171n6; "Mass
Culture as Woman: Modernism's
Other," 45, 171n6
hypnotherapist, 53
hysteria, 25–26, 48–54, 95, 117, 136,
151, 182n5
*Hystories: Hysterical Epidemics and
Modern Media* (Showalter), 49–50

icons: Goddess, 40; Native American,
18
idealization: of black women, 11; multiracial, 166
identity: assumption of, 63, 65;
authority on, 76; change, 4, 12, 78,
130–31; cultural, 59; feminist, 12;
formation, 25, 35, 56, 110; gender, 6,
10, 12, 57, 61, 86, 91, 104, 107, 111,
130, 131, 163–67, 177n10; ideas of,
30, 163; Indian, 63–64, 72–85,
through memory, 76, 131; national,
24, 179n9; New Age, 27; personal,
84; politics, 147, 161; racial, 6, 72,
79, 80, 86, 108, 131, 167; rational,
130; religious, 6; sale of, 4; source
of, 77; white, 29; woman's, 85, 141
"Identity, Recovery, and Religious
Imperialism: Native American Women and the New Age" (Kasee), 85

ideology: cultural, 18, 49–50, 147, 168;
domestic, 100; dominant, 110;
gender, 18, 24, 25, 90, 107; macrobiotics, 92; national, 18; political, 37;
prehistorical memory, 119–24, 132;
self-help, 4
"Ideology and Ideological State Appa-
ratuses" (Althusser), 92
"Imaginary Indians in Modern Times"
(Shoemaker), 85
immigrants, 162
imperialism: cultural, 10, 60–61,
176n6; racial, 73, 167; religious, 85;
spiritual, 44
"Importance of Being Oprah, The"
(Harrison), 138
impotence, 104–105
*In a Different Voice: Psychological
Theory and Women's Development*
(Gilligan), 154
"In the Interest of Public Good? New
Questions on Feminism" (Albert),
174n14
"In Person: Unlocking the Energy
Within" (Kannapell), 54
"In Search of a Definition: New Age
Theory" (Long), 31
In Search of New Age Spiritualities
(Possamai), 38
*In Search of White Crows: Spiritual-
ism, Parapsychology, and American
Culture* (Moore, L.), 14–16
incest, 155
Independent Women's Forum, 155
India, 123
Indian: history, 68, 77, 175n3, 176n9;
language, 68, 77, 80; organizations,
82; politics, 68; symbols, 65, 68, 80
Indianness: and Lynn Andrews, 60,
67–68, 72, 85, 165; and Mary
Summer Rain, 60, 75, 77, 79, 82–83,
85, 165; and women, 19, 87
"Indians America Loves to Love and
Read: American Indian Identity and
Cultural Appropriation, The"
(Shanley), 57, 68–69, 73